Economic and Social Commission for Asia and the Pacific

Asian and Pacific Decade of Disabled Persons: mid-point ~ country perspectives

United Nations

New York, 1999

This publication has been issued with the generous financial support of the Government of the Republic of Korea.

ST/ESCAP/2014

UNITED NATIONS PUBLICATION
Sales No. E.00.II.F.17
Copyright © United Nations 1999
ISBN: 92-1-119965-4

This publication has been issued by the Social Development Division of the ESCAP secretariat. It has not been formally edited.

For further information, please contact:

Director

Social Development Division, ESCAP, United Nations Building Rajadamnern Nok Avenue, Bangkok 10200, Thailand

Tel: (662) 288-1513; Fax: (662) 288-1030
E-mail: dgs.unescap@un.org

INTRODUCTION

The present publication is a companion to *Asian and Pacific of Decade Disabled Persons: mid-point ~ regional perspectives on multisectoral collaboration and national coordination* (ST/ESCAP/2004). This volume contains country and area perspectives concerning the implementation of the Agenda for Action for the Asian and Pacific Decade of Disabled Persons up to 1997, the mid-point of the Asian and Pacific Decade of Disabled Persons, 1993-2002. They are drawn from the papers presented to the Meeting of Senior Officials to Mark the Mid-point of the Asian and Pacific Decade of Disabled Persons held in Seoul from 26 to 29 September 1997.

CONTENTS

CHAPTER I

Australia

A. National overview

Australia has a federal system of government with origins in the British system of government and law. The Constitution of Australia established a commonwealth (federal) government with specific powers. Each of the states and territories has a parliament with powers in all areas not specified in the constitution as commonwealth powers.

The commonwealth, state and territory governments operate on the Westminster system, in which the political party or coalition with the majority of elected members in the lower house of parliament forms the government. Ministers with executive powers are drawn from these elected members of the Government of Australia. However, not all state/territory parliaments have an upper house. Within states there are local governments such as municipal and shire councils.

B. Policy measures

1. National coordination

In 1991, Australia introduced the Commonwealth/State Disability Agreement, which represents an effort on the part of all governments to develop a coordinated, rationalized and integrated approach to disability services in Australia.

The agreement is an arrangement between state, territory and commonwealth governments covering the funding and administration of employment, accommodation and other disability support services for people with disabilities. Total commonwealth, state and territory government funding for these services amounts to $A1.7 billion.

Following the development of the Commonwealth Disability Services Act 1986, there has been considerable overlap and confusion in the funding arrangements for disability services by the different levels of government. The agreement rationalized these arrangements, making state and territory governments responsible for accommodation and related services and the commonwealth responsible for employment services. Advocacy and research are joint responsibilities.

The Agreement also provided for the establishment of Joint Advisory Bodies in each state/territory to advise the commonwealth and state and territory ministers on the planning, delivery and evaluation of services. The Joint Advisory Bodies have been set up in each state and territory except Victoria, and they are expected to continue to operate in their present format until 30 June 1998. In 1996, the agreement was evaluated and a new one is currently being considered.

In addition, the Disability Services Subcommittee, a group of commonwealth and state/territory officials who administer disability services meet regularly to coordinate issues affecting people with disabilities across all states and territories.

2. Legislation

Australia has both national and state legislation to address discrimination against people with disabilities. There are also a number of other acts which promote the rights of people with disabilities, both at a commonwealth and state/territory level.

(a) *Commonwealth Disability Discrimination Act 1992*

The Commonwealth Disability Discrimination Act 1992 is the principal piece of legislation discharging the commonwealth's responsibility to people with disabilities. This legislation constitutes the legal basis for the protection and promotion of the rights of people with disabilities and makes it an offence to treat someone less favourably because of their disability in a number of areas of public life, including access to places and facilities. The Disability Discrimination Act 1992 overrides state legislation.

The Commonwealth Disability Discrimination Act 1992, is a complaints-based legislation, similar to other forms of anti-discrimination legislation in Australia pertaining to sex and race. A Disability Discrimination Commissioner within the Human Rights and Equal Opportunity Commission administers the Act.

The Act also provides for the formulation of standards in relation to employment, education, accommodation, public transport and the administration of commonwealth laws and programmes. Standards equate with mandatory levels of minimum access. Once a standard is established it will be unlawful not to comply with it. Work is currently under way on looking at developing standards under the Disability Discrimination Act 1992 in the areas of public transport, employment, education, commonwealth government information and communications and access to premises.

The Commonwealth Disability Discrimination Act 1992 allows for the development of action plans, which identify barriers for people with disabilities within an organization, and sets a time frame for addressing them. The benefits of developing a disability action plan are threefold:

(i)   It demonstrates a commitment to anti-discrimination principles for people with disabilities;

(ii) It can be given to the Human Rights and Equal Opportunity Commission be taken into account if a complaint is made against an organization;

(iii) It provides a tool to plan for change.

Many organizations, including commonwealth, state and local government bodies as well as private providers have submitted action plans to the commission.

(b)   Disability Services Act 1986

The Commonwealth Disability Services Act 1986 was created to help meet the commonwealth's obligations to people with disabilities. The objectives of the act are to assist people with disabilities to participate fully and be integrated as members of the community, and achieve greater independence, employment opportunities and self-esteem. Each state and territory has developed complementary legislation, which mirrors this commonwealth act.

(c)   Human Rights and Equal Opportunity Commission Act 1986

The Human Rights and Equal Opportunity Commission Act 1986 provides for complaints of discrimination according to the International Labour Organization Convention (111) which covers race, colour, sex, sexual preference, religion, political opinion, national extraction or social origin. This act also provides for the rights of people with disabilities.

(d)   Hearing Services Administration Act 1997

This act provides the legislative authority for the implementation of a voucher system for the delivery of government-funded hearing services to eligible adults. This system is scheduled to begin on 1 November 1997.

Under the voucher system consumers will be entitled to receive one or more specified hearing services, including assessment of their hearing loss, the provision and fitting of hearing devices, provision of rehabilitation advice and maintenance of the devices. The level and complexity of each service will depend on an individual's clinical need, as assessed by qualified staff of the service provider in consultation with the client.

A particular feature of the voucher system is that consumers can choose their hearing services provider – either Australian Hearing Services, the public sector provider, or select one of over 120 private providers. A scheme for accreditation of suitable service providers, rules of conduct for service providers, and rules surrounding the nature, extent and use of vouchers are provided for in the act.

(e) State/territory legislation

A number of acts at the state/territory level also govern the rights of people with disabilities. For example, the Intellectually Disabled Persons' Services Act 1986 in Victoria said that the objective of the government is to provide a range of high quality services to enable intellectually disabled persons to remain with their families or in their local communities, and to promote integration into the community.

C. Progress made in the first half of the Asian and Pacific Decade of Disabled Persons

1. National coordination

(a) National Disability Advisory Council

The National Disability Advisory Council was established on the International Day of Disabled Persons on 3 December 1996. It is Australia's national coordination committee on disability. One performance indicator it has identified in its strategic plan is the achievement of goals for the Asian and Pacific Decade of Disabled Persons, 1993-2002.

The council helps to strengthen the links between the Government of Australia and the disability field, and to work with the Minister for Family Services to improve the lives of people with disabilities. It also provides consumer views to the Government of Australia and will also refer to the minister issues requiring further investigation and consultation with consumers before a decision can be reached by the government. Members of the council include people with personal experience of disability, people with experience as carers and service providers.

(b) Commonwealth Disability Strategy

In November 1994, Australia adopted the Commonwealth Disability Strategy – a ten-year plan of action for commonwealth departments and agencies to remove barriers in commonwealth programs, services and facilities for people with disabilities. It is due to be evaluated in 1998 to look at ways of making it more effective.

The strategy was developed in consultation with the disability community and the Government of Australia. As such it reflects the priorities of people with disabilities while also having a commitment from commonwealth public service organizations. It is divided into core and target areas. The core areas reflect fields of administrative responsibility common to all commonwealth organizations while the target areas refer to specific portfolio responsibilities.

All commonwealth organizations are expected to report against the strategy's action every two years. The first progress report was published in November 1995. It provides a number of good and best practice examples to assist other organizations to think about providing equal access for people with disabilities. The next progress report is due to be tabled in parliament in 1997.

(c) *Hearing Services Advisory Committee*

To coordinate the administration of the voucher system under the Hearing Services Administration Act 1997, Australia is establishing the Hearing Services Advisory Committee, which will provide the Parliamentary Secretary to the Minister for Health and Family Services with advice on aspects of the operation of the new voucher system for the delivery of hearing services to eligible adults. The committee will comprise individuals selected on the basis of their skills and expertise.

The role of the Hearing Services Advisory Committee will evolve over time, but it is anticipated that, in the first 12 to 18 months, the advisory committee will focus mainly on quality assurance matters.

(d) *Options coordination*

In Australia, each state and territory has its own mechanisms for coordinating services for people with disabilities within that state/territory. For example, in South Australia, the implementation of Options Coordination in September 1995 was part of the recommendation for a widespread reform of the disability sector in South Australia.

The aim of Options Coordination agencies is to provide local client services coordination and to make the disability sector in South Australia more equitable, effective, efficient and accessible. Options Coordination provides a single entry point to the service system for people with disabilities and will ensure the consistent determination of eligibility, assessment of need and allocation of resources for the purchase of services across all disability areas.

In Queensland, the establishment of the Disability Directions Committee in 1993 brought together 13 departments and agencies, which offer programmes that impact on people with disabilities. This became the focus of a whole of government approach to disability services.

2. Information

(a) *National data collections and analysis*

On an annual basis data is collected about services directly provided or funded by commonwealth, state and territory governments under the Commonwealth/State Disability Agreement. This collection covers a wide variety of service types: accommodation, community support, community access, respite, employment, and other commonwealth/state disability agreement services.

The data collected relates to both services provided and characteristics of consumers. The purpose of this collection is to enable exchange, between jurisdictions, of standard core items with nationally agreed definitions. This information is also increasingly being used in the assessment of the performance of government funded service provision in the disability sector.

The Commonwealth Department of Health and Family Services also collects more detailed information about employment services administered by the commonwealth under the Commonwealth/State Disability Agreement. This collection occurs on a quarterly basis and provides nationally consistent information about employment services, their consumers and the jobs they obtain.

The Australian Bureau of Statistics conducts a Disability, Ageing and Carers survey every five years. The next one is due in 1998. This survey collects data on basic demographic characteristics of people with disabilities. The bureau is also exploring the possibility of including a question on disability in test questions for the 2001 census.

The objectives of the disability services unit of the Australian Institute of Health and Welfare are to describe the need for, provision and use of disability services in Australia, to inform community debate, and to support the development of public policy in the area of disability by relevant and timely data development, collection, analysis and publication.

In 1996, the Institute established the Disability Data Reference and Advisory Group, to advise it as it works towards the goal of greater consistency in concepts and definitions underpinning national data on disability services.

The group comprises government and non-government representatives as well as independent experts. It includes representation of the three Disability Task Force departments and the Australian Bureau of Statistics. The group has established a programme of work on both national and international developments, including the development of nationally consistent data definitions and the revision of the International Classification of Impairments, Disabilities and Handicaps.

Under the Privacy Act 1988, commonwealth agencies may not collect information about individuals except for a lawful and relevant purpose and may not use it for a purpose other than that for which it is collected without the individual's consent. Individuals have a general right of access to information about themselves, and information about individuals may not be disclosed except in very limited circumstances, such as where it will lessen an imminent and serious threat to life and health or where it is necessary for the enforcement of the law.

(b) National data development

The Commonwealth Department of Health and Family Services is also very interested in improving national information about people with disabilities and the demand for disability services in Australia. In cooperation with other common-wealth agencies such as the Australian Bureau of Statistics, the Australian Institute of Health and Welfare, the department works toward obtaining, better information about people with disabilities and disability services. The department is involved in working groups and committees promoting a nationally consistent definition of disability. One issue of particular interest is obtaining nationally consistent and reliable information about indigenous peoples with a disability.

(c) Internet homepage

The Office of Disability has a homepage on the world wide web, which can be found at http://www.health.gov.au/ood. This homepage includes information about programmes, special events, publications, media releases and speeches and links to other relevant sites. It is updated regularly to include information about reforms and changes to the Disability Services Programme.

(d) Print disability services

The commonwealth funds 14 national print disability services. For the past five years the total funding allocated has been in the order of $A1.2 million annually. The services produce documents in alternative formats for people who cannot obtain access to information in the printed form. The majority of services produce documents in Braille and large print or on audio tape and computer disk. One of the services produces audio cassette/book kits, which are narrated at slower than usual speeds for people with literacy problems, including those with an intellectual disability.

The services register their material on an Australian Bibliographic Network preventing duplication in production and ensuring the documents are available nationally. In consultation with all national print disability services and other interested parties a reassessment of the Print Disability Programme will be undertaken during 1997-1998. It is envisaged the commonwealth and service providers will be developing uniform quality assurance mechanisms following the reassessment.

(e) *Captioning*

Since 1990, the commonwealth has provided funding for the captioning of the Australian Broadcasting Commission's late edition news. Funding is also provided for captioning of commercial videos, including news releases.

In the 1996-1997 budget, $A7 million, over four years was provided through the Commonwealth Department of Communications and the Arts for captioning the Australian Broadcasting Commission's early evening news service and the Special Broadcasting, Service's World News.

(f) *Research*

The Disability Services Programme funds research and development projects under Section 12 of the Disability Services Act 1986. The programme is currently reviewing its priorities in the context of the federal government's commitment to support for families, partnership between the commonwealth and state and territory governments, an improved focus on individual clients rather than on providers, and microeconomic reform to improve the quality, choice and financial sustainability of programmes. Research and development should provide data and information to inform evidence-based policy and planning for the delivery of its services.

(g) *Research conducted by the Department of Social Security*

The Department of Social Security has recently commissioned a number of research projects to improve understanding of the needs of people with disabilities.

(i) *Unmet demand*

The report from this study quantifies the actual level of unmet demand and the potential for additional workforce opportunities. It also examines the characteristics of clients who are getting assistance compared with the characteristics of clients who are missing out on assistance and determines reasons why clients miss out on assistance or have their assistance deferred and assesses the availability of programmes in the community.

The information collected in this report is presently being considered by the Department of Social Security.

(ii) *Costs of disability*

Currently, the basic income support payment for people with disabilities, the Disability Support Pension, is paid at the same rate as other pension payments. However, most people with disabilities incur additional costs associated with their disabilities. They also find it generally more difficult and expensive to enter the labour market and, should they find work, it is generally in a lower paid occupation.

Research under way should provide a clearer picture of which people with disabilities incur additional costs and the nature and level of those costs. The results from this will be discussed with representatives from the disability community and professionals in the health and medical fields to inform government policy making.

(iii) Long-term adequacy of payments

Work to examine the long-term adequacy of payments to people currently receiving the Disability Support Pension has begun. Given that most of these people receive some form of income support from the day they get a disability until the day they die, the ability of these customers to meet long-term costs of living on a pension payment needs to be considered.

While many people going on to an aged pension have had the chance to accumulate assets, or in the case of those unemployed or on sole parent pension are able to put off major purchases until circumstances change, people with disabilities have little opportunity to accumulate funds to replace household items or make significant repairs to a house or vehicle.

This project will compare the length of time people on various payments spend on income support, opportunities for accumulating assets and lifestyles of recipients.

3. Public awareness

In 1996, a series of information guides and a staff training kit were developed as part of the Commonwealth Disability Strategy to assist commonwealth departments to make their services inclusive of people with disabilities. The information guides are titled: "Better Employment Practices"; "Planning Better Services"; "Better Physical Access"; "Better Communication Practices".

In addition, the Office of Disability in the Department of Health and Family Services provided support and assistance to other areas of the commonwealth public service in preparing Disability Action Plans prepared under the Disability Discrimination Act 1992.

In 1997, the commonwealth government is undertaking market research to aid in the development of a community campaign and related information programmes on disability discrimination issues. The objectives of the research are to examine community attitudes towards people with disabilities, propose target audiences for a possible campaign looking at changing attitudes, and develop a campaign strategy which provides a range of communication options.

(a)   International Day of Disabled Persons

Each year, the United Nations International Day of Disabled Persons, is marked around the world with activities on 3 December.   In 1997, events in Australia will be coordinated by the Commonwealth Office of Disability and the National Information Communication Awareness Network and feature specific activities at a regional level as well as a National Photographic Exhibition Project. The focus of these projects is the promotion of a broad range of positive images of people with disabilities participating in various aspects of community life and an increased awareness of disabilities throughout the community.

(b)   Prime Minister's Employer of the Year Awards

The Prime Minister's Employer of the Year Awards are an annual, ongoing event designed to recognize employers who have made significant efforts to include people with disabilities in their workforce.   Publicity surrounding the Awards provides a valuable means of encouraging all employers to consider employing people with disabilities.   By showcasing best practice in this area, we are able to overcome some of the attitudinal factors which can create barriers for people with disabilities.

(c)   State/territory initiatives

In Western Australia community education is one of nine major goals in the Disability Services Commission's Five-Year Business Plan.   This goal aims to enhance community understanding and acceptance of people with disabilities as equal members of Western Australian society.   A major community education campaign will be undertaken during 1998.

State government of Queensland agencies have implemented a number of public awareness strategies.   Among them are broadcast of a radio programme *Barrier Beat* throughout Queensland on 13 community radio stations.   The programme focuses on issues relevant to people with disabilities and launch of the Disability Awareness Kit, *Just Like Me*, which focuses on helping children to develop a positive understanding of people with disabilities.

4. Accessibility and communication

(a)   Access to premises and the built environment

The Australian Building Codes Board is currently engaged in a process designed to bring the Building Code of Australia up to the standards required of anti-discrimination law.   That process involves two committees, one, a technical advisory committee and the other a policy committee both reporting to the board.

The hope is that this process may lead to the adoption of a suitably revised Building Code as a disability standard. This is currently not possible as the provisions of Section 31 of the Disability Discrimination Act 1992, dealing with disability standards, do not allow for standards in this area. The Government of Australia is currently considering an amendment to expand the power to make standards to include this area.

In addition, the Human Rights and Equal Opportunity Commission issued a document, *Advisory Notes on Access to Premises*, giving the Commission's view of what those designing and building new buildings should consider to ensure adequate access for people with disabilities. The document also touched on what level of access is necessary to comply with the Disability Discrimination Act 1992. In addition, it also addresses not only physical access to building, but extend to areas such as signage, hearing augmentation facilities, appropriate fitments and infrastructure.

(b) National Relay Service

The Government of Australia provided funding of $A26 million over four years to implement the National Relay Service and operate the Telecommunications Equipment Access Programme to improve telephone access for people who are deaf, or who have a hearing, speech or communication impairment. The National Relay Service started operation in May 1995.

The service allows people to make telephone calls whether they use a telephone typewriter (TTY), modem or regular handset. A human relay operator converts text conversation to voice and relays the voice caller's conversation in text. The Telecommunications Equipment Access Programme provides financial assistance to eligible consumers to purchase equipment to access the relay service.

In its first two years of operation, the National Relay Service has facilitated over 700,000 telephone calls. From 1 July 1998, it will be funded through the Universal Service Levy to which all licensed telecommunications carriers will contribute.

(c) National Relay Service Advisory Council

The National Relay Service Advisory Council, established in December 1995 for a term of two years, ensures that the Government of Australia receives effective feedback and advice from consumers on the operation of the relay service. Its responsibilities include assessing the performance of the relay service operator, advising on changes to current and future relay service requirements, and ensuring that all target groups of the service are treated fairly and equitably. The Council comprises seven members: five consumer representatives and two commonwealth representatives.

(d) *Telecommunications*

Over the years, Telstra, Australia's major telecommunications corporation, has had a strong involvement in meeting the needs of people with disabilities. In 1981, "The International Year of Disabled Persons", Telstra introduced a range of specialized products to assist people in using the standard telephone.

Telstra now has disability programmes which provide support in the form of funding and sponsorship for disability groups, concessions on a range of disability products and services, and support services. For example, Telstra has a free call TTY Enquiry Line for deaf and hearing impaired people, a free call Disability Enquiry Hotline which provides specialist telecommunications information for people with disabilities, and modified pay-phones, including TTY pay-phones already in place.

(e) *Transport*

Draft Standards for Accessible Public Transport, to be adopted under the Commonwealth Disability Discrimination Act 1992, have been developed as a technically feasible way of implementing access for people with disabilities to public transport. Before they are adopted, however, they have been referred to the Attorney-General with a request that the Attorney-General produce a regulation impact study concentrating on the likely costs and benefits of implementing the standards and on the likely market for the introduction of such standards.

At a state/territory level many steps have been taken to improve access to transport for people with disabilities. For example, in Queensland, strategies to improve accessibility for people with disability to transport include funding by local government of a project aimed at increasing accessibility of private bus usage for people with disabilities. Its taxi drivers must also undertake training to improve communication and assistance to people with disabilities. The state also runs a pilot programme to make bus stops accessible to people with disabilities.

(f) *State/territory initiatives*

Access and communication issues are also a priority of state and territory governments. For example, in Western Australia, the Disability Services Act 1993, Sections 28 and 29 relate to the preparation and implementation of disability service plans by public authorities. These plans aim to improve access to services and facilities.

In New South Wales, Section 9 of the Disability Services Act states that each state government agency is required to prepare and implement a disability plan providing for improved accessibility of services for people with disabilities. These Section 9 plans include, for example, strategies by government agencies to make buildings more accessible, public transport more user-friendly and provide for an increase in the provision of communication aides such as TTY and publications in Braille.

5. Education

Key stakeholders such as non-government schools, universities, private training providers and representatives of people with disabilities have joined commonwealth and state/territory representatives on a task force to consider whether to proceed with Disability Discrimination Act Education Standards.

In 1997, there will be a first round of national consultations. Disability Discrimination Act Education Standards have the potential to clarify existing obligations and rights under the Disability Discrimination Act 1992 to enhance opportunities for people with disabilities in education and training.

(a) *Schools*

The areas of concern regarding education identified in the Agenda for Action for the Asian and Pacific Decade of Disabled Persons (hereafter referred to as the Asian and Pacific Agenda for Action) are addressed by both the commonwealth and state/territory governments under various programmes of assistance for children and students with disabilities.

State and territory governments provide significant financial assistance to students with disabilities to support their mainstream education, special classes and units and special schools. The commonwealth also seeks to improve the educational participation and outcomes of young people with disabilities through the provision of assistance targeted at schools, organizations, community groups and non-school organizations. To this end the commonwealth provides supplementary funding to assist children and students with disabilities under the Special Learning Needs Programme.

In 1997, approximately $A92 million is available specifically for children and students with disabilities. Commonwealth funding assists with the participation of children and students with a range of disabilities into mainstream education, and is provided to state and territory education authorities (government, Catholic and independent), as they are in the best position to determine need at the local level.

It is these education authorities that are responsible for directing funds to those children most in need of additional support, according to state priorities and within broad commonwealth guidelines. Areas of priority include funds for specialist and professional personnel, support for early intervention services, capital grants to assist with building access and equipment, and the dissemination of teacher resource materials for use with children with special needs.

The states/territories have a number of initiatives to increase access to education for people with disabilities. For example, the Education Department of Western Australia promulgated its document "Social justice in education – policy and guidelines for the education of students with disabilities" in late 1993.

Over the last five years, 50 per cent of all students with disabilities in Victoria were integrated into regular schools and it is proposed that in the next five years the number of students will reach 80 per cent. All schools in Victoria are provided with additional resources for the support of students with disabilities. This includes teachers, teachers aides, equipment and paramedical support.

(b) Higher education

The Government of Australia provides funding to universities to encourage the successful participation in higher education of members of disadvantaged groups, including people with disabilities. Each year over $A5 million is allocated through the Higher Education Equity Programme for this purpose. The Programme supplements the expenditure of institutions on equity initiatives.

Host institutions in each state and territory are also provided with an allocation under the Higher Education Equity Programme for cooperative projects for students with disabilities. In 1997, $A575,000 was provided for this purpose.

The Programme has recently been reviewed. The review found that the projects have produced good outcomes, including development of information materials for students with disabilities, seminars aimed at raising staff awareness and research into issues affecting the successful participation of students with disabilities in higher education. They have also encouraged the development of better links between institutions.

The Regional Disability Liaison Officer initiative was established at the end of 1994 to coordinate disability services nationally across geographic regions in the technical and further education and higher education sectors. Around $A2 million was allocated over 1994-1996 to support the establishment of 15 Regional Disability Liaison Officer positions. A further $A750,000 was allocated in the 1996 budget to continue the initiative into 1997.

The Government of Australia is also funding the development of a higher education code of practice for students with disabilities, which draws together existing guidelines and information to form a good practice guide for all tertiary institutions in the provision of services for students with disabilities. The code is expected to be available towards the end of 1997.

The merit-based equity scholarship scheme, which began in 1997, provides scholarships for selected new undergraduate students from disadvantaged groups, including students with disabilities.

Australian universities utilize funding received as operating grants from the federal government of Australia and other sources, to provide support services for students with disabilities. They provide many forms of assistance for these students, including flexible admission, counselling, seminars and information designed to raise awareness of disability issues among staff, special arrangements for examinations and alternative forms of assessment, specialist adaptive equipment such as voice synthesisers and Braille embossers, as well as note-taking and interpreting services and course materials in alternative formats.

A number of reports on participation of people with disabilities in higher education have been commissioned over the last five years. These include:

(i) *Additional Costs of Education and Training for People with Disabilities (1992)*

Research on additional costs of education and training for people with disabilities was pursued through a qualitative examination of experiences of people with disabilities in universities and colleges of technical and further education (TAFE), and through a survey to establish the number of people with disabilities in TAFE colleges and universities, along with their characteristics and support needs.

(ii) *Guidelines for Disability Services in Higher Education (1994)*

This document was published by the National Board of Employment, Education and Training, which was an independent advisory body to the then Minister for Employment, Education and Training. The guidelines provide advice on good practices, which may assist higher education institutions to provide better opportunities for students with disabilities. They cover matters such as outreach and recruitment, admissions and enrolment, support programmes, physical access, personal assistance and vocational guidance and placement.

(iii) *Financial Benchmarking of Students with Disabilities (1994)*

The study on financial benchmarking of students with disabilities looked at a support model operating in one university and designed an instrument to track the costs incurred in providing individual support to students. It found that two factors affected the cost of providing support to students, type and level of disability and amount and type of contact hours in the student's area of study. A formula has been developed to calculate the cost of support for any individual student.

(c) *Links between education and employment*

The Post-school Options Programme is a state and commonwealth government funded programme that was initiated in 1990 to assist school leavers with disabilities in Western Australia to access appropriate employment and community access and recreation regardless of the extent and severity of their disabilities. To date there have been in excess of 1,000 school leavers assisted through the programme. The commonwealth funds the employment component of the programme and the state funds community access and recreation.

The state government of Western Australia has made a forward commitment that all young people with disabilities leaving school up to 1999 will be assured of a place in a community access program, if employment is not an option for them.

The Ageing and Disability Department in New South Wales funds the Post-school Options Programme to provide a range of services and supports to bridge the gap for school leavers with disabilities between their departure from school and their participation in the wider community as adults. Funding for the programme has grown from $A7,543,000 in 1994-1995 to $A23,198,000 in 1997-1998 and has been used by 1,200 eligible school leavers since it began.

In South Australia, in response to the need for appropriate vocational and non-vocational support options for young people with disabilities on leaving school, the Disability Advisory Council has recommended a number of strategies to improve the coordination of existing services. Draft protocols have been prepared for referral between agencies and to ensure that school leavers are assessed and appropriately linked to the disability service system on leaving school.

6. Training and employment

(a) Vocational education and training

The Government of Australia provides assistance to people with disabilities through the entry level training incentives programme. The prime element of the programme, which provides assistance to people with disabilities, is the Disabled Apprentice Wage Support.

The Disabled Apprentice Wage Support was introduced on 1 July 1983 to increase employment opportunities in apprenticeships for people with disabilities. This support consists of a weekly payment of $A104.30, which may be provided for up to the duration of the apprenticeship. Extra help may also be granted to allow necessary workplace modifications or the hire or purchase of special equipment, tutorial assistance or interpreter services. This support is available to employers who take on and indenture, in an approved trade, a person who has been assessed as having a disability.

While trainees with disabilities are currently unable to attract this wage support, they may be eligible for assistance to allow necessary workplace modifications or the hire or purchase of special equipment, tutorial assistance or interpreter services under the Job Seeker Preparation and Support Programme. Trainees may also attract wage subsidies if they meet the normal employer incentive criteria.

(b) Employment services

The Government of Australia provides employment services through arrangements provided by the Department of Health and Family Services, which provides specialized employment assistance to people with disabilities who require ongoing assistance or support to maintain employment, and the Department of Employment, Education, Training and Youth Affairs which provides assistance to job seekers.

People with a lower level of disability are able to access these mainstream employment services. The mainstream employment services include some assistance targeted specifically towards people with disabilities.

(c) Specialized employment assistance for people with disabilities

Commonwealth funded employment services provide support for people with disabilities to gain and maintain employment. This may include pre-employment training and support, job search, and on-the-job support.

Commonwealth funded employment services fall into two main categories:

(i) Open employment services

In an open employment service, consumers receive support from a service outlet but are directly employed by another organization not funded under the Disability Services Act 1986. This includes competitive employment, training and placement services, individual supported job services, and some enclave services.

(ii) Business services providing supported employment

In business services providing supported employment, consumers are employed by the same organization that provides the employment support. These include business services, work crews and some enclave services.

(d) Supported wage system

Most Australians who have a disability and participate in the open workforce do so at full award rates of pay. However, there are some people who are unable to obtain and/or maintain employment at full award rates due to the effects of a disability on their workplace productivity.

With the availability of the supported wage system, people in such circumstances can now choose to access a reliable process of productivity-based wage assessment and related workplace-specific assistance in order to access appropriate jobs in the open workforce. For example, an eligible person who elects to participate may be independently assessed as having a productivity level of 70 per cent, compared to the productivity of co-workers who are performing the same, or similar duties and are receiving a full award wage. In such circumstances the eligible worker and the employer can agree to an ongoing employment relationship whereby the rate of pay will be at 70 per cent of the full rate.

The supported wage system has been developed in close consultation with employer, trade union and disability peak bodies, and with peak bodies and specialized employment agencies for people with disabilities.

(e) Disability Reform Package

The Disability Reform Package was introduced in 1991 to target people with a significant level of disability, which rendered them unable to work full-time. The package is jointly administered by the Department of Social Security, Department of Employment, Education, Training and Youth Affairs and Department of Health and Family Services.

The package emphasized reintegration into the labour force and the promotion of employment through the provision of rehabilitation and training. It also aimed to facilitate the transition to employment for those who could work part-time, provide a more appropriate payment structure for those with long-term conditions and restore the short-term nature of sickness benefit.

As a result of initiatives being undertaken by the Department of Social Security and other departments, and the finding of an evaluation of the Disability Reform Package, the operations of the Disability Reform Package are currently being reviewed.

In the 1996-1997 budget, the Government of Australia announced significant changes to labour market assistance arrangements in the country. As a result of these changes, assistance under the Disability Reform Package will continue to be available until May 1998, when the new employment services market is established, which will provide individualized assistance to all clients including people with disabilities.

On 1 May 1997, the Commonwealth Services Delivery Agency (Centrelink) was established with functions and staff from the Department of Employment, Education, Training and Youth Affairs and the Department of Social Security. This new arrangement has brought together the services provided by two of the departments participating in the Disability Reform Package, and as a result, identification of potential Disability Reform Package clients is now undertaken by the specialist disability officer in Centrelink.

(f) Pilot programme on more intensive and flexible services

This pilot programme has been implemented by the Department of Social Security to test the feasibility of providing intensive and flexible services to people with severe, unstable or multiple disabilities. It aims to maximize the work outcomes for Disability Support Pension customers who are currently not accessing programmes because the Disability Reform Package does not meet their specific needs. Participation in the pilot is voluntary.

Under the pilot programme, each participant receives case management services which assess customer needs, develop an action plan to meet customer needs, facilitate access and coordination of required services and support the customer through the change process.

Service providers are responsible for providing secondary rehabilitation services such as occupational therapy, physiotherapy and psychiatric and psychological services; pre-vocational training such as personal presentation, motivation skills, budgeting, English as a second language, literacy and numeracy skills, independent living training, transport assistance and/or training; and support services such as alcohol and drug support services providing alcohol and drug-free recreational activities, counselling and support, and mental health support services.

Results obtained through the pilot to date have been positive. An evaluation is expected to be finalized by the end of 1997.

(g) Current labour market programme assistance for people with disabilities

Labour market assistance is available in four main areas:

(i) Employer incentives

Incentives for employers to employ and train eligible job seekers and to arrange placements for more disadvantaged clients.

(ii) Enterprise and adjustment

Assistance for individual job seekers, enterprises and regions.

(iii) Training for employment

To assist unemployed job seekers to gain employment through the provision or enhancement of vocational skills linked to specific employment opportunities.

(iv) Job seeker preparation and support

To help job seekers access employment and training and address barriers which may be preventing this.

(h) Future employment assistance for people with disabilities

In the 1996-1997 budget, the Government of Australia announced significant changes to labour market assistance arrangements in the country.

Key elements of the reforms, which impact upon the provision of employment assistance to people with disabilities, and which are due to be implemented by May 1998 include the establishment of a Commonwealth Services Delivery Agency (Centrelink), which will combine the income support facilities of the Department of Social Security with the employment services functions of the Departments of Employment, Education, Training and Youth Affairs, and contracting private and community-based organizations, including a corporatized public provider to provide flexible labour exchange (FLEX) services. These services may involve canvassing employers for jobs, placing people in those jobs and providing additional assistance to disadvantaged job seekers who cannot be matched immediately with available jobs.

Providers of assistance will have a clear focus on getting outcomes for their clients because they will be paid for placing job seekers into employment. Providers will have maximum flexibility in how they choose to meet the needs of their disadvantaged clients, including people with disabilities.

To reflect the particular needs of special groups in the employment services market, the government will provide specialist contact officers, including disability support officers, in Centrelink. The Government of Australia will also ensure disadvantaged groups receive an equitable share of assistance, broadly equivalent to the shares of assistance received under the current employment services arrangements.

Other programmes, such as the Community Support Programme, assist those people with disabilities who would not be in a position to benefit from even the most intensive form of assistance under the new employment services market.

(i) Income security

Australia has a comprehensive set of income security payments for people who are sick, injured or have a disability. For example, sickness allowance may be paid if a person cannot work or study because of illness or injury. The Disability Support Pension may be paid if an illness, injury or disability will stop a person from working for at least two years. If a person is permanently blind, he/she will automatically get the Disability Support Pension.

7. Prevention of the causes of disability

Australia has a number of public health initiatives to reduce accident, illness and disability. Amongst them are:

(a) *Expansion of immunization coverage with special emphasis on the control of measles and poliomyelitis*

On 25 February 1997 a package of measures designed to achieve a significant increase in the immunization coverage of Australia's children as rapidly as possible was announced. The measures proposed in *Immunise Australia: The Seven Point Plan* are:

(i)   A range of initiatives directed towards parents;

(ii)   Incentives for general practitioners;

(iii)   Improved monitoring of immunization targets;

(iv)   Immunization days;

(v)   Measles elimination;

(vi)   Education and research;

(vii) Introduction of school entry requirements to ensure that parents submit details of children's immunization history prior to enrolment in schools.

Of particular significance is the commonwealth's commitment to a measles elimination programme, which will be developed in consultation with states and territories and draw on the expertise of countries such as the United Kingdom, which conducted an extremely successful campaign during 1995. It is anticipated that this programme will be conducted during 1998.

Australia has also made significant progress towards the elimination of poliomyelitis. There have been no notifications of wild-type poliomyelitis in Australia since 1986 and in accordance with the global commission certification of poliomyelitis eradication, Australia will be working towards documenting the eradication of poliomyelitis by meeting established criteria set for the certification of regional poliovirus elimination.

(b) *Activity to reduce drug-caused disability*

Australia is seeking to manage the adverse health, social and economic consequences of drug misuse, including drug-caused disability, through the National Drug Strategy. The National Drug Strategy brings together the federal and state governments of Australia regardless of political affiliation. It is a comprehensive policy incorporating a balance of measures aimed at reducing the demand for drugs while at the same time limiting its supply.

Action to address drug use occurs in the areas of education, prevention, rehabilitation, treatment, enforcement and research.

In 1993, the National Drug Strategy replaced the National Campaign Against Drug Abuse, which had been in operation since 1985. Although the campaign was hailed as a major achievement in drug policy, campaign evaluations suggested that there was a need for, among other things, improved strategic direction and for closer cooperation between law enforcement and health. The National Drug Strategy was adopted to build on the strengths of the campaign, but with improved strategic direction and with a closer cooperation between law enforcement and health.

At the July 1997 Ministerial Council on Drug Strategy, it was agreed that a five-year national drug strategic framework will be developed in consultation with key stakeholders and this framework and future National Drug Strategy advisory structures would be considered at an extraordinary meeting of the council to be held in November 1997.

(c) Injury prevention

Much of the responsibility for injury prevention lies with state and territory governments. The commonwealth's role focuses more on capacity building, including research, funding the collection, analysis and dissemination of injury statistics.

In Victoria, for example, the Community Child Health programme provides funding for the development and publication of literature to promote child accident injury prevention. This was recently extended to include farm safety and children aged five to seven years old.

(d) Prevention of road accidents

Since the late 1980s, Australia has undertaken a concerted effort to reduce the economic and social implications of road trauma. The number of deaths and serious injuries has fallen by around 30 per cent. The annual economic savings have been in the vicinity of $A2 billion.

During this period, Australia's national safety standards for new vehicles have been upgraded to match the best standards of the world. A reduction in serious injury will reduce the number of people who sustain permanent disabilities each year through accidents.

Road transport injury was, until recently, the most common form of injury death, but death rates have been declining since 1970, and there was particularly rapid decline from 1988 to 1992.

Progressive introduction and enforcement of seat belt wearing in 1970, random breath testing in 1978, and speed limits played a major part in the steep decline in the road toll. In addition, other significant features in reducing the road toll over this period included continuing improvements in vehicle design and improved roads.

(e) Firearms

In an unprecedented legislative action, in the 12 months between May 1996 and May 1997, approximately 400,000 firearms were removed from communities across Australia and approximately $A200 million paid to gun owners in compensation. The federal and state governments of Australia have banned self-loading rifles, shotguns and pump action shotguns, and introduced comprehensive registration systems for all firearms.

The following requirements have also been set, that people must establish a genuine reason to own or possess or use a firearm, that a permit be obtained to acquire a firearm with a 28-day waiting period, and that all first time applicants undertake training.

The federal and state governments of Australia have also agreed on the grounds for refusal and cancellation of firearms licences, the regulation of mail order and transport of firearms and setting minimum standards for security and storage of firearms.

(f) State/territory initiatives

State and territory governments have a large responsibility for the provision of public health programmes which prevent disability. The Queensland Health Department has enhanced the prevention of causes of disability through health promotion programmes, improved professional training, school based programs for children with learning difficulties and specific programmes for at risk populations, particularly addressing folate deficiency (deficiency of folic acid).

Its strategies have focused on neonatal screening, postnatal follow-up services and home visitation services, child health services, pool drowning prevention strategies, burns prevention, immunization and mainstream paediatric services.

8. Rehabilitation services

(a) Commonwealth Rehabilitation Service (CRS)

The CRS is the leading vocational rehabilitation provider in Australia. It assists people with an injury or disability to gain or keep employment. It is funded by the Government of Australia to provide vocational rehabilitation programmes to persons in receipt of social security pensions and benefits and to other persons who can not afford to pay for a rehabilitation programme.

CRS' objective to reduce the personal, social and financial cost of disability to the individual and the community through the direct provision of rehabilitation services. In doing so the CRS aims to provide high quality, accessible rehabilitation services to people with disabilities between the ages 14 to 65 throughout Australia. Such services also aim to assist people with disabilities obtain or retain employment or make substantial gains toward employment.

(b) Hearing Services Programme (HSP)

The Government of Australia provides a range of hearing rehabilitation services to meet the needs of eligible hearing impaired people. Acoustic testing and equipment supply and training are fundamental components of this service.

More than 130,000 adults and 22,000 children received a government-funded hearing service in 1996-1997, through Australian Hearing Services (AHS), a government authority.

The Government of Australia in the 1996-1997 budget announced reforms to delivery arrangements for government-funded hearing services under the HSP. The principal reforms are the separation of purchasing of hearing services from the provision of hearing services, and the introduction of a voucher system for adult clients of the HSP including consumer choice of service provider.

AHS will continue to operate as a commonwealth statutory authority after 1 July 1997 and will be the principal public sector service provider for children and prescribed public sector clients. It will also meet essential community service obligations on behalf of the government. The latter include hearing services to eligible people in certain remote areas, eligible aboriginal and Torres Strait Islander peoples, people with complex hearing rehabilitation needs, hearing and noise related research, and hearing loss prevention activities.

(c) Australian Hearing Services (AHS) – services to aboriginal and Torres Strait Islander peoples

AHS has provided specific programmes to meet the special needs of Aborigines and Torres Strait Islander peoples for over 40 years. In 1996-1997, specially trained Australian Hearing Services audiologists made over 350 visits to more than 180 remote aboriginal and Torres Strait Islander communities across Australia. Service delivery efforts, in particular, focused on children because of the educational problems caused by otitis media-related hearing loss.

AHS also focuses on non-clinical activities designed to strengthen and expand cooperation with community organizations, and to build a multidisciplinary team approach to hearing health care with state government health and education departments.

Training about ear health is also provided to aboriginal and Torres Strait Islander health workers. Through training and the provision of the equipment necessary for the early detection of ear disease in infants, it is anticipated that the adverse effects of endemic hearing complaints will be reduced. AHS will also provide mainstream hearing services to eligible adults, those under 21 years old, aboriginal and Torres Strait Islanders through the hearing services programme.

9. Assistive devices

A wide range of assistive devices are produced in Australia. These range from relatively small and inexpensive aids to major pieces of equipment such as lifting hoists and electric wheelchairs. Australia has a network of independent living centres which have many aids and appliances on record.

These can be categorized as aids to daily living in areas such as the kitchen, laundry, bathroom and bedroom, mobility aids, including wheelchairs, walking frames and crutches, and communications aids, such as computers, telephone typewriters and flashing alarm clocks.

In Australia, assistive devices are produced by a number of small private firms, non-profit organizations, hospitals and government agencies.

Technical Aid to the Disabled is a non-profit organization using volunteers dedicated to the design and construction of assistive devices for people with disabilities. Members of organization comprise a broad range of design, engineering, medical, paramedical and other professional and technical skills.

Technical Aid to the Disabled will develop devices when the commercial equipment is not available, provide technical information and advice to people with disabilities about devices and the appropriate technology, and disseminate information on devices and technology to the rehabilitation and engineering professions, governments and the community.

(a) State/territory initiatives

The state governments of Australia are primarily responsible for the provision of aids and appliances. The arrangements for delivery of assistance for people with disabilities by the states and the eligibility of people with disabilities vary between and within states. These services range from loans to full subsidies for the purchase of aids or rental schemes.

The Programme of Aids for Disabled People is administered at a state level. For example, in New South Wales, it is administered by the New South Wales Department of Health.

Many activities are occurring at the state/territory level to improve the availability of equipment. For example, a full review of the Home Medical Aids Programme was undertaken by the Queensland Health Department.

New policies and guidelines have been prepared to ensure statewide consistency in access, items available, subsidy levels and prioritization of applications. A framework has also been developed for the rationalization of the scheme with other programmes providing aids, to enable people to remain living in the community.

The Government of Australia funds specific equipment programmes, including the provision of equipment assistance for people of working ages to facilitate their participation in the workforce and programmes directed towards enabling people with disabilities to live independently in their own home, thereby avoiding premature entry to nursing home care.

Goods designed and manufactured expressly for use by people with disabilities are exempt from the sales tax. In special circumstances a person with a disability may also claim exemption on goods that would ordinarily be subject to the sales tax.

(b) *Continence Aids Assistance Scheme*

The Continence Aids Assistance Scheme provides assistance to people with a permanent continence condition, and a permanent disability, to manage the costs of incontinence, which can constitute a significant barrier to their participation in training, education and employment. The scheme currently helps around 11,000 Australians with disabilities.

Started on 1 January 1993, the scheme was developed in response to consultations with the disability community, which indicated that the cost of continence aids presented a major barrier to the participation of people with disabilities in employment, education and training.

10. Self-help organizations

The majority of disability groups are represented formally or informally at the federal, state and local levels.

The Office of Disability in the Department of Health and Family Services provides a link for members of the disability community to express their views, aspirations and needs to the Government of Australia. An important role for the office is to disseminate information to the disability community and provide opportunities for them to communicate with ease to the Government of Australia.

There are a number of ways in which the Office of Disability is facilitating consultation with people with disabilities. The establishment of the National Disability Advisory Council is an important avenue through which the voices of families, carers and disability service providers will be heard. The Office of Disability funds several national peak disability bodies to represent the views of their members to the Government of Australia.

It also provides funding to the National Caucus of Disability Consumer Organizations to be proactive on issues which impact on the lives of all people with disabilities. Caucus members include the ten peak consumer groups in the disability sector. Its functions include information sharing and networking amongst its members, and collective campaign action and representation to government on issues affecting people with disabilities.

(a) *Advocacy services*

The Government of Australia is committed to providing people with disabilities and their families with a greater array of genuine choices and opportunities – the contribution of families is seen as integral to maintaining a strong, cohesive and compassionate society. One way the Government of Australia has contributed to this is to continue to fund a number of disability advocacy services.

Advocacy services assist people with disabilities, including young people, their families and supporters to become informed about their rights and how to exercise those rights. Advocacy services represent the interests of people with disabilities in the community, either individually or as a group.

Under the current Commonwealth/State Disability Agreement, responsibility for advocacy is shared by both levels of government. The commonwealth currently administers funding to 77 advocacy services at an annual cost of approximately $A10 million each year with the states and territories contributing approximately $A3.8 million.

The Government of Australia is concerned to support advocacy services for people with disabilities in areas which are currently not as well represented by existing services because of, in particular, distance, ethnic background, multiple disability or an inability to provide self-advocacy.

The National Disability Advocacy Programme is currently being reviewed to ensure that commonwealth resources committed to disability advocacy are targeted and utilized in the most effective manner and are in line with the Government of Australia's social policy agenda.

(b)   State/territory initiatives

At a state and territory level there are a number of mechanisms for enabling people with disabilities to influence policy.

In Western Australia, people with disabilities, their carers, family members and advocates are involved in a variety of committees and boards.   These include Board of the Disability Services Commission, Advisory Council for Disability Services, Regional Advisory Forums, Standards Reference Group, Post School Options Working Party, Council of Funded Agencies, the boards of many government funded non-government agencies and various ad hoc groups such as the Carers' Task Force.

In Queensland, a number of initiatives have been established as part of the institutional reform agenda to improve advocacy for people relocating from residential to community accommodation.   These include the establishment of a Family Support Network which provides an independent source of information and support to families, and the Independent Representative Service.   This links people with disabilities in residential care to a person who supports them in decision-making about their accommodation choice and ensures that appropriate planning takes place for relocation into community-based accommodation.

The Ageing and Disability Department in New South Wales is supportive of the role of advocates and self-help organisations and has undertaken consultations across the state with a view to developing an Advocacy Plan.

The development of an Advocacy Plan has two major objectives: to develop principles and protocols for the operation of advocacy for people with disabilities in New South Wales; and to investigate imbalances and deficits in the provision of advocacy across the state.

11. Regional cooperation

Australia has contributed to the Asian and Pacific Decade of Disabled Persons, 1993-2002, through:

(a) Signing the Proclamation on the Full Participation and Equality of People with Disabilities in the Asian and Pacific Region signalling a commitment to the Asian Pacific Agenda for Action;

(b) The attendance by the Assistant Secretary, Disability Planning and Quality Assurance Branch, at the meeting to launch the Asian and Pacific Decade of Disabled Persons, 1993-2002, held from 1 to 5 December 1992 in Beijing;

(c) Contributing funds totalling $A70,000 to support the Asian and Pacific Decade of Disabled Persons. This money was placed in the Technical Cooperation Trust Fund for the Asian and Pacific Decade of Disabled Persons, which amounted to over US$260,000 in April 1996;

(d) Hosting the 1994 Disabled People's International World Assembly and providing $A250,000 financial assistance to enable the attendance of delegates from less developed countries;

(e) Contributing to the secretariat costs of the South Pacific Disability Council;

(f) Agreeing to host the 1995 visit of a delegation from the China Disabled Persons' Federation and providing $A30,000 financial assistance. A cultural exchange visit to Australia by the China Disabled People's Performing Art Troupe occurred at the same time and was sponsored by the private sector at a cost in excess of $A120,000;

(g) Preparing a presentation for representatives of the Ministry of Civil Affairs, China, who were on a study tour hosted by the Department of Social Security.

CHAPTER II

Bangladesh

A. National overview

One of the least developed countries in the world, Bangladesh has a population of about 120 million over an area of 147,570 square kilometres. It has a population density of 797 person per square kilometre and a per capita income of US$280.

Poverty is the biggest problem that the country is facing. The other major challenges are lack of adequate productive employment and widespread illiteracy. Solving these problems is therefore, high on the country's agenda for comprehensive economic, social and human development. Human welfare is the central theme of Bangladesh's agenda as is the issue of people with disabilities and their welfare.

Bangladesh does not have any comprehensive data about the number of disabled persons. According to a sample survey made by the World Health Organization and some non-governmental organizations (NGOs), the prevalence of disabilities is close to 10 per cent or about 12 million people. If these figures include other affected people, families and their dependents, the number of people with disabilities in the country will be very high.

The Government of Bangladesh is conscious about the need to formulate appropriate policies, plans and laws for the education, training and rehabilitation of the people with disabilities. A National Policy on Disabilities and People with Disabilities has been finalized by the government and is awaiting legislative approval.

B. Progress made in the first half of the Asian and Pacific Decade of Disabled Persons

In Bangladesh, the programmes and activities undertaken during the first half of the Asian and Pacific Decade are aimed at promoting the cause of people with disabilities in different fields.

1. National coordination

The country has formulated a comprehensive national policy in the first half of the Decade. The policy includes measures to ensure the rights of disabled persons, equalizing their opportunities, education, training, rehabilitation, creation of employment opportunities, income maintenance, social security, accessibility to the physical facilities and public information (Braille, sign-language, audio-visual aids), fixation of quota for employment and provision for employment of persons with disabilities.

The Government of Bangladesh has adopted a unique policy for employment of persons with disabilities by fixing a 10 per cent quota for vacancies in the public sector. The government has also permitted tax-free import of assistive devices for disabled persons. It has set up a 53-member National Coordination Committee of the Disabled headed by the Minister for Social Welfare. The committee reviews and coordinates disability-related activities run by NGOs.

To provide the necessary suggestions and guidance to the government and NGOs about disability-related issues, a central organization, the National Disability Trust, was established. Its members are representatives from the government and NGOs.

Despite various limitations such as the scarcity of resources, lack of professionalism and intervening technology, Bangladesh has attached high priority to the disability agenda. The country's efforts are in accordance with the Agenda for Action for the Asian and Pacific Decade of Disabled Persons, 1993-2002. Bangladesh also follows the objectives and guidelines of United Nations Declaration on the Rights of Disabled Persons and has signed the Proclamation on Full Participation and Equality of People with Disability in the Asian and Pacific Region. However, the lack of adequate resources is limiting the successful implementation of these programmes.

2. Legislation

The Government of Bangladesh is conscious about the need for appropriate policies, laws and plans for the education, training and rehabilitation of people with disabilities. Various measures have been taken to meet their needs. Over the past few decades, the government has set up a number of institutions for people with disabilities. Of late, NGOs have demonstrated keen interests on their educational, training and rehabilitation needs. Most of the current efforts have been institutional in approach and nature.

The Parliament of Bangladesh has given its legislative approval for the National Policy on Disabilities and People with Disabilities.

3. Education

The education, training and rehabilitation programmes in Bangladesh are currently institutional in nature due to inadequate facilities in regular educational services, insufficient skilled manpower and the largely ignorant parents and guardians, most of whom are illiterate and poor. In Bangladesh, both the government and the NGOs are active in the field of education, training and rehabilitation of people with disabilities.

The numbers of institutions run by the government were as follows:

(a)	Schools for hearing-impaired persons	7
(b)	Schools for visually-impaired persons	5
(c)	Schools for intellectually disabled persons	1
(d)	Integrated educational programme for visually-impaired persons	47

Initiated by the government in 1974 and integrated into the normal education curriculum, some 5,000 people with disabilities have received training and/or are being rehabilitated annually under this scheme. However, the programme still does not meet total needs.

(e)	Vocational rehabilitation centres	2
(f)	Employment Rehabilitation Centre for Physically Handicapped	1
(g)	National Centre for Special Education	1
(h)	Industrial Unit	1

The institutions run by NGOs were as follows:

(a)	Schools for hearing impaired persons	12
(b)	Schools for visually impaired persons	3
(c)	Schools for intellectually disabled persons	1
(d)	Integrated educational programme for visually impaired persons	40
(e)	Vocational rehabilitation centre for hearing impaired persons	1
(f)	Vocational rehabilitation centre for visually impaired persons	3
(g)	Vocational rehabilitation centre for intellectually disabled persons	2
(h)	Vocational rehabilitation centre for orthopaedically disabled persons	3
(i)	Sheltered workshop for blind persons	1
(j)	Computer training for orthopaedically disabled persons	1
(k)	Job placement programme	1

4. Training and employment

The Government of Bangladesh has adopted a unique policy for the employment of people with disabilities. Some 20 per cent of public sector jobs are reserved for them. Among the various institutions and programmes for the training and rehabilitation of people with disabilities, four stood out for their services offered as well as their areas of specialization. They are:

(a) *Employment Rehabilitation Centre for the Physically Handicapped (ERPH)*

The ERPH at Tongi, Gazipur, is a government-run institution and was established in 1981, as a joint project between the Department of Social Services and the Swedish International Development Authority through the Swedish Free Mission. It is the only centre of its kind in the country.

The ERPH is specially designed to provide training to disabled persons (deaf persons, speech-impaired persons, and blind persons) so that they may also work and live as equal members of society. The aim is to train and rehabilitate through waged- and self-employment, and also to inculcate in the trainees self-reliance and self-respect. It trains some 105 people with disabilities each year.

The ERPH provides both theoretical and vocational training, including the following:

(i) A mechanical workshop which trains 30 students, over a 12-month period, in trades such as lathe, welding, milling and grinding;

(ii) Handicraft training for 35 students per year, in tailoring 25 students, and woodworks for 10 students;

(iii) A six-month training course that prepares 20 students per year for self-employment in duck and poultry farming;

(iv) A six-month training programme that helps prepare 20 people with disabilities for self-employment in nursery;

(v) Mobility training for blind students; arrangements are being made to train them in cane and bamboo work.

Music classes are also held regularly for blind persons and mobility-impaired students under the guidance of a blind music instructor.

Training in different games, sports and physical fitness is conducted regularly by trained teachers, and trainees participate in games and sports held at different levels.

In addition, the ERPH also provides a number of specialized support services for people with disabilities. These include a hearing centre which is supported by the government. The hearing centre provides hearing tests and other services to students from various centres for physically disabled persons and schools for deaf and speech-impaired persons run by the Department of Social Services. The hearing centre also provides hearing aids for deaf students. A health clinic has been set up to provide preventive health care and first-aid to students. It is staffed by a full-time nurse and a part-time doctor. ERPH trainees are also given free residential accommodation and board.

The Government of Bangladesh also provides follow-up services for trainees who have completed their courses at the ERPH. These include a rehabilitation grant of Tk4,000 for each trainee who would use it as seed money, and job placement programmes where placement officers would help find suitable employment for the trainees in different mills and factories, and other industrial units. The officers also are in constant contact with them and provide continuous help, counselling and advice.

Over the years, the ERPH has established itself as a viable and sustainable institution for training people with disabilities. The government plans to set three more such centres in Khulna, Chittagong and Rajshahi.

(b) *Industrial Production Unit (Maitry Shilpa)*

In 1983, the government with the assistance from the Swedish Free Mission established a plastics factory named Maitry Shilpa, which is run by people with disabilities on a commercial basis. The unit has been producing various types of plastic products and providing a regular income for disabled persons.

Products from the factory entered the National Export Fair in 1984 and came up tops, winning the first prize under the government stalls category. Since it started operations, several hundreds of apprentices have been rehabilitated and are employed in different mills and factories.

(c) *Vocational Training Centre for the Blind (VTCB)*

VTCB is an NGO established in 1976 jointly by the government and a Germany-based NGO. It is the only institution for blind persons in the country that offers 100 disabled persons per year skills training for different trades, including chalk making, weaving, carpentry, jute and handicraft-making. It also has a sheltered workshop for blind persons and offers rehabilitation package programmes for self-employment to 20 blind persons each year.

5. Rehabilitation services

(a) *National Centre for Special Education (NCSE)*

The NCSE was established in 1991 with the assistance of the Norwegian Association for the Blind and Partially Sighted, Norwegian Association of the Deaf and Norwegian Association for the Mentally Retarded. The NCSE aims to train staff, assess, train and rehabilitate people with disabilities, develop assistive devices and provide counselling. It is a composite institution consisting the following institutions:

(i) *Teachers Training College for Special Education*

The college offers 30 vacancies for its year-long diploma programme. Special education courses at Bachelors and Masters levels will start from the coming academic session at the Bangladesh National University.

(ii) *Residential/day primary schools for people with disabilities*

These schools provide seven years of primary education, including pre-school and pre-vocational classes. The schools for visually impaired persons and hearing impaired persons each offer 70 vacancies while the school for intellectually disabled persons offers 50.

(iii) *Resource unit*

The unit provides services such as assessment for hearing and vision, develops special teaching aids and methods and distributes special aids and teaching aids. It also provides services such as repair of hearing and other technical aids, distribution of special aids for the schools for persons with disabilities, information on disabilities and special education.

In addition, the NCSE provides special training such as activities of daily living for all three institutions, Braille, low vision training and mobility for visually impaired persons, communication and use of hearing aids for hearing impaired persons as well as speech training and physiotherapy for intellectually disabled persons.

There are also refresher and special courses for teachers, courses for parents and guardians, social and health workers and staff. The NCSE has residential facilities for students, guardians and trainee teachers.

(b) Other rehabilitative and training institutions

(i) Department of Special Education, Institute of Education and Research at the University of Dhaka: the Department recently introduced a diploma and a post-graduate course in special education. It aims to train teachers to specialize in teaching disabled students. The curricula have been designed and developed according to international standards.

(ii) Braille press and other assistive devices: The Government of Bangladesh runs a Braille press which will soon be computerized. An assembling unit for hearing aids has also been established. In Bangladesh, there is a private company which manufactures Braille writing frames, abacus and white canes and supplies these to the local market at a much lower cost compared to that of imports.

(iii) Rural Rehabilitation Centre (RRC); one RRC has been established at Fakirhat, Bagerhat to train and rehabilitate disabled persons living in the rural regions. It has 40 vacancies per year, providing training in tailoring, mechanical workshop, animal husbandry and coir-making.

(iv) Bangladesh Protibondi Kalyan Samity (BPKS) job placement service: established in 1985, the BPKS is a front-ranking organization for disabled persons. It runs a job placement programme where a trained officer helps in matching people with disabilities and prospective employers.

(v) Computer training: NGOs such as BPKS have started offering free computer training for educated youths with disabilities. This has proven to be immensely effective in helping them gain jobs as such skills are in high demand.

C. Activities planned for the second half of the Asian and Pacific Decade of Disabled Persons

Disabilities and people with disabilities are given much attention in all of the development plans of the Government of Bangladesh. Currently, a number of them are being implemented with greater emphasis on the training and rehabilitation of people with disabilities. A special feature is that NGOs are increasingly involved in implementing these plans.

The key strategy of these plans is that existing special schools and rehabilitation centres will be gradually converted into resource centres for special education. Steps are also being taken to extend the integrated programme for blind persons countrywide. Community-based rehabilitation (CBR) programmes are also being launched in selected areas and a proposal to start a national training institute is being considered.

D. Trends and issues

The major issue involved in the training and rehabilitation of people with disabilities is equalization of opportunities. In a slow-growth economy with a less-developed private sector, the government has to bear the responsibility of providing these services. However, in the recent years NGOs have increasingly been extending these services for people with disabilities. Some of them have been delivering services, including the CBR programmes, effectively.

Another key issue is priority. As a general policy, the government gives equal attention to each individual sub-group of people with disabilities. It is a difficult task for the government. NGOs are perhaps better suited for the purpose. The Government of Bangladesh encourages NGOs and the private sector to extend services for people with disabilities at a faster pace. Due emphasis in this regard will be given in the national policy.

On employment for people with disabilities, the role of the private sector needs to be emphasized. But, this area has so far not been sufficiently explored. NGOs are showing more interests in the issue. However, in some cases, NGOs have succeeded in persuading greater private sector participation.

Globally, technological advancement is racing ahead in the field of training and rehabilitation of people with disabilities. However, this has made it harder for developing countries such as Bangladesh to keep pace. Therefore, there should be a global commitment for easy transfer of technology so as to enable receiving countries to adopt the technology appropriately.

The number of people with disabilities is increasing due to accident, diseases, malnutrition, ignorance and lack of consciousness about proper security measures. Some might become a burden on their families and if not gainfully employed, they might also stand in the way of Bangladesh's economic development.

If they are trained in different skills according to their abilities and aptitudes, they can also participate in nation-building activities. The country has the same obligations to them as it has to other citizens. Bangladesh needs their active participation and contributions for its economic and social development. The principle of equality and participation is both a question of human rights and a condition for the welfare and progress of all citizens.

The main thrust of the Government of Bangladesh is to design and implement programmes for people with disabilities in accordance with United Nations strategies and guidelines. However, due to resource constraints, lack of job opportunities, negative attitudes and a host of other problems, there still remains a gap in the services and provisions for people with disabilities. These issues can only be overcome through the mutual cooperation of the international community by way of sharing ideas, experiences and resources.

CHAPTER III

Brunei Darussalam

A. National overview

Brunei Darussalam is situated on the northern coast of the island of Borneo with an area of 5,765 square kilometres and a population of just under 300,000. With a small population, the people, irrespective of their abilities, are the main and most precious asset of the country.

1. National coordination

There are three government ministries and two voluntary organizations directly involved with the affairs of disabled persons in Brunei Darussalam.

(a) The Ministry of Welfare, Youths and Sports is mandated to recommend, develop, administer and implement welfare programme and services primarily to promote the well-being of the country's needy population, uplift their living conditions and social functions.

(b) The Ministry of Health (MOH) is involved in providing medical and health needs of people with disabilities. A MOH unit, the Handicapped Playgroup, provides leisure and play nursery classes to pre-school children or children below five years old under the direct supervision of paediatric specialists. The specialists also monitor their health and growth. The children are taught activities to suit their needs such as simple colouring and drawing. They are then assessed whether they could continue their education in regular schools. The MOH also trains and counsels recovered disabled patients, helping them lead normal lives by providing rehabilitation services and teaching them new job skills.

(c) The Ministry of Education is now providing programmes to integrate disabled children into regular schools. Specially trained teachers will be attached to the regular schools where disabled children are enrolled.

(d) The Paraplegic and Physically Disabled People's Association addresses and helps tackle the problems faced by people with disabilities. It then formulates a set of programmes to help disabled persons integrate into society.

(e) The Association for the Disabled Children is concerned with the care and welfare of disabled children in Brunei Darussalam. It is run by volunteers, mostly government officers to help the children in recreation and other activities.

Both non-government organizations (NGOs) aim to create greater awareness in society that there are people with special needs but are traditionally kept isolated from the community by their families. It is either because the families are ashamed of having a disabled family member or are overly protective. It is hoped that through the various activities organized by the NGOs that the public will become more aware of and accepting of disabled persons in the community, to mix freely without facing any fear or prejudice.

2. Legislation

In 1987, the Government of Brunei Darussalam issued a circular, Number 26/1987, through the Public Works Department of the Ministry of Development, that all necessary facilities for persons with disabilities are to be incorporated in the design of present and future public buildings. These facilities include public walkways, signboards, signs and signals, parking facilities, ramps, zebra crossings, entry doors, handles, handrail for steps and stairs, escalators, lifts, reception counters, telephones and toilets.

A legislation to safeguard the rights of disabled persons, protect them from exploitation and to ensure that they receive equal pay is currently being drafted.

3. Welfare assistance for people with disabilities

The first welfare assistance was given to disabled persons by the Department of Welfare, Youths and Sports in 1967, where scholarship grant were extended to seven blind persons for training in established schools for blind persons in Singapore and Malaysia. The trainees were taught Braille reading and typing, mobility, and basket making. One trainee underwent further specialized training to becomes a telephone operator. All the trainees were successful in their undertakings and when they returned to Brunei Darussalam, they were employed by the government according to their skills and training.

In 1975, the department organized its first special education for blind persons in Brunei Darussalam. More blind people became interested in the training and enrolment increased. The training centre eventually expanded and moved into larger premises. More volunteers and teachers were recruited to run the training courses. The curriculum consisted orientation and mobility, household activities, which is also known as skills of daily living, Braille reading and typing, the Malay and English languages, fundamental teachings of Islam, mathematics and music.

Four years later in 1979, the disability programme was expanded to include children and youths who are deaf and intellectually disabled, all paraplegics and recovered patients who still need continuous rehabilitation.

In 1983, more children, from all over the country, enrolled in this special education programme. The training centre was further expanded to accommodate all the trainees. Then in 1997, the Ministry of Education declared that disabled children would be integrated into regular schools if their paediatricians deemed it suitable.

B. Progress made in the first half of the Asian and Pacific Decade of Disabled Persons

1. Education

A special education programme for disabled children was initiated by volunteers from the Department of Welfare, Youths and Sports and the hospital staff from the Ministry of Health. The aim was to provide special classes for the children, to stimulate their mental, emotional and social functioning, and help them adjust to and eventually become accustomed to the activities and behaviour of other children and the community. They were also taught activities that meet their needs, and basics on health care and hygiene. These classes were conducted four times a week.

Another new development was the restructuring of the educational curriculum for disabled persons. Previously, all students with disabilities were placed together in one class, irrespective of their disability and individual needs. However this was later restructured to help meet the individual needs of the trainees.

The Ministry of Education and the Ministry of Welfare Youths and Sports allocate three specially-trained teachers to assist in the restructuring of the training curriculum, implement the new teaching method at the training centre as well as teach the students. Skilled and knowledgeable trainers and instructors from abroad are also recruited to provide additional manpower support and help. As disabled children are now accepted in regular school, a new special education programme is being drafted and this is especially for disabled children who are unable to attend regular schools.

2. Rehabilitation services

The Government of Brunei Darussalam feels that people with disabilities have the full potential, if developed, to contribute to and become productive members of society. To achieve this goal, the Ministry of Welfare, Youths and Sports initiated a development rehabilitation programme, which caters to blind persons, deaf persons, intellectually disabled persons, paraplegics and other physically disabled persons as well as those whose disabilities still require rehabilitation and training.

The Ministry of Health through its Occupational Therapy Section teaches paraplegic persons and recovered patients to be self-reliant and it provides job training according to the extent of their disability. The trainees are encouraged to strive towards improving their living conditions, become confident and lead normal lives in society.

The rehabilitation facility of the Ministry of Welfare, Youths and Sport is at Kampong Pulaie Centre. The basic thrust of this rehabilitation programme is to provide training services enabling disabled persons to become economic assets to themselves, their families and the country. Such skills also enable them to assume greater responsibilities in the community. Currently the centre conducts four major rehabilitation programmes: basic orientation training; vocational training; special academic training and selective employment training programmes.

(a) The basic training programme aims to provide orientation on mobility, general cleanliness and skills for daily living activities so that the disabled persons will be able to share the responsibilities at home without requiring much assistance.

(b) The vocational training programme aims to provide skills development through youth and adult vocational skills training courses, and prepare them for gainful employment. Much help and guidance are given to help the trainees select the courses that best suit their needs and abilities. Currently, training is provided to those who are 18 years and older. The vocational training courses offered include basket making, loom weaving, knitting and crochets for women, and carpentry, wood-work, furniture repair and agricultural training for men. Trainees interested in motors and electronics are enrolled in technical schools run by the Ministry of Education.

(c) The academic training programme provides the academic studies and special education catering to their individual needs. Blind persons are taught Braille reading and typing, English and Malay languages, arithmetic and Islamic studies. Deaf persons are taught sign language and lip reading. Intellectually disabled children are separated from the others and given specialized activities to suit their interests, needs and abilities.

(d) The selective employment programme aims to provide services that will enable disabled persons to find suitable jobs. It also assists those who want to start their own businesses, work at home or in sheltered workshops.

3. Training and employment

In Brunei Darussalam, disabled government employees also receive the same salaries as their counterparts. Since 1983, three trainees have been working at Public Works Department's Furniture Section while two are involved in small-scale business activities such as basket making. A few disabled persons are also working as receptionists and telephone operators at the Ministry of Health.

With recommendations from the Ministry of Welfare, Youths and Sports, one former trainee now running his own business, supplies waste paper baskets to several government departments. Another former trainee now runs a small grocery shop.

On certain occasions, the products made by people with disabilities are put on display especially during public festivities. They are also invited to display their finished products for public viewing and this in turn will encourage the public to buy the products.

A monthly allowance is given to each trainee enrolled in the training courses. The allowance, which is given after the trainee has completed a three-month probation, is adjusted according to the category or grade attained by the trainee. The minimum monthly allowance is B$40 and the maximum is B$180. An incentive of B$240 is extended to trainees who consistently obtain high grades in all their subjects.

Brunei Darussalam offers overseas training scholarship if the courses are not offered in the country. For example two blind trainees were sent overseas for their agricultural studies.

The allowance paid per month are graded according to their grade-alphabet category and duration of study:

Grade/month	Category	Duration of study	Allowance (B$)/month
Probation period	E	3 months	None
Beginner	D	3-6 months	40
Elementary	C	8-12 months	72
Intermediate	D	8-12 months	120
Advanced	A	8-12 months	180
Incentive	High Grade		240

For disabled children and youths, the classroom method of grouping is preferred compared to open workshop teaching. The disabled students are also taught extra-mural activities, brought to places of historical interests, and encouraged to watch documentaries and experience the excitement and joys of excursion and picnics.

4. Supportive therapy

Supportive therapy is extended to the parents or families of the disabled trainees. Social workers would help families with disabled children better understand the conditions of their child. This emotional, moral, social and educational support shared with the families helps alleviate unwarranted fears and anxieties that parents may have toward the child. Through supportive counselling, parents are able to acquire more positive attitudes and feelings which facilitate their acceptance and understanding of the child's condition. The social worker also helps the disabled family members enrol into the various rehabilitation programmes and services available. Counselling is either done by staff from the Ministry of Health or the Ministry of Welfare, Youths and Sports, wherever applicable.

5. Sports programme

Apart from looking after the sports programme and activities of the general public, the Ministry of Welfare Youths and Sports also runs activities and programmes for persons with disabilities in Brunei Darussalam. The Ministry of Health, through voluntary services by staff member, also plays an important role in the promotion of sports for disabled persons.

Brunei Darussalam's first disabled sport team participated in the Fourth FESPIC Games in Surakarta Indonesia in 1986 as well as other important sporting events.

Medal tally of Brunei's disabled participants in the following sports events from 1986-1992

Year	Gold	Silver	Bronze	Place/country
1986	–	2	–	The 4th FESPIC Games in Surakarta, Indonesia
1987	2	–	–	The 23rd National Sports Games for the Disabled, Okinawa, Japan
1989	–	3	2	The 5th FESPIC Games, Kobe, Japan
1990	3	6	3	Sport Games for the Disabled, Melakah, Malaysia
1992	6	2	–	The 28th National Sports Games for the Disabled in Yamagata, Japan (18-19 October)
1994	–	4	2	FESPIC Games, Beijing, China
1996	6	4	2	Sukan Orang-Orang Tidak Berupaya, Kuching, Malaysia
Total	**17**	**21**	**9**	

6. Public awareness

The general public of Brunei Darussalam are now more accepting people with disabilities. This change in attitude is because of various awareness campaigns through the mass media such as radio, television and newspapers, pamphlets, workshop seminars and religious talks carried out by the government and NGOs. As both bodies are under the royal patronage, any programmes or activities conducted do receive greater publicity and are given higher profile.

Parental participation in the training of a disabled person is of utmost importance especially where trainers are in short supply. A family support system, including a group of caregivers such as therapists, volunteers and parents themselves is being formed to provide emotional support.

C. Activities planned for the second half of the Asian and Pacific Decade of Disabled Persons

Brunei Darussalam hopes to set up more facilities or centres to better deliver rehabilitation services straight to those who need them. In this way any help, activities or programmes are more accessible to disabled persons. Community outreach will be made easier. It would also be easier to mobilize and recruit volunteers for the centres.

With close cooperation among the three ministries and the two NGOs, Brunei Darussalam hopes to better address and meet the needs of disabled persons, enabling them to integrate into the community and become assets to themselves, their families and the country.

CHAPTER IV

Cambodia

A. National overview

The Ministry of Social Affairs, Labour and Veterans Affairs (MSALVA)[1] of Cambodia is preparing a document on the progress it has made in implementing the Agenda for Action for the Asia and Pacific Decade of Disabled Persons, 1993-2002. Cambodia has been trying to fulfil its commitment to achieve the aims of the Decade.

With large numbers of people with disabilities in the country, both the Government of Cambodia and non-government organizations (NGOs) share a strong interest in enhancing their social welfare. In Cambodia, it is estimated that there are 120,000 people with disabilities, or close to 1.4 per cent of the total population. Although much work was done to enhance the social welfare of people with disabilities, many obstacles remain and these have to be tackled before the country could achieve the desired results.

B. Progress made in the first half of the Asian and Pacific Decade of Disabled Persons

1. National coordination

Cambodia has made concerted efforts to improve rehabilitation and welfare services for people with disabilities and to effectively and efficiently implement the Agenda for Action. This is especially so over the past year. Several sectoral groups covering all levels of involvement in disability issues were set up to coordinate the concerned NGOs and to coordinate and collaborate with the MSALVA.

A task force was set up, comprising representatives of the sectoral groups from all rehabilitation services, people with disabilities and government personnel. The task force is a consultative grouping which provides ample opportunities for all interested and potentially affected groups to contribute to the development of a national strategy on rehabilitation and disability issues.

---

[1] Current name is the Ministry of Social Affairs, Labour, Vocational Training and Youth Rehabilitation (MOSALVY).

The task force's four subcommittees meet regularly, and develop their programmes according to guidelines developed by the coordinator. Once a month, from September 1995 to September 1996, the members met to review the progress of each group, discuss the issues raised and kept everyone mutually informed and updated.

The process covers essentially six steps:

(a) Formation of the task force;

(b) Assessment of the current situations through distributing a general questionnaire, a questionnaire on training and making site visits;

(c) Drafting the guiding principles;

(d) Analysis of the information gathered and identification of the main issues;

(e) Prioritization of the main issues;

(f) Development of recommendations and action plans to address each of the main issues.

The recommendations from the task force are intended to guide the NGOs and the MSALVA to continue their efforts to coordinate, improve upon and expand the programmes and activities for and with Cambodian people with disabilities. The recommendations are complemented with a few action plans. After the task force has accomplished its mission, a new coordinating body, the disability action committee (DAC) will be formed to monitor and implement the recommendations and action plans.

2. Legislation

During the first half of the Decade, several regulations relating to the social welfare of people with disabilities have been issued. The first is an act that permits people with disabilities to receive medical and vocational rehabilitation services, training and employment. The second is a directive to implement the first regulation.

Within the task force, a small working group has been focusing on legislation related to issues on people with disabilities. It is hoped that the work of this group will eventually result in the passing of legislation supporting and protecting the rights of people with disabilities. It is hoped that during the Decade, a basic law for disabled persons could be enacted.

3. Information

Nationwide statistics are not available. However, a survey conducted by the Rehabilitation Department from the MSALVA, in cooperation with NGOs in several provinces, shows that the number of people with disabilities accounts for an estimated 120,000 people, or close to 1.4 per cent of the total population of Cambodia. Several directories on rehabilitation services for people with disabilities are available, although none is complete. With 90 per cent of Cambodians living in rural areas, most do not have access to these directories.

Work to develop and enhance the database on disabilities has been on-going especially in the Department of Rehabilitation and several NGOs. A National Resource Centre, within the National Centre of Disabled People (NCDP) has recently been established and is expected to provide resources and information to those interested in disability issues.

4. Information and public awareness

It is absolutely necessary for Cambodia to develop a public awareness programme to educate and change public misconceptions about people with disabilities. Educating influential groups such as teachers, monks, healthcare workers, government institutions and NGOs are also helping to change the people's attitudes.

Awareness campaign activities such as the celebration of the National Day of Handicapped Sports, with contests and games in which all the participants are disabled, have been very successful. Every year the level of participation doubles, and it is becoming a regular and popular cultural event that focuses public attention on people with disabilities, as active and equal citizens. The participants themselves enjoy psychological as well as physical benefits from such sports days and other similar activities.

Public awareness is enhanced through periodical press releases, the printed media as well as radio and television broadcast on the services available and the rehabilitation of disabled persons.

5. Accessibility and communication

In Cambodia, the issues of accessibility, communication and other regular supporting facilities are not being adequately addressed by the public and the community. The tremendous problems include the lack of awareness in the public and private sectors and of strong legislative support. Many changes must be made to rectify the situation of Cambodia. One main concern is the lack of security. Some areas are simply inaccessible and too dangerous.

Other changes required involve the overall development of the country such as widespread basic health services, power stations, water systems, roads and other facilities and services.

Except for the production of wheelchairs, no other action has been taken to improve accessibility for people who are mobility-impaired. The same void exists with regards to communication systems for deaf people, for whom there is no widely used sign language and no sign language interpreters. The Cambodian Disabled People's Organization is currently working on developing a programme to address these issues. There is only one blind school in Phnom Penh, run by a local NGO called Kruasa Thmey Organization, where Braille is taught. It also conducts a small centre-based programme for young blind students. However, no services are available for people with intellectual disabilities.

At the end of the Decade, there will be a vast improvement in accessibility and communication, where awareness campaigns will create a deeper understanding among the various government departments, especially institutions which have the authority to determine regulations on accessibility, including accessibility for public buildings, roads and transportation as well as the people and community.

6. Education

The DAC, together with the MSALVA and NGOs, have been trying to promote the integration of children with disabilities in public schools. While there is no law restricting their enrolment, children with disabilities often do not go to schools for the very same reasons as other children. These include poverty, inaccessibility of schools, fear of being treated badly by other children, and that they are needed at home to help supplement family income.

7. Training and employment

The MSALVA, in accordance with part of the previous 1987 national rehabilitation programme, works jointly with the NGOs and international organizations to establish 11 vocational training centres in the country. In future, one such vocational training centre will be set up in each province in Cambodia. There are three main components of these vocational training centres:

(a) Pre-training activities

This includes vocational assessment, guidance, student selection and preparatory courses. Vocational assessment or guidance is meant to help potential students choose to learn the most advantageous skill. Student selection is the central process of choosing the best possible students among the applicants. Potential students need to discuss their situations with the counsellors, social workers or other knowledgeable persons to determine their needs to learn the skill. They must also assess the potential of successfully using one skill versus another, given the particularities of the local labour market, and the potential impact of the student being away from his/her normal environment for an extended period of time. These training centres need students who can follow through and complete the courses. They also need to enrol a certain number of students per semester to make it viable for them, in terms of usage of equipment and trainer and supporting staff strengths, to continue conducting the courses.

(b) Skills training

This usually consists of some classroom-style courses, including theoretical topics, followed by or concurrent with, a longer period of supervised hands-on practical experience in a workshop located on the premises of the centre. Often, these workshops are operated as actual businesses, both to give students practical experience in business management and to generate revenue for the centres.

(c) Post-training follow-up

The majority of disabled graduates need some follow-up action upon completion of their training courses. Activities to assist the graduates in making the transition from the classroom to the workplace are absolutely essential to achieve the ultimate goal of skills training, which is to increase their self-esteem and for them to be financially independent and enjoy an improved quality of life.

Ever since the MSALVA started its vocational rehabilitation programmes in collaboration with the NGOs and international organizations, some 2,161 students with disabilities have been trained and over 1,400 who have graduated have found paid jobs or started small self-employed businesses in their villages.

However, the projects can only meet a small percentage of needs. Job placement cannot be completely guaranteed after the training, partly because there are no specific incentives or quota systems to encourage employers to hire people with disabilities, and currently the labour market in Cambodia remains unfavourable.

8. Prevention of the causes of disability

Mines are a primary cause of disability in Cambodia. It is estimated that there are more than 20,000 people with limb amputations, and 250-300 new amputations per month are performed.

One method to prevent this type of disability is through the mines awareness campaigns. Mines awareness is taught throughout the country and particularly in provinces that are at high risk. Anti-personnel mines in the ground must be removed and the laying of new ones stopped.

Polio creates as many cases of disabilities as mines. The high incidence of polio is the result of a prolonged period of conflict and the breakdown of infrastructure, healthcare and immunization services in Cambodia. A recent nationwide immunization programme is underway, where some 1.7 million children under the age of five have been immunized.

Leprosy is another disabling disease prevalent in Cambodia. The International Federation of Leprosy Association through an NGO, funds a National Leprosy Control Programme implemented by the Ministry of Health and the National Centre of Dermatology and Leprosy.

Eye problems are also a cause of disability. In Cambodia there are only four specialist centres for eyecare; three are in Phnom Penh and the fourth is in Battambang. People in the rural provinces, therefore, do not receive treatment for very simple eye problems such as cataract, trachoma and conjunctivitis, resulting in thousands of cases of blindness which could have been prevented. Children become blind through lack of Vitamin A and measles.

During the Decade, much effort has gone into developing programmes on the prevention of disabilities due to accidents, diseases and malnutrition, especially through job safety procedures, immunization, better medical treatment, improved nutrition, distribution of Vitamin A capsules and vaccination campaigns for children under five.

9. Rehabilitation services

Basically, rehabilitation services are executed through two systems, institutional service and non-institutional service.

The institutional system is provided at the rehabilitation centres, where people with disabilities are given social, vocational and limited medical rehabilitation. Food and accommodation are also provided at the centres. In Cambodia there are several rehabilitation centres, where prosthetics, orthotics, wheelchairs, and other adaptive equipment are produced. There is also a school of physiotherapy, which has 91 graduates to date. These physiotherapists are based in provincial hospitals, rehabilitation centres and are part of the national health system.

Non-institutional system of rehabilitation is provided through several activities such as community workshops at the village level, productive cooperation groups, and especially community-based rehabilitation (CBR). Community-based services are opening up in many provinces. Some are outreach services to follow-up on people with disabilities who have been through the centres. Some are truly CBR services, in that they focus on one geographically limited area and attempt to lead the community in developing local solutions to the problems that people with disabilities face. Some are somewhere in between where trained rehabilitation agents would go from house to house, offering counselling, referrals to other services, and direct assistance for basic therapeutic needs and for income generation.

10. Assistive devices

There is an orthopaedic component factory, a national school for prosthetics and orthotists, and 15 workshops that produce and repair assistive devices in Cambodia. Three prosthetic workshops are in Phnom Penh and 12 are in the provinces. Only three workshops provide orthotics for disabled persons and all but four use the same technology. Three different technologies have been used, polypropylene technology, aluminium technology, and leather with combination of wood technology.

The technological capability for producing assistive devices in Cambodia is very good, but there are two main difficulties in this area: one is coordinating and standardizing the work of NGOs; and the second is following-up on the prosthetics and orthotics users over time. Travelling from the countryside to a town costs money. Being away from agricultural activities for several days is difficult for people living on a subsistence level, and so far, there are few follow-up services which reach people with disabilities in their rural homes.

In the first half of the Decade, much effort has been made to fulfil the needs for assistive devices. By now, the production of assistive devices is just able to meet around 25 per cent of the need. By the end of the Decade, it is hoped that this capacity will be increased by 40 per cent.

11. Self-help organizations

The Cambodian Disabled People's Organization (CDPO) was formed in September 1994. It is an important voice for Cambodian people with disabilities and represents most groups that are involved with disability issues. CDPO is a self-help, self-representation, cross-disability organization.

Its mission statement reads: "CDPO is an organization of people with disabilities so as to support, protect, serve and promote their rights, achievements and interests, in order to bring about their fuller participation and equality in Cambodian society".

The National Centre of Disabled People was established in 1996. This is a resource centre, a place for training, for information collection, for holding meetings, and a retail outlet for the products made by people with disabilities. It is anticipated that an employment service for people with disabilities will be established in the near future with the cooperation of MSALVA.

12. Regional cooperation

National cooperation between government, NGOs and international organizations related to the rehabilitation services for people with disabilities has been very satisfactory. It is important that this be maintained and further developed.

Cambodia has the capacity to enhance regional cooperation with more commitment and enthusiasm than ever before, and the country has actively participated in several regional activities. In the first half of the Decade, the government and NGOs of Cambodia have actively participated in every major related event, meeting, conference, sports event, festival and exchange of information in the region. These include those organized by ESCAP, Rehabilitation International and Disabled Peoples' International.

C. Activities planned for the second half of the Asian and Pacific Decade of Disabled Persons

During the first half of the Decade, much has been achieved in often very difficult circumstances, but there is still a vast amount of work to be done. Cambodia will certainly need more than the next five years to meet the objectives of the Agenda for Action.

What has been achieved are the most important components. It is expected that not only the government, but also the NGOs will have increased capabilities in developing the basic goals to provide equalization of opportunities and social integration of all people with disabilities in Cambodia.

Both the government and people of Cambodia are striving to develop a just and equal society. This will be achieved by treating people with disabilities with dignity, and supporting their rights to equal opportunities within the community. The result will be growth in national pride and enhancement in the quality of life for all Cambodians.

CHAPTER V

China

A. National overview

People with disabilities are entitled to equal rights in political, economic, cultural and social life. However, due to their own disabilities and other external obstacles, many are still disadvantaged and play marginal roles in society.

In China, the liberation of people with disabilities is just as important as the national liberation and women's liberation movements. It has emerged as a pressing task for the government and the international community.

During the United Nations Decade of Disabled Persons, 1983-1992, the situation of disabled persons in many countries has improved, though as varying extents in different parts of the country. However, the goals of equality, participation and sharing are far from being fully achieved.

In the Asian and Pacific region, governments, disabled persons and their related organizations went further to recognize the rights of people with disabilities. They are clearly aware that a dynamic economy and relative political stability are prerequisites for social development, including the development of disabled persons. The prosperity and stability should be reflected in the efforts devoted to people with disabilities.

The Government of China proposed a regional decade of disabled persons after the United Nations Decade. Regional governments, disabled persons and their organizations, thus adopted and declared the period 1993 to 2002, as the Asian and Pacific Decade of Disabled Persons. An Agenda for Action for the Asian and Pacific Decade of Disabled Persons, was also adopted to set the goals for the Decade.

B. Progress made in the first half of the Asian and Pacific Decade of Disabled Persons

1. National coordination

China is a developing country and is undergoing rapid economic development and much social transition. The country has adopted an overall development policy in its work for people with disabilities. The government takes the lead in this initiative and society offers its support with the full participation of disabled persons. This policy has proven to be sound and effective.

The State Council Coordination Committee on Disability was set up in September 1993. A state councillor heads it and its members include leaders from 34 government ministries and commissions and other civil groups. It plays a very important role in planning, coordinating and implementing the policies and programmes for people with disabilities.

After having successfully implemented the work programme for disabled persons during the Eighth Five-year Plan period, the work programme for disabled persons during the Ninth Five-year Plan period was formulated. In the past five years, the following have been achieved:

(a) About 2.25 million disabled persons have been rehabilitated through key projects;

(b) Immunization campaigns for the prevention of polio have been conducted;

(c) More than 97 million women of childbearing age, pregnant women and new-born babies have been given iodine capsules to prevent intellectual disability;

(d) Enrolment rates of disabled children have risen from less than 20 per cent to 62.5 per cent;

(e) Employment rates for disabled persons have risen from less than 50 per cent to 70 per cent;

(f) Accessible facilities are being set up;

(g) Six million people with disabilities are living in improved conditions;

(h) Cultural and sports activities for disabled people have become more colourful.

2. Legislation

In China, the basic legislation framework on the protection of the rights and interests of people with disabilities is already in place in the form of the Law of the People's Republic of China on the Protection of the Disabled Persons. In addition, by-laws have also been formulated and implemented in all provinces, autonomous regions and municipalities.

In 1993, the State Council issued and enacted the Regulations on the Education of People with Disabilities. The National People's Congress reviews the laws every four years. The Ministry of Justice and legal service institutions also provide legal services to further safeguard the rights and interest of disabled persons.

3. Public awareness

Society has become more understanding, respectful and caring of people with disabilities. With higher self-respect, self-confidence, they become more aware of self-improvement and are more self-reliant. Disabled persons are participating more actively and are contributing to society.

4. Education

Special education for disabled children is incorporated into the local compulsory education programmes. Integrated education will become common practice. Special education classes are established at the township level and more are being set up in counties with more than 300,000 people and with many disabled children. A special education network provides integrated education.

Visually-, hearing-, and mild and moderately intellectually-disabled students also receive special education. As such, the enrolment rate of disabled students is almost on par with that of non-disabled students. The enrolment rate of students with visual, hearing and intellectual disability is expected to reach 80 per cent and above. The pre-school education of disabled students is also developing well. Employable disabled persons also receive vocational training. China is currently running high school and college education for disabled students on a trial basis.

5. Regional cooperation

In the first half of the Decade, the Government of China has fulfilled its promises and supported many activities of the Decade. They include the following:

(a) The China Disabled Persons' Performing Art Troupe paid visits to Australia, Indonesia, Malaysia, New Zealand, the Philippines, Republic of Korea, Singapore and Thailand, and its performances have helped raise awareness of the rights of people with disabilities;

(b) It hosted the Sixth Far East and South Pacific (FESPIC) Games for Disabled Persons in 1994;

(c) Representatives from China participated in the Meeting to Review the Progress of the Asian and Pacific Decade of Disabled Persons, 1993-2002, held in Bangkok in 1995 and also played an active role;

(d) It provided financial assistance to the ESCAP secretariat in printing Decade documents;

(e) It cooperated with the Governments of India and Malaysia and the ESCAP secretariat, and successfully carried out intergovernmental cooperation projects which promoted multisectoral collaboration on disability;

(f) China, in close cooperation with ESCAP, has been conducting a pilot project on the promotion of non-handicapping environments for disabled persons.

C. Activities planned for the second half of the Asian and Pacific Decade of Disabled Persons

China has the largest disabled population and the development of services for people with disabilities still lags behind its economic and social development. Many disabled persons still live in poverty and face difficulties. In the process of reform and modernization, China will carry out its promises to safeguard the human rights of disabled persons and to improve their living conditions by implementing the goals of the Agenda for Action for the Asian and Pacific Decade of Disabled Persons and the United Nations Standard Rules on Equalization of Opportunities for Persons with Disabilities.

1. Legislation

In the second half of the Decade, the country plans the following:

(a) Draft the Regulations on the Employment of Persons with Disabilities;

(b) In compliance with the Law of the People's Republic of China on the Protection Disabled Persons, provinces, autonomous regions and municipalities will implement by-laws of the Regulations on the Education of Persons with Disabilities, and Regulations on the Employment of Persons with Disabilities;

(c) The cities, countries and towns will draft regulations to assist disabled persons;

(d) A complete legal system for the protection of the rights of disabled persons will be formulated.

To raise public awareness of legislation, China will step up publicity and education on the Law on the Protection of Disabled Persons. Disabled persons are also gradually becoming more aware of the laws protecting their rights. The country also provides legal services to disabled persons in the urban and rural areas. More legal assistance organizations for disabled persons will be established.

2. Rehabilitation services

In the second half of the Decade, China plans to form a comprehensive social rehabilitation services system, based on the community and family, so that disabled persons can benefit. It also plans to implement key projects so that more than 3 million disabled persons can receive the following services:

(a) 1.2 million will receive sight-restoring cataract surgery;

(b) 50,000 will receive orthopaedic operations;

(c) 300,000 will be fitted with artificial limbs and orthopaedic devices;

(d) 40,000 low-vision persons will receive vision aids;

(e) 60,000 deaf children will receive hearing and speech training;

(f) 60,000 intellectually disabled children will receive training;

(g) 100,000 physically disabled persons will receive systematic training;

(h) 1.2 million mentally ill persons will receive comprehensive treatment.

There are also plans to develop 2.4 million pieces of 100 types of user-friendly assistive devices. These are urgently needed for the self-reliance, information, functional training, education, employment and recreation of disabled persons.

3. Education

In China, there are plans to develop double-spelling Chinese Braille and Chinese sign language will be popularized.

4. Training and employment

The employment services network for disabled persons will be completed and the quota scheme for the hiring of people with disabilities will be implemented. The care-giving system will be strengthened. Disabled persons are also encouraged to start their own business and rural production. The employment rate of disabled persons is aimed at 80 per cent.

More poverty alleviation loans will be given to help disabled persons find jobs. This will help resolve the basic living problems of 15 million poverty-stricken disabled persons. Special relief assistance will be provided in urban and rural areas to guarantee the basic living for three million disabled persons in abject poverty. Activities assisting persons with disabilities will be implemented by individual work units.

5. Information

In China, all channels, including public education, press and publication organizations, will publicize disability concerns and contribute towards creating a good social environment. Television programmes with sign language will be broadcast in all medium-sized cities. Radio services at the county and district levels will also broadcast the various issues and concerns on disability.

The National Day of Assisting Disabled Persons will be observed more effectively. Voluntary services to assist people with disabilities, including programmes such as Young Pioneers Assisting Disabled People and Young Volunteers, will be better organized. Outstanding individuals and units involved in providing services to and assisting disabled persons will be recognized and rewarded.

Publicity promotion committees for disability will be mobilized at all levels to seek and recognize role models in self-reliance and progress. To encourage greater publicity, a scheme called prizes for good news on disability, is being planned.

6. Accessibility

China will implement fully the design code of urban road and public building for accessibility for disabled people. It will enforce the regulations in its capital construction projects and make sure that the stipulated facilities are available. It will also widely publicize and promote accessible facilities.

7. Prevention of the causes of disability

The Government of China will coordinate and work towards improving the current disability prevention system. Statutory agencies and civic groups will also work with each other and coordinate their efforts on this issue. The aim is to gradually form a sound and well-managed disability prevention system that provides accurate information and effective monitoring and uses scientific methodology in tackling the issues.

China will run and implement key projects by 2000 to help eradicate the most prevalent causes of disability. These include:

(a) Providing pre-natal and post-natal care should be provided to decrease congenital disability by one-third;

(b) Increase immunization to ensure that up to 90 per cent of the population is immunized to help minimize polio;

(c) To substantially reduce disabilities caused by malnutrition and cerebral diseases;

(d) Strengthen the management of ear-affected medical problems to reduce occurrence rates by one-third;

(e) Control the problem of iodine deficiency to help eradicate iodine-deficiency disability;

(f) Reduce work and road accidents to a minimized rate to cut down the occurrence of disability caused by such incidents.

8. Regional cooperation

China will continue to assume its international responsibilities and duties in line with its own national development, and actively support and participate in the activities of the Decade. It will work towards enhancing China-India cooperation on assistive devices by inviting leading Indian experts to visit China and hosting a Sino-India seminar on multisectoral collaborative action on disability in Beijing in 1998, at mutually convenient dates in the near future.

China will continue to support regional and subregional cooperation in the second half of the Decade. It will continue to attach great importance to disability issues and will make further efforts to contribute to disability causes. It will also strengthen the framework to achieve the goals of the Agenda for Action for the Asian and Pacific Decade of Disabled Persons.

It will continue to work towards equalization to help people with disabilities be on a par, in terms of national, economic and social development, with their non-disabled counterparts. China aims to achieve the goals of "equality, participation and sharing" to enable people with disabilities to aid social progress and contribute to society.

CHAPTER VI

Fiji

A. National overview

The development of services for disabled persons in Fiji began in the mid sixties through the efforts of the pioneering organizations that were providing some services then, namely the Fiji Crippled Children Society, the Fiji Society for the Blind and the Fiji Red Cross Society.

Momentum started to build up in the seventies and the need to diversify into vocational training programmes became apparent as there was the need to train teachers to meet the educational demands of the country's disabled children. This was organized through the Ministry of Education.

However, the services and the established vocational training programmes were reviewed in the late eighties and found to be inadequate because they favoured those in the bigger urban centres but were inaccessible for the rural disabled population. The need to identify ways and areas of improving these services was inevitable.

The declaration by the United Nations General Assembly of the year 1981 as the International Year of Disabled Persons greatly assisted the attempts to reorganize disability development for Fiji, more so with the focus on the establishment of a central authority with powers under legislation to spearhead this development. The failures of the past had been identified.

The responsibility to organize and implement the much-needed changes fell to the Department of Social Welfare. Through the guidance of the department, a subcommittee was appointed in 1989, comprising government, disability non-governmental organizations (NGOs) and disabled persons. It recommended the establishment of a central authority to meet the needs of disabled persons and disability development in the country.

Through the Ministry of Women, Culture and Social Welfare the Cabinet in September 1992, approved the establishment of the Fiji National Council for Disabled Persons (FNCDP) as the central authority and the national coordinating body for disability development in Fiji.

It could therefore be said that Fiji was already moving in the right direction in establishing its national coordinating mechanism. The meetings held in Beijing in April and in December 1992 merely reinforced the development that was already taking place. The Proclamation on the Full Participation and Equality of People with Disabilities in the Asian and Pacific Region adopted in Beijing therefore became the framework and the springboard Fiji needed to carry out its commitment to disability development, in a planned and comprehensive manner. Fiji therefore became a signatory of that proclamation in July 1993.

Since then, the country has developed its infrastructure and has been a willing co-sponsor of the above instrument by using the Agenda for Action as its guiding document.

B. Progress made in the first half of the Asian and Pacific Decade of Disabled Persons

1. National coordination

Although it was formally established in September 1991, the FNCDP was not fully operational until mid-1993 with a budgetary grant from the Department of Social Welfare. This grant continued to be provided until 1996, when the Ministry of Health and Social Welfare took over.

The FNCDP comprises members from the government ministries and departments that have direct input into disability development and the NGOs that are providing services for disabled persons.

Under the FNCDP Act, Advisory Committees have been formed, whose members are appointed by the Minister for Health and Social Welfare to advise and make recommendations either for research, implementation of policies or legislative amendments within the individual policy categories of the Agenda for Action, relevant to Fiji.

(a) Enactment of the FNCDP Act of December 1994;

(b) Formation of eight district disability committees;

(c) Registration of 24 disability organizations under the FNCDP;

(d) Inclusion of the FNCDP requirements into the Fiji Population Census in 1996;

(e) Strengthening of the rights and treatment of disabled persons under Fiji's Amendment Constitution Act of July 1997; the FNCDP contributed to this process through a submission to the Constitution Review Commission in 1996; the FNCDP is also drafting plans to build its headquarters which will also house some NGOs.

2. Legislation

The most important legal work now is the review of Fiji's National Building Code. The FNCDP Advisory Committee is preparing its submission to the Ministry of Urban Development and Housing on the need to provide accessibility to Fiji's disabled population. A significant development was the submission made by the FNCDP to the Constitution Review Commission in 1996.

Fiji has just enacted its much-awaited Constitution of 1997. This contains amended clauses and provisions to benefit the disabled population of Fiji. It is expected to greatly enhance disability development especially in the areas where discriminatory provisions existed previously. It will form the basis from where more positive provisions could emerge.

3. Health

The Ministry of Health and related NGOs currently provide the various services aimed at meeting the health needs of people with disabilities. The Ministry also provides the facilities for institutional-based rehabilitation services in Suva.

Most of the equipment required for daily living is imported and this is expected to be so in future. However, attempts were made recently to start the production of wheelchairs in Fiji. Project discussions are on-going between Fiji's related NGOs, and New Zealand and Australian producers.

In August 1997, the FNCDP will meet with an Australian organization to discuss the production of assistive devices, with the aim of extending the services of the O&P Laboratory based in the capital, to the western and northern divisions of the country.

A national workshop on community-based rehabilitation (CBR) involving the Ministry of Health, NGOs and the FNCDP is being planned for October 1997. This will be the forerunner to many such collaborative programmes in the future.

It is still somewhat difficult to gauge the level of success for these three areas:

(a) Prevention of the causes of disabilities;

(b) Production of assistive devices;

(c) Formulation of a National Plan for community-based programmes.

However, there are positive indications that more dialogue and cooperation will take place between the Ministry and the FNCDP in the second half of the Decade on these key areas.

4. Education

The FNCDP, in pursuance of the work of its Advisory Committee on Education, continues the uphill task of convincing the Ministry of Education of the need for more positive changes in the education of disabled children in the country. These include the following:

(a) Develop a clear policy on education of disabled persons, including integration into the mainstream education system;

(b) Provide qualified special education teachers;

(c) Provide remedial teachers and the admission of disabled children into the secondary education system;

(d) Provide proper curriculum for vocational training;

(e) Provide Braille facilities for visually-impaired children;

(f) Establish a separate unit with resources to look after special education;

(g) Provide scholarships for teachers and disabled students for further training and higher education.

The FNCDP will continue its dialogue with Ministry of Education with the keen hope of achieving more positive results during the second half of the Decade.

However, the country did achieve some success in education with the introduction of the caregivers certificate course at the University of the South Pacific and with FNCDP's participation at the Careers Exposition in Suva in 1996 and 1997.

5. Information and public awareness

Public education through the wide dissemination of disability information has continued to be the responsibility of individual disability organizations, each focusing on its own area of specialization.

A national disabled persons' association runs an aggressive advocacy programme, taking advantage of the tremendous support from the Fiji media such as radio, television and newspapers.

The FNCDP has been organizing disabled persons' participation in the various national celebrations since 1995, however, it is the active involvement of the disabled people themselves, working through their respective NGOs in awareness raising, fund-raising and sports programmes, that has led to wider public awareness on their needs and aspirations.

The celebration of the International Day of Disabled Persons, for the first time in 1996, was a resounding success. The day was celebrated in eight main centres, organized by the FNCDP's district disability committees.

6. Training and employment

For training and employment, FNCDP's work is supported by the appointment of an Advisory Committee, whose members comprise experts in human resource development. The involvement of the Ministry of Labour, the Fiji Institute of Technology and the Fiji National Training Council in this Advisory Committee was initially very encouraging.

However, progress has been slow and very little has been achieved. The absence of qualified personnel and an established curriculum by the Ministry of Education, has been one of the main reasons for the failure of vocational training for disabled persons. As a result, the system has not been providing young disabled people with the basic knowledge and skills to become more employable nor are they in a position to organize their own work or be self-employed. However, it is refreshing to note that through the pre-vocational training in a few of the "special schools", they have been able to produce some arts and crafts, toys and furniture which they have sold to keep these programmes running.

The FNCDP is reviewing the current situation and is hopeful that during the second half of the Decade, a breakthrough will take place which would lead to the establishment of a national training institution and programme to undertake vocational training for persons with disabilities into 2000 and beyond.

7. Accessibility

The issue of accessibility, especially in the built environment, is presently receiving a lot of interest. Fiji is in the process of finalizing its National Building Code which will cover construction of houses, public amenities and renovations.

The FNCDP advisory committee responsible for this policy is presently working on a plan which the FNCDP will put forward to the ministry concerned. It will cover all areas of need for disabled persons within the built environment.

Suva's City Council, responding to FNCDP request, has started to show its support in the construction of public toilets in the city centre with provisions for wheelchair users and other disabled persons. In addition, there have been provisions for car parks for disabled persons and signboards. There are also plans for appropriate zebra crossings and other access features that have yet to be provided.

Through FNCDP's networking with the district disability committees, assurances have been received that other urban centres are also planning to make their cities and towns more friendly for people with disabilities. Currently, more organizations have become aware of the need for access for persons with disabilities, especially at the Fiji Institute of Technology and the local University of the South Pacific where no provisions were considered initially.

The FNCDP is optimistic that with the current level of interests, more will be achieved in terms of housing, transport and communication during the second half of the Decade.

8. Sports and recreation

Disabled athletes have always made Fiji proud in the many international competitions they have attended. Although devoid of proper facilities and funding, Fiji is a sport-loving nation and disabled sports persons have always shown their interests to participate in most sports and recreational activities.

Although the Advisory Committee of the FNCDP have not met regularly to work out a policy for disabled persons sports, disabled persons are organizing their own annual sports tournaments through self-help efforts.

The present situation is far from satisfactory and much more can be achieved through the involvement of the Ministry of Youth and Sports, in terms of formulating a national policy on sports for disabled persons, incorporating the provision of sports facilities, equipment and annual funding. In this respect the FNCDP will pursue further dialogue with the ministry.

9. Self-help organizations

Organizations of disabled persons in Fiji have continued to organize their own affairs. Their autonomy is protected under the FNCDP Act. However, their efforts to be united have not been quite so successful. There is no doubt, that if the disabled persons of Fiji do come together, irrespective of their disabilities, they would form a forum that would be effective in supporting the FNCDP in its work and thereby inform society fully of their needs and aspirations.

10. Regional cooperation

FNCDP hosted the training workshop on the management of self-help organizations of persons with disabilities in the Pacific in February 1996, where participants from Tonga, Samoa, Vanuatu, Solomon Islands and Fiji took part. The ESCAP funded training programme was held at the South Pacific Commission Training Centre.

The NGOs that took part expressed concerns over their governments' non-recognition of their needs and development. They also expressed the need for closer cooperation and exchange of information.

The involvement of regional organizations such as the South Pacific Commission, University of the South Pacific, Forum Secretariat and others will certainly enhance the recognition of disabled persons' development, laying the foundation for regional cooperation and the sharing of resources among the disabled population of the Pacific. The FNCDP is committed to strengthening regional cooperation in the second half of the Decade.

C. Conclusion

Since its humble beginnings, the FNCDP has been striving to bring recognition, improved facilities and quality of life to people with disabilities.

The FNCDP has contributed much to what Fiji has achieved in the development of disabled persons both under its own plans and the Agenda for Action for the Asian and Pacific Decade of Disabled Persons, although a lot more needs to be done to bring In affirmative policies, legislation and resource-allocation to this segment of the population.

No doubt, this has demanded much hard work and perseverance on the part of the NGOs, parents and guardians, teachers and school management to keep the schools operating. The people with disabilities, the supportive communities and the government which is diversifying its efforts and resources to an area that was previously overlooked and neglected.

FNCDP's experience and information gathered thus far and the promise that the results of the 1996 National Population Census Survey will be available from December 1997, help ensure that there will definitely be clearer guidelines to pursue now, than in the formative years of the council.

An action plan for the second half of the Decade will be an absolute priority for the FNCDP by the end of 1997. The Fiji Government – through the FNCDP – sees the next five years as crucial to disability development and is now poised to meet the challenges ahead.

However, it is also painfully aware that it needs to double its efforts to ensure that the momentum generated during the first half of the Decade is not lost. It must ensure that all parties in the equation – the disabled people themselves, the services of the self-help organizations, support groups for disabled persons and all government agencies – come together to support the FNCDP in achieving the objectives of the Decade.

CHAPTER VII

Hong Kong, China

A. National overview

Hong Kong became a special administrative region of China on 1 July 1997. In Hong Kong, a well-established network is in place for coordinating the planning and provision of rehabilitation services by government, statutory bodies and non-governmental organizations (NGOs). The aim of Hong Kong, China, is to help integrate an estimated 370,000 people with disabilities into the community and to help develop their potential to the fullest.

B. Progress made in the first half of the Asian and Pacific Decade of Disabled Persons

1. National coordination

The Commissioner for Rehabilitation, who reports to the Secretary for Health and Welfare in the Government of the Hong Kong Special Administrative Region (HKSAR), is responsible for developing policy goals on rehabilitation and coordinating efforts to implement them.

In 1995, Hong Kong published its new long-term policy on rehabilitation services for people with disabilities in a white paper, titled *Equal Opportunities and Full Participation: A Better Tomorrow for All.* This document sets out the plans of the Government of Hong Kong, China, to further develop rehabilitation services over the next 10 years and beyond.

A year later in 1996, Hong Kong published a new rehabilitation programme plan, which presents a comprehensive picture of the current and planned rehabilitation services for people with disabilities over a five-year period. This plan provides a comprehensive picture of the current rehabilitation services being provided and the ones in the pipeline. It is also used as the basis for the government to formulate the budget and the manpower needs for implementing these services. The plan, published in 1996, covers the period from 1994-1995 to 1998-1999. A review is scheduled to begin in 1998.

When formulating these two policy documents, the Government of Hong Kong, China, has sought input and feedback from service providers, people with disabilities and their families. It also consults the local community regularly about major policy issues. In addition, an advisory body, the Rehabilitation Advisory Committee, has been set up to advise the Government of Hong Kong, China, on:

(a) Development and phased implementation of rehabilitation services in Hong Kong and study of the proposals in the White Paper and the rehabilitation programme plan;

(b) Training of rehabilitation services personnel;

(c) Definition of the respective roles of government departments and NGOs to maximize available resources.

The committee chairman comes from the private sector and committee members include representatives from the various concerned parties such as service providers, parent support groups, self-help groups, professionals, businesses and government departments.

Within the committee are five subcommittees, chaired by non-governmental officers. The subcommittees would study and recommend proposals on employment, education, accessibility, recreation, transport, public education and application of information technology for people with disabilities.

The Government of Hong Kong, China, also works with the NGOs to plan and implement rehabilitation services for people with disabilities. Currently, more than 70 NGOs are working with 14 government departments to implement the rehabilitation programme plan.

The Joint Council for the Physically and Mentally Disabled helps facilitate and coordinate communication between the government and the NGOs.

In 1997-1998, Hong Kong's expenditure on rehabilitation services is expected to reach nearly US$1.33 billion, an increase of about 126 per cent over the 1992-1993 figure.

2. Legislation

Hong Kong fully recognizes the importance of legislative measures in the rehabilitation process. In recent years, it has made significant progress by introducing new laws and amending existing ones to improve the well-being of people with disabilities.

In 1995, Hong Kong amended some existing laws to protect and to facilitate mentally disabled persons in giving evidence in court. These new amendments include:

(a) Use of the local dialect instead of English in court proceedings;

(b) Conduct of trials in settings similar to that of juvenile courts;

(c) Giving of evidence via television links;

(d) Acceptance of video recordings as evidence in chief.

In 1996, the Disability Discrimination Ordinance came into force, as did the Equal Opportunities Commission (EOC), which plays a key role in enforcing the provisions of the ordinance.

The ordinance contains provisions to make discrimination on the grounds of disability unlawful in areas such as employment, education, accessibility, and the use of buildings and accommodation. It also gives people with disabilities the legal means to fight against discrimination and harassment, and to fight for equal opportunities. Any person who is discriminated or harassed on grounds of a disability may lodge a complaint with the EOC. The EOC will process the complaint initially through a reconciliation process. If both sides are unable to reach a settlement, the EOC may assist the aggrieved person in instituting legal proceedings.

In 1996, Hong Kong also amended some existing laws to provide the court with additional options to deal with cases in which the accused are unfit to plead in criminal proceedings by reason of mental disability. These options include guardianship orders, and supervision and treatment orders. It also made amendments to prevent arbitrary interference into the privacy and freedom of patients in mental hospitals.

In June 1997, Hong Kong introduced major improvements to the Mental Health Ordinance with a view to providing better legal safeguards for mentally disordered and mentally handicapped persons, as well as for their care-providers. The improvements provide a better guardianship scheme for mentally disordered and mentally handicapped persons. It is now in the process of drafting a subsidiary legislation and setting up an independent guardianship board.

3. Information

Currently, Hong Kong has a central registry for rehabilitation to collect and collate data on people with disabilities. New computers were installed to facilitate data retrieval and compilation of statistics. It will continue to consider ways to improve the effectiveness of the system as a tool to help provide rehabilitation services in the future.

4. Public education

Public education helps create positive attitudes towards people with disabilities and inculcates a better understanding of their special needs. In Hong Kong, major public education activities have been, and will continue to be, planned and organized to reach out to the community at large. A total of US$5.6 million has been allocated for public education activities between 1993-1994 and 1997-1998. The money to be spent in 1997-1998 is close to US$1 million. It is hoped that this will help develop an environment in which the community takes pride in accepting people with disabilities.

5. Accessibility and communication

Hong Kong recently published *Design Manual: Barrier Free Access 1997*, which sets out the mandatory and recommended requirements on the provision of access facilities in buildings for people with disabilities. Taking the lead, the government will continue with its ongoing refurbishment programme to improve the accessibility of the existing government buildings.

From 1992 to 1996, the Government of Hong Kong, China, organized four summit meetings between representatives of people with disabilities and public transport operators to discuss measures to improve the accessibility of the public transport system for people with disabilities.

In Hong Kong, public transport operators have been providing a wide range of facilities for their disabled passengers. These include low-floor buses with access ramps for wheelchair users, tactile guide paths and step edges marked with contrasting colours for visually-impaired persons, as well as induction loops and electronic information displays for hearing-impaired persons.

Hong Kong also expanded the operation of a territory-wide *Rehab* bus network for people with disabilities. Its scheduled and on-call services have expanded by 56 and 133 per cent, respectively, since 1992.

Accessibility also encompasses communication. Through donations from charitable funds, it was able to help hearing- and vision-impaired persons buy facsimile machines and computers for communication purposes. It has also succeeded in enlisting the help of local television broadcasters who provided captioning for hearing impaired persons.

6. Education

Hong Kong provides pre-school services to children with disabilities aged below six years. Since 1992, it has increased by nearly 54 per cent, the number of pre-school places to about 4,000 by 1997. To meet additional demand, it has also secured funds to provide some 300 extra places by 2000.

Hong Kong provides nine years of compulsory and free education to children with disabilities aged six years old onwards. It provides special education for those who are unable, even with additional support, to benefit from mainstream education.

The Board of Education reviewed its special education for students with disabilities and published its findings and recommendations in a report in 1996. Some of the recommendations, such as improving staff provisions in special schools, have already been looked into. It has also launched a two-year pilot project to integrate children with disabilities into ordinary schools from the school-term beginning September 1997.

From 1998, access facilities for physically disabled children will be provided in all new schools. Provisions are being made to improve accessibility in existing schools. A conversion programme is under way to ensure that each school district has at least one school that is accessible for physically disabled students.

A special admission scheme was started in 1997 for students with disabilities studying in tertiary institutions. Counselling and assistance are made available to disabled students to help them integrate into their new learning environment.

7. Training and employment

Hong Kong remains firmly committed to strengthening job opportunities for people with disabilities. From 1994 to 1996, the Government of Hong Kong, China, organized three summit meetings between representatives of persons with disabilities and employers associations to discuss measures to improve the employment opportunities for people with disabilities.

It is making progress in achieving the targets agreed to at these meetings. For example, a large-scale seminar, held in October 1996, to promote the working abilities of people with disabilities, attracted some 950 employers.

As the largest employer in Hong Kong, the government is committed to taking the lead in employing people with disabilities. It aims to employ a total of 4,400 people with disabilities by end-1997 in the civil service, that is, about 2.4 per cent of the entire civil service workforce. As of end-1996, there were 4,390 employees with disabilities.

To promote the employability of people with disabilities, the Hong Kong Special Administrative Region (HKSAR) provides vocational assessment service and vocational training courses for them. Since 1992, it has expanded the vocational assessment service and training service at the skills centres by 116 and 45 per cent, respectively. It has also offered more commercial and service courses to replace traditional industrial and technical ones to meet the needs of the labour market. Tailor-made part-time and short courses are also provided.

As of 31 March 1997, there were 845 full-time training places. With the completion of two new skills centres, an additional 456 full-time training places will be available by 1998-1999, representing a 46 per cent increase.

8. Prevention of the causes of disability

Vigilant anti-epidemic measures and surveillance have managed to keep the levels of many communicable diseases low in Hong Kong. A comprehensive immunization programme for infants has succeeded in significantly reducing the incidence of disabilities caused by poliomyelitis, congenital rubella and other diseases. Immunization is available free at maternal and child health centres and it is also provided by private medical practitioners.

A multidisciplinary approach with active community participation is being adopted in formulating preventive health programmes. As chronic diseases become the predominant causes of morbidity and mortality in the population, the emphasis of health education programmes is on prevention through healthy life-styles.

9. Rehabilitative services

Hong Kong, China, continuously provides social rehabilitation services to help people with varying degrees of disabilities to realize their full potential. To improve the quality of life of people with disabilities and that of their carers, it has expanded substantially day and residential services for disabled adults.

By end-1997, it will have more than doubled from the 1992 figure, the number of residential places to some 7,500 places. During the same period, the number of day places will also be increased by about 65 per cent to some 10,900 places. Extra places will be provided to meet demand. The HKSAR has already secured funds to provide some 2,500 additional day and residential places by 2002.

While institution-based rehabilitation services are currently being improved upon, Hong Kong has also put emphasis on community-based rehabilitation. It has set up two community rehabilitation network centres in 1995 and the third one in May 1997 with a view to enhancing the quality of life of chronically-ill persons and their families. This is achieved through the provision of social work and allied health services, the promotion of self-help and advocacy, training, and the launching of educational as well as community programmes.

10. Assistive devices

The Jockey Club Rehabilitation Engineering Centre set up in 1987, works on fusing science and technology in the rehabilitation process. Over the years, it has contributed towards optimizing the use of rehabilitation technology, which already exists, and ensuring that there is greater awareness of the existence of this technology among front-line workers and users.

A disability allowance of HK$1,200 per month, which is non-means-tested and non-contributory, is payable to people with disabilities to help meet the additional expenses arising from their conditions. A higher disability allowance of HK$2,400 per month is payable to those who require constant nursing care. They may use the allowance to purchase equipment or aids which they require. Since 1992, the total amount of disability allowance paid has increased by 72 per cent from some US$74.7 million to US$128.2 million.

11. Self-help organizations

In recent years, self-help groups are becoming increasingly popular in Hong Kong as effective and cost-efficient stress-buffering mechanisms, and for enhancing the abilities of people with disabilities to cope with their daily activities.

These organizations not only provide meaningful social, education and leisure activities, but also promote a spirit of mutual help among people with disabilities. Through seminars, the mass media and campaigns, they foster a positive image of and promote the rights of people with disabilities. Where the nature of disability prevents people from expressing and advocating their rights, parents or relatives may form organizations to represent their interests on their behalf.

Hong Kong will continue to further develop self-help organizations by enhancing their participation in policy formulation and supporting their activities which promote the well-being of persons with disabilities.

Parents resource centres provide a place for parents to discuss matters of mutual interests and to meet others facing similar problems. The centres also offer enquiry and referral services to parents and organize recreational and educational facilities for families with disabled children. Since April 1994, there are six government subvented parent resource centres and a few others supported financially by charitable funds.

12. Regional cooperation

Both the Government of Hong Kong, China, and the NGOs have participated actively in international as well as regional activities on disability issues. In July 1994, it was present at the Manila Conference on Campaign' 94 on the Asian and Pacific Decade of Disabled Persons, 1993-2002. In June 1995, Hong Kong attended the Economic and Social Commission for Asia and the Pacific (ESCAP) meeting in Bangkok, and in September that same year, it attended the regional conference of Rehabilitation International in Indonesia. In 1996, it attended the Rehabilitation International World Congress in New Zealand. In September 1998, Hong Kong will host the 11th Asian and Pacific Regional Conference of Rehabilitation International. The Government of Hong Kong, China, and its NGO partners do share the same vision and are looking forward to closer cooperation with ESCAP members.

C. Activities planned for the second half of the Asian and Pacific Decade of Disabled Persons

Over the past five years, Hong Kong has made substantial achievements in the provision of rehabilitation services and has moved much closer to the goals of full participation and equal opportunities for people with disabilities. It understands that there may be concerns over whether the commitment to achieving these goals will remain after the hand-over of Hong Kong's sovereignty to China. The basic law already recognizes the success it made in building its social welfare systems and explicitly recognizes its right to continue to develop them as it sees fit in the light of the current economic and social conditions.

In compliance with the basic law, Hong Kong will continue to implement the approved policies. Expansion of various rehabilitation services will continue to meet new demand. As mentioned above, it has already secured funds to provide some 300 extra pre-school places by 2000 and some 2,500 extra day and residential places by 2002 to meet new demand. Hong Kong also plans and provides rehabilitation services through a well-established network among the government, statutory bodies and NGOs. With the concerted efforts of these parties, it is confident that it will maintain the momentum in improving the quality of life of people with disabilities in the years ahead.

CHAPTER VIII

India

A. National overview

India is a sovereign socialist, democratic republic with a parliamentary system of government. The Constitution of India, which is the fundamental law of the country, enshrines equality, freedom, justice and the dignity of the individual as basic goals in the preamble. In addition, provisions such as the directive principles of state policy and fundamental rights, enshrine and re-emphasize India's tradition of being an inclusive society where its people are the critical resource for building the nation.

India has a federal structure with 26 states and six union territories with a total estimated population of 950 million. Some 25.7 per cent of the people in India live in urban areas while the rest in the rural areas. The states are divided into 507 administrative units or districts.

India ranks among the oldest civilizations in history with a rich and varied heritage. Taking care of older persons, the sick, and disabled people has been a part of the fundamental social ethos of the country with its strong roots in familial and community bonds. However, organized rehabilitation services for people with disabilities have been largely a post-independence phenomenon. The beginnings were often small, with personal or family commitments, but these have gradually blossomed out into organizational endeavours in the governmental as well as non-governmental sectors.

The earlier Ninth Five-year Plan of the Government of India made a modest beginning in formulating and implementation of schemes and programmes for the welfare of people with disabilities. It was, however, during the seventh (1985 to 1990) and eighth (1992 to 1997) plans that significant strides in providing for programmes and services for disabled persons were made in different sectors.

In the past 15 years, there has been a growing awareness and several significant landmarks in the sector of disability both at the national and at the international levels. 1981 was declared as the International Year of Disabled Persons. Following this, the period 1983 to 1992 was proclaimed by the General Assembly as the United Nations Decade of Disabled Persons. The major outcome of the United Nations of Disabled Persons was the emergence of a global movement recognizing the importance of integration of people with disabilities into society through a world programme of action.

The Economic and Social Commission for Asia and the Pacific (ESCAP) proclaimed 1993 to 2002 as the Asian and the Pacific Decade of Disabled Persons at its Beijing Session held in 1992. The aim is to give a fresh impetus to the implementation of the world programme of action in the ESCAP region beyond 1992. Other significant global events were the declaration of 1993 as SAARC Year of Disabled Persons, the World Summit on Social Development in Copenhagen and the United Nations Conference on Women held in Beijing, both held during 1995. These Conferences specially focused on issues and concerns relating to the lives of people with disabilities.

These international trends as well as indigenous endeavours have had a direct impact on the thinking of policy makers, professionals, people with disabilities and non-governmental organizations (NGOs) working in India. There has now emerged a clear shift from the earlier concept of welfare for disabled persons to a demand for equal participation. The new emphasis has led to the concept of people with disabilities as partners in nation building rather than as objects of charity and welfare and as a burden on the country's economy. People with disabilities are increasingly being perceived as valuable contributors to the socio-economic development of the country.

B. Progress made in the first half of the Asian and Pacific Decade of Disabled Persons

The first half of the Decade has been characterized by some landmark developments in India. The Persons with Disabilities (Equal Opportunities, Protection of Rights and Full Participation) Act was enacted in 1995. This is a comprehensive piece of legislation which treats rehabilitation as a right and aims to eliminate discrimination and create a society which provides opportunities for development of people with disabilities to their fullest potential. Action on implementation of the Act has started in right earnest and is an ongoing process.

Another crucial factor in recent times has been the liberalization of the Indian economy with implications on employment opportunities in the governmental and public sectors and the greater role of competitive and market forces. The recent legislation prescribes a 3 per cent reservation (1 per cent each for physically-, visually- and hearing-impaired persons) in identified posts in all government and public sector offices.

In order to empower people with disabilities to cope with the new challenges and to develop the necessary entrepreneurial skills and initiatives, the National Handicapped Finance and Development Corporation was set up to support self-employment projects for people with disabilities.

With the shift in emphasis from providing welfare to ensuring the rights of disabled persons, the importance of convergence of policies and programmes in different sectors, so as to provide synergy, has emerged to the forefront. The efforts of the government, non-governmental and other agencies in the welfare sector need to be more structured and concerted in approach. India must also ensure linkages between programmes in all connected sectors such as education, vocational training and employment, rural and urban development, health, and women and child development. There must also be optimum utilization of available resources and holistic rehabilitation for people with disability.

1. National coordination

The Persons with Disabilities (Equal Opportunities, Protection of Rights and Full Participation) Act, 1995 which has been enforced from 7 February 1996, calls for the formation of the Central Coordination Committee by the Central Government of India.

The members of this committee include members of parliament, officials of ministries and departments of the central government and state governments and NGOs. This body is the apex authority for taking policy decisions regarding implementation of the Act. The committee was officially inaugurated in February 1997.

The Act also calls for the formation of the State Coordination Committees by the state governments. These committees were represented by officials from the state government ministries and departments, members of state legislative assemblies and NGOs.

In addition, the Act also provides for the formation of the Central Executive Committee and State Executive Committees. These are in the process of being formed with the deadline set by December 1997.

An intercountry (India-China) seminar for evolving suitable mechanism to ensure multisectoral collaborative action for disabled persons was convened in March-April 1997. To give a thrust to the process of implementation of the Act, various regional inter-state workshops followed with the state-levels multisectoral workshops are being planned. They will be held in various states within the next year. One of the aims is to develop successful models of service delivery at the district levels to ensure the fulfilment of the objectives as laid down in the Act and to replicate the same in all parts of the country.

The Act provides reservation of 3 per cent benefits to the people with disabilities in all poverty alleviation schemes. The Ministry of Rural Areas and Employment has already taken an initiative in this direction in 1996 by ensuring suitable amendments in the integrated rural development programme under which the groups of disabled persons will be given a revolving fund of 25,000 rupees for income-generating activities. All the ministries and departments which are operating the poverty alleviation programmes and projects shall identify the schemes under which participation of disabled persons may be ensured.

2. Legislation

The comprehensive Act can aptly be described as a progressive and modern piece of legislation. It deals with both the prevention and promotional aspects of rehabilitation such as education, employment and vocational training; the creation of barrier-free environment; provision of rehabilitation services for people with disabilities; institution for persons with extensive disabilities and social security measures such as unemployment allowance and a grievance mechanism both at the central and state levels.

The Constitution of India is the basic law of the country and it provides various rights to all the citizens. Article 14 of the constitution said that the "State shall not deny to any person equality before the law or the equal protection of laws within the territory of India".

Any law or executive orders can be challenged in the supreme court at the national level and high courts at the state level on the grounds of violating any provisions of the constitution. In the case where any law or executive order is found to be violating any provision of the constitution, that particular law or executive order can be declared null and void. No Indian law discriminates against people with disabilities. There are various provisions in the constitution which make the government take affirmative actions for the weaker sections of society, including people with disabilities.

The matter relating to the examination and identification of all substantial and procedural laws is being taken up with the law commission with a view to repeal the provisions that restrict full participation and equalization of opportunities or provisions which are discriminatory to people with disabilities. A task force under the Law Commission is expected to be set up by December 1997.

The Parliament of India had earlier enacted a law for the setting up of the Rehabilitation Council of India (RCI). Its main responsibility is the standardization of curriculum and training facilities of various professional courses on rehabilitation of people with disabilities and to inspect the facilities to monitor compliance.

The RCI is playing an important role in ensuring the quality of services in the crucial area of manpower development. So far, a total number of 91 organizations have been recognized by the RCI for running certificate, diploma and degree courses in the area of disability.

The Government of India has also given various income-tax deductions from the total income taxes from people with disabilities. The limit under Section 80-U has been raised from Rs20,000 to Rs40,000 and deduction of Rs20,000 from the taxable income of the parents or guardians of people with disabilities has been allowed provided this amount is deposited in any scheme of Life Insurance Cooperation (LIC) and United Trust of India (UTI).

3. Information

The Asian and Pacific Decade Agenda for Action has been circulated to various central government ministries and departments, state governments, district rehabilitation centres and voluntary organizations for wider dissemination, including through translations into local languages.

Periodically, India undertakes, through the National Sample Survey of India (NSSI), data collection concerning people with disabilities. In 1991, the NSSI conducted a country-wide survey covering disabilities, including visual, hearing, speech and physical disabilities.

About 16,150,000 people are estimated to have one or the other of the four types of disabilities mentioned above. This constitutes 1.9 per cent of the total estimated population in the country. It has been observed that for the country as a whole, the prevalence of physical disability was 20 per 1,000 persons in the rural sector and 16 in the urban sector. Between the two sexes, the prevalence is marginally more among males than females.

For this survey, intellectually disabled persons were excluded. However, a sample survey, conducted by NSSI in 1991 for persons with delayed intellectual development between 0-14 years old estimates that about 3 per cent of the estimated child population have delayed intellectual development. On the basis of some random sample surveys, it has been estimated that about 2 to 2.5 per cent of the population in India is intellectually disabled.

A National Survey on Blindness, conducted during 1986 to 1989 under the aegis of the Ministry of Health and Family Welfare, estimated that 11,920,000 persons are blind as against 3,470,000 estimated by the NSSI survey in 1981.

The NSSI survey conducted in 1991 reported that there has been a marginal decline in the incidence of blindness. It has also been observed in the report that (NSSI 1991) "experts are of the opinion that with greater pace of development and urbanization, the disability prevalence rate is also likely to rise".

However, with better health care and advancement of medical sciences during the decade (1981 to 1991), the incidence of some types of disabilities have shown a decreasing trend, although the overall impact of these factors is a marginal rise in the prevalence rate.

According to national programme for control of blindness (WHO report 1989), about 28,560,000 persons have low vision. A study conducted by Indian Council for Medical Research estimated that 6.8 per cent of the people in urban areas and 10.8 per cent of the people in rural areas have significant hearing losses.

The number of leprosy-affected persons is estimated to be about 4 million, of whom about one-fifth are children. About 15 to 20 per cent of the cases is with deformities. In 196 districts in the country, the prevalence rate is more than five per one thousand persons. About 430 million persons live in these high endemic districts.

The NSSI in its forty-sixth round (July to December, 1991) organized a sample survey on disabilities, literacy and culture. On the availability of special facilities for disabled persons such as integrated education, special schools, vocational training, institutions and organizations, the survey found that only 10 per cent of Indian villages had an integrated education centre within a distance of less than 10 kilometres. The situation is much worse in respect of other types of facilities.

The facilities of special schools for visually-, speech- and hearing-impaired and intellectually disabled persons were non-existent in more than 97 per cent of the villages in India even within a distance of 10 kilometres. About 96 per cent of the villages did not have the facility of vocational training within that distance. Only 6 per cent of the villages have rehabilitation services and these are provided by organizations which either move from one village to another in vans or have set up camps at different villages.

The National Information Centre of Disability and Rehabilitation (NICDR) was established in 1987 by the Ministry of Welfare. Its basic objective is to build up Information database on disabled persons' situation and disability related issues. The database is structured to provide information to policy makers, planners, researchers, institutions and individuals.

The NICDR also periodically publishes the directory of institutions and directory of professionals. The NICDR has also set up a technical library to assist the professionals. Recently, it published a directory of institutions working for disabled persons in India.

It also proposed that NICDR should be integrated with the National Centre of Disability Rehabilitation (NCDR) to work as a resource centre for all the institutions working for people with disabilities. This new centre will undertake various research and development activities as well. Currently, an agreement is being worked out between the government and National Institute for Disability Rehabilitation and Research (NIDRR), Washington.

The six national institutes and apex level institutions have published directories of institutions and professionals focusing on each area of disability.

A full census of disabled persons is also being planned for 2001 along with the general census. The needed manpower training for this purpose will be arranged through the national institutes of disabilities.

4. Public awareness

The Ministry of Welfare places great emphasis on public awareness of disability-related issues. The NICDR also plays an important role in sensitizing the media towards the various disability-related issues, generating awareness among the people in general and the intelligentsia in particular, about the potential of disabled persons and de-mystifying disability among the general masses.

The Ministry of Welfare, and national institutes and apex level institutes have prepared a number of documentary films and spots on issues relating to disability. The national broadcaster, *Doordarshan*, has also produced a number of films with the support of the Ministry of Welfare.

Constant contacts are maintained with various government and non-government media channels such as the print media, All India Radio, *Doordarshan*, Directorate of Advertising and Visual Publicity, Field Publicity Department and the State Information Department, to ensure a sustained media campaign. *Doordarshan* has agreed to produce a series of documentaries on disability.

Currently, the Ministry has printed a calendar with the theme "Trust the Abilities of People with Disabilities" to highlight the potential of disabled persons.

For the annual International Day of Disabled Persons, the President of India presents the following national awards: the most efficient disabled employee; the outstanding employer of disabled persons; the individual doing work for the cause of disabled persons; the best institution working for disabled persons; the best placement officer of disabled persons; the technology awards for inventions in the field of disability.

The ceremony was telecast live on the national network for greater public awareness in 1995 and 1996.

The six national institutes have also undertaken various public awareness measures through films, print media and radio. They are the National Institute for the Visually Handicapped, Dehradun; National Institute for the Hearing Handicapped, Mumbai; National Institute for the Orthopaedically Handicapped, Calcutta; National Institute for the Mentally Handicapped, Secunderabad; Institute for the Physically Handicapped, New Delhi; National Institute of Rehabilitation Training and Research, Cuttack.

The use of traditional media such as theatre and folk groups is being encouraged by the government to bring out the potential of people with disabilities. India has a rich cultural heritage and varying folk arts and it is the constant endeavour of the government to make the best use of such traditional media to create public awareness and counter deep-rooted superstitions about disability and people with disabilities.

There are also various grant-in-aid schemes, in which NGOs provide up to 90 per cent (95 per cent in the rural areas) funding for the rehabilitation services. Certain provision for the production and distribution of public awareness materials and holding camps have great potential for creating awareness among the public.

There is a proposal to produce various films for training the parents of intellectually disabled children, for broadcast on *Doordarshan* during the regular programmes of National Council for Education Research and Training and Central Institute of Educational Technology.

5. Accessibility and communication

The Act has a chapter on non-discrimination which provides for barrier-free environment in transport and in the built environment. There is also one chapter which provides for barrier-free environment in educational institutions.

The Ministry of Urban Affairs and Employment, in collaboration with Municipal Corporation of Delhi and ESCAP, has started the New Delhi Pilot Project. This selected project, which was inaugurated in December 1996, aims to make barrier-free all the public buildings and offices in the localities which are frequently used by people with disabilities, and situated within a kilometre radius of Indra Prastha Estate. The project is expected to have a demonstration effect and play an important role in extending technical guidance and the necessary motivation to other cities towards the promotion of non-handicapping environment.

In 1996, the Ministry of Urban Affairs and Employment has also undertaken the task of formulating model building by-laws which will provide for easy access to public buildings by persons with disabilities. The model building by-laws have been circulated to all the state governments for adoption and implementation.

A national-level workshop will be convened in 1997 to facilitate the implementation of the provisions relating to creation of barrier-free environment as contained in Act. The administrators, town planners, architects, constructors and officials from surface transport, railways and communications ministries will be invited to work out the strategies and suitable models for adoption in making the existing buildings and infrastructure barrier-free, and finalizing the modifications in existing building by-laws.

The Government of India set up a core group in 1997, consisting of government officials, technical experts and voluntary organizations, to examine the relevant provisions relating to the creation of barrier-free environment. The group's recommendations are expected to be received and finalized by December 1997.

Doordarshan also telecasts once weekly, a special news bulletin for the people with hearing disability.

The Ali Yavar Jung National Institute for the Hearing Handicapped in Mumbai developed a loop induction system which will facilitate communication of hearing impaired persons at crowded places such as railway stations. The Delhi Railway Station has already been fitted with one such device. Another 15 major railway stations are expected to be fitted with the system in 1997.

6. Education

The Act places a statutory obligation on the government to provide free education to disabled children in an appropriate environment till the age of eighteen. It also provides for establishment of special schools, facilities for imparting non-formal education and education through open schools and universities to disabled children, organizing teacher training programmes, taking steps for adaptation of curriculum, reform of examination system, promoting research and providing various facilities to disabled children at the national level.

The objective is to integrate the people with disabilities with the general community at all levels as equal partners, to prepare them for normal growth and to enable them to face life with courage and confidence.

The Scheme for Integrated Education of Disabled Children (SIEDC) provides educational opportunities for disabled children in the general school system so as to facilitate their retention and ultimate integration in the system.

SIEDC is implemented through the education departments of the state governments, and autonomous and voluntary organizations. Over 53,000 disabled children in 13,674 schools have been covered so far. Under SIEDC, 100 per cent financial assistance is provided. These include allowances for books and stationery, uniforms, transport allowance, readers allowance for blind children, escort allowance for severely disabled children particularly those with lower extremity disability, boarding and lodging charges for disabled children residing in hostels.

In addition, the Government of India also sets up and equips resource rooms with aids and assistive devices, provides teacher support in the ratio of 1:8, pays resource teachers as applicable in the state/union territory, pays helpers and attendants and gives special pay for resource teachers.

It also funds a survey to identify disabled children in the blocks/districts and assess the children via a team comprising a doctor, a psychologist and a special educator. It also buys and produces instructional materials, pays for the training and orientation of resource teachers and the salary of an administrative cell at the state level to implement and monitor the programme.

During Ninth Five-year Plan commencing from 1997 to 1998, the Government of India proposed to expand the coverage of the SIEDC into the "unreached" areas. The total proposed allocation for SIEDC during Ninth Five-year Plan has been kept at Rs one billion with a view to expand the coverage of the programme and making it more effective.

Another programme, the Project Integrated Education for the Disabled (PIED) was introduced with United Nations Children's Fund assistance in 1987. PIED was started in a selected block in 10 states of Haryana, Madhya Pradesh, Maharashtra, Mizoram, Nagaland, Orissa, Gujarat, Rajasthan, Delhi and Tamil Nadu.

Under PIED, a block is taken as a project area and all the schools in that block are converted into integrated schools. An external evaluation of PIED in 1994 showed that not only had the enrolment of disabled children increased considerably, the retention rate among disabled children was very high, about 95 per cent. The figure was even higher than that for normal children in the same block. The PIED programme, which is being run through 1,382 schools – benefiting over 6,000 children – has now been merged into the SIEDC programme.

Under the holistic, community-based and innovative District Primary Education Programme (DPEP), which was launched in 1994 and covers 60 districts, integrated education for all children with mild to moderate disabilities is being given special emphasis. The programme will eventually be introduced in 120 districts.

The project board of the National Elementary Education Mission, which is part of the Department of Education in the Ministry of Human Resource Development, has already approved the revised guidelines to incorporate integrated education for the disabled children in the DPEP. DPEP covers the areas of environment building, community mobilization and early detection, teacher training, development of innovative designs for primary schools and removal of architectural barriers in existing schools, provision of education aids and appliances and resource support at block/district level.

The Government of India has already set up a core group comprising government officials, technical experts and voluntary organizations to examine the relevant provisions of the Act relating to pre-school education, integrated education and special education. It will give its recommendations, which are expected to be submitted and finalized by December 1997.

A workshop on the implementation of the relevant provisions of the Act was convened on 29 August 1997 in New Delhi. State Education Secretaries participated in the workshop and worked out action plans to strengthen the existing programmes and to ensure the participation of all children with disabilities in formal and non-formal educational programmes on an equal basis.

A special scheme covering the establishment and development of special schools has been implemented since the period 1993-1994. Under the scheme, voluntary organizations are given the necessary assistance of up to 90 per cent to set up special schools. A special scheme of manpower development has also been introduced (1991-1992) under which 100 per cent assistance is provided for running training courses for teachers in the area of cerebral palsy and mental disability.

The Central Board of Secondary Education (CBSE) has set up a committee to look into means of modifying the examination system so as to make it easier for disabled children to take examinations. The CBSE already allows provision of the facility of amaenuensis for blind and physically disabled children when they sit for the tenth standard and twelfth standard board examinations. It also opened a cell for parents to lodge the grievances of parents regarding placement of disabled children.

The national institutes of disabilities under the Ministry of Welfare have been organizing training programmes for special teachers. The University Grants Commission (UGC) has taken an initiative by opening universities and colleges to cater to the needs of disabled children. UGC is implementing a scheme under which financial assistance will be provided to the universities for organizing special education programmes for teacher who hold Bachelor of Education and Master of Education degrees, to enable them to teach disabled children. UGC also reserves 30 research associateships every year for disabled students and scholars.

7. Training and employment

The Act of 1995 has recognized the special need to support individuals whose prospects of securing, retaining and advancing in suitable employment are substantially reduced as a result of a duly recognized physical or mental impairment.

The Government of India has set up a core group to examine the existing facilities and infrastructure available for vocational training and employment for people with disabilities. It will also make recommendations for restructuring, strengthening and expanding these facilities so as to realize the objectives as laid down in the Act.

The emphasis is being given to ensure the inclusion of people with disabilities in the mainstream facilities that are already available. The core group has already given its recommendations to the Government of India in July 1997 and they are still under consideration. The recommendations include the setting up of a mechanism for identification of new employment opportunities in the formal and non-formal sectors for people with disabilities.

The Act has a 3 per cent reservation rate to people with physical disabilities in government jobs and public sector undertakings. The necessary administrative instructions for this issue have already been issued in February 1997 by the Department of Personnel and Training.

The Ministry of Labour through the Directorate-General of Employment and Training (DGE&T) extends its services to persons with disabilities through a number of schemes. There is a conscious effort to integrate such persons in nation building.

There is also a network of 915 employment exchanges which cater for the registration and placement of job seekers including those with disabilities. Besides registering and placing in salaried job, the general employment exchanges also provide vocational guidance and employment counselling, organize career guidance and provide useful career information for disabled job seekers.

The employment market information programme of the employment exchanges gives basic information concerning the employment market which is used by various sponsoring agencies working for disabled persons. Thus, the employment exchanges also provide vocational guidance and help persons with disabilities take up self-employment ventures.

There are 47 special employment exchanges and 41 special cells in general employment exchanges with the specific objective of helping persons with disabilities get gainful employment. About 53,000 persons with disabilities have been employed through these special employment exchanges and special cells throughout the country.

The National Council of Vocational Training, an apex non-statutory body set up by the Ministry of Labour, has formulated a policy of reserving 3 per cent of seats for trainees with locomotor disability in all industrial training institutes (ITIs) – in both engineering and non-engineering groups of trades. The standards of training and norms of trade testing are uncompromised. However, some relaxation in medical standards is provided. All ITIs, which currently number some 3,000, are located in different parts of the country. They offer admission to disabled persons in different trades as per their suitability.

Under the Apprenticeship Act, 1961, which aims at the development of human resources through skills training based on the latest technology. Some 3 per cent of vacancies are reserved for persons with disabilities. So far about 610 physically disabled persons have been trained in 13 designated trades. These trades have been divided into 29 trade groups. The Apprenticeship Training Scheme currently covers only persons with locomotor disability. It has agreed in principle that people with hearing disability will also be under the programme.

A committee of experts has been set up to identify various trades in which hearing and speech disability will not be a serious handicap. Accordingly, under the Act, the subcommittee of the Central Apprenticeship Council (CAC) has recommended that 18 trades for apprenticeship training for people with hearing disability. However, the details for imparting related instructions (trade theory) through sign language are yet to be evolved. The Ministry of Labour is also considering a scheme of incentives to encourage establishments to hire physically disabled persons as apprentices.

The DGE&T runs 17 vocational rehabilitation centres (VRCs), throughout the country for the different categories of disability. The VRCs have arrangements to assess residual capacity, training, evaluation and placement of persons with disabilities.

The above training is provided free. The Indian government also lends support to the VRC training programmes by providing stipends to the trainees. This also serves as a catalyst for non-governmental agencies which assist persons with disability in vocational rehabilitation.

Skill training workshops are conducted in seven of the 17 VRCs for entirely non-formal training according to the suitability of the candidates. In 1996, about 19903 disabled persons were admitted in various VRCs.

The government is planning to establish at least one VRC in each state during the Ninth Five-year Plan and also assist the state governments and local authorities, and NGOs in establishing vocational rehabilitation centres to cater to disabled persons.

Statistical appreciation of performance of VRCs since their inception till December 1996

Description	VH	HH	OH	NL	MH	Total
Number of clients admitted	27,809	27,285	258,312	3,002	2,796	319,204
Number of clients evaluated	26,683	26,173	246,630	2,846	2,610	304,942
Number of clients rehabilitated	8,934	11,543	73,701	956	808	95,942

In order to implement the Agenda for Action for the Asian and Pacific Decade of Disabled Persons (hereafter referred to as Asian and Pacific Decade Agenda for Action), the Ministry of Labour has drafted very ambitious plans to strengthen the vocational rehabilitation services for disabled persons.

It is setting up 10 more VRCs with skill training workshops and rural rehabilitation extension centres. These centres will be equipped with modern and sophisticated instruments, training aids and will be housed in buildings exclusively designed for disabled persons, keeping in view the government's commitment to provide barrier-free and easily accessible structure for them.

Out of the total allocation for plan schemes of the employment directorate about 37 per cent is proposed to be provided during the Ninth Five-year Plan exclusively for rehabilitation of disabled persons.

A large number of non-governmental agencies are working in the area of training, employment and economic rehabilitation of persons with disabilities throughout the country. There is also a conscious effort to change over to modern trades suited to new technologies and market demand.

Opportunities for training, however, are limited in the rural areas and unevenly spread in the country. The Ministry of Labour has a programme of Rural Rehabilitation Extension Centres (RRECs) where the services of the VRCs are extended to rural areas through mobile camps and 11 RRECs set up under the VRCs at Mumbai, Calcutta, Kanpur, Ludhiana and Chennai.

The Ministry of Labour is fully aware of the need to provide equal opportunities for vocational training and employment for women and girls with disabilities. Much effort has been made to increase the intake of women and girls with disabilities in vocational training and integrate them with the requisite support services into existing vocational training facilities.

A vocational rehabilitation centre for disabled women has been set up exclusively for rendering vocational rehabilitation services to disabled women job seekers. There are plans to turn this centre into a regional vocational rehabilitation centre. India also plans to set up nine more such centres in different parts of the country. These centres will function as integrated training centres utilizing the facilities available with the regional vocational centre for women.

The Central Institute for Research and Training in Employment Service (CIRTES) is responsible for training officers of the national employment service to sensitize them about the special placement needs of people with disabilities and for research-related to placement activities.

CIRTES has organized 10 training programmes, which covered the special placement needs of disabled persons, during 1996 to 1997. In addition, training programmes for personnel involved in the vocational rehabilitation of disabled persons are being organized. CIRTES has also developed career literature for disabled job seekers and their parents. The posters developed by CIRTES depicting the employability of disabled persons are being used in campaigns to assess their potentials and vocational skills.

The Ministry of Rural Areas and Employment recently took an initiative to help disabled rural poor to carry out suitable economic activities of their choice. Some 3 per cent of the total subsidy budget under the Integrated Rural Development Programme will be earmarked for providing revolving fund assistance of Rs25,000 each to groups or sangams of the disabled rural poor for such activities. This will be in addition to the existing provisions of 3 per cent reservation of benefits for individual beneficiaries. The Viklang Bandhu scheme under the Ministry of Welfare will implement this proposal.

Under the *Indira Awas Yojana,* a housing scheme for the rural poor, 3 per cent of the benefits have been reserved for the physically disabled persons living below the poverty line in rural areas. Similarly, under the *Jawahar Rojgar Yojna,* a major wage employment programme for the rural poor, 3 per cent of the funds has been earmarked for the creation of barrier-free infrastructure for disabled persons in rural areas.

The National Handicapped Finance and Development Corporation has been incorporated in January 1997 as a non-profit company fully funded by the Ministry of Welfare. The paid up share capital of the Corporation is Rs2 billion and the authorized capital is Rs4 billion. It is envisaged that the state governments would set up such corporations of their own or identify channelling agencies for the national corporation in order to ensure that people with disabilities get full advantage of the new initiative. The main objectives of the corporation are to promote and support entrepreneurial and self-employment ventures by people with disabilities. A consultation meeting was held on 10 July 1997 with the participation of state government officials, officers from financial institutions and non-voluntary organizations to discuss the draft guidelines for disbursing the loans to the disabled entrepreneurs. The corporation is expected to begin operations by December 1997.

8. Prevention of the causes of disability

In a survey conducted in 1991, the national sample survey organization found that old age and injuries are the major causes of visual disability. Ear discharge, old age and other illnesses are important causes of hearing disability. Paralysis and other illnesses are the major reasons for speech disability. For locomotor disability, polio is the cause of one-third of the cases, burns and injuries in nearly one-fourth of the cases and leprosy is responsible for 2 to 3 per cent of the cases.

Health and human development form integral components of socio-economic development of the nation. As per the Constitution of India, public health, sanitation, hospitals and dispensaries fall in the state list while the central Government of India is responsible for implementing programmes of national importance.

India is a signatory state to the Alma Alta declaration which envisages health for all by the year 2000. The national programme for control of blindness, national goitre control programme, national mental health programme, national programme on Japanese encephalitis, leprosy, nutrition, maternal and child health care programmes constitute the main plank for disability prevention services through the network of primary health centres, subcentres, district and teaching hospitals.

There are 22,229 primary health centres, 131,379 sub-centres and 1,923 community health centres. Disability prevention services, which form part of the health care scheme, are provided by 599,000 trained *dais* (mid-wives) and 417,000 health guides. Child development, nutrition, infant care and immunization form essential components of the curriculum for training *dais* and health guides.

Early detection in the field level is carried out by multi-purpose health workers attached to primary health centres, auxiliary female child minders, mid-wives attached to sub-centres, *anganwadi* workers and *balsevikas* (female child minders) of the ICDS Programme, village rehabilitation workers and community-based rehabilitation programmes of the government and NGOs. There are 290 *anganwadi* training centres for imparting training to *anganwadi* workers and helpers while there are 20 middle-level training centres for imparting training to supervisors and child development project officers. Started in 1961 to 1962, the *balsevikas* training programme implemented welfare programmes for pre-school children. There are 25 *balsevikas* training centres, each conducting one academic year training course for 50 trainees. Training programmes for each of these functionaries have adequate inputs for the early detection of childhood disabilities including mental retardation.

Also in place are early intervention services for infants at-risk and children having delayed development. With lower infant mortality rates, babies with genetic defects have greater chances of survival. The early intervention programmes, being carried out at more than 50 centres in the country over the last decade, have shown that early intervention helps improve the physical and mental functioning of the child. It also enables and encourages parents in the care and management of such babies in the home setting, with periodic consultation provided by early intervention centres. It is expected that, within a decade, such services would be available nationwide.

The major factors leading to various types of disabilities have already been identified and prevention measures initiated. Such measures are managed by Department of Women and Child Development, Ministry of Human Resource Development and Ministry of Health and Family Welfare, which initiated various programmes that provide enough micro-nutrients to the mother and child and other immunization programmes. These programmes will be strengthened during the period 1997-2002. Public education programmes through the mass media will be enhanced.

9. Rehabilitation services

There is a recent thrust towards reaching rehabilitation services to people with disabilities living in the far-flung rural areas. Here the importance of community-based rehabilitation (CBR) is well established as it is logistically difficult and expensive to provide institutional rehabilitation services. The strategy is to take a multisectoral and decentralized approach in the provision of services within the community, with appropriate inputs from various sectors.

India has a tradition of family and community-based initiatives in rehabilitation. This provides an inherent strength and a basis on which successful community initiatives can be built upon. It is further reinforced by NGOs who have made significant contributions in the area of community-based rehabilitation, particularly in the southern areas of the country where considerable expertise and experience have been built up. Another factor is the 73rd and 74th amendments of the Indian Constitution which has conferred powers and responsibilities to elected local bodies at the rural *(panchayats)* and municipal levels which could be constructively utilized and integrated into programmes for community-based rehabilitation.

The Ministry of Welfare has proposed a national programme for rehabilitation of persons with disabilities during the Ninth Five-year Plan. It is envisaged that at the national level, a national centre for disability rehabilitation will be established. At the state level, a state institute will serve as a resource centre and also undertake manpower development, research and provide model services.

At the district level, a district rehabilitation centre will provide specialist services in rehabilitation and work in tandem with district hospitals and other bodies concerned with rehabilitation. At the block level, which comprises 50,000 people, two multi-purpose rehabilitation workers (MRW) will provide services to people with disabilities, their families, and the community. The officers will also network with education, labour, social welfare and health personnel, and NGO agencies in the area. At the *Gram Panchayat* or local government level, which comprises a cluster of villages, two CBR workers – one male and one female from the area – will be suitably trained to cater to about 50,000 people.

They will be supported by elected local government as well as grass-roots functionaries of the concerned departments and non-governmental agencies. Strategies for implementation at the field level are flexible to enable state governments to utilize various methods – government, *panchayat* or non-government – suited to local conditions.

The comprehensive national rehabilitation programme thus formulated was discussed in a meeting held on 30 June 1997 where the representatives of the state governments, central government and voluntary organizations participated. The national level programme will be implemented during the next five years in a phased manner.

The Ministry of Health and Family Welfare has taken-up a pilot project of community-based rehabilitation in five states – Maharashtra, Andhra Pradesh, Madhya Pradesh, Tamil Nadu and Kerala. The all India institute of physical medicine and rehabilitation in Mumbai is acting as the main implementing agency and the training of personnel for both professionals and grass-roots level functionaries is underway. This programme utilizes the existing infrastructure of health, women and child development, welfare and local government sectors in implementing the programme.

Persons with intellectual disabilities are at a greater risk of exploitation and physical/social abuse by the unscrupulous elements of society. It has been a major cause of worry to the parents of children with intellectual disability as to "what will happen to their children after their deaths?" A committee formed under the chairmanship of Justice Baharul Islam suggested the formation of a national trust for intellectual disability with the following objectives:

(a) To provide guardianship and foster care;

(b) To strengthen and support the welfare process of families, foster families, parent association, voluntary organizations and the community;

(c) To provide legal aid to the mentally disabled persons and their families;

(d) To receive, own and manage the bequeathed properties by parents to maintain their intellectually disabled children after their deaths.

The Government of India has decided to set up a statutory trust to achieve the above objectives. The proposed bill is being drafted with inputs from voluntary organizations and the parent associations of children with intellectual disability. Consultation meetings were held in June 1997. After the final round of discussions, the bill is expected to be formally introduced in the Lok Sabha in 1998.

The Ministry of Welfare has assisted in setting up the Indian Spinal Injury Centre in collaboration with Italy. The government has contributed Rs25 million towards the construction of the centre as a one-time grant. It is the first institute of its kind in the country for the spinal injury patients.

The Government has set up 47 special employment exchanges and 41 special cells in the normal employment exchanges. The aim is to help disabled persons get gainful employment. Some Rs60 million has been allocated for this project under the Ninth Five-year Plan. About 53,000 disabled persons have been given placement through these special employment exchanges and cells. In addition, there are 17 vocational rehabilitation centres. Under the country's Apprentices Act, 1961, trainees are trained in various industrial establishments with 3 per cent of the vacancies reserved for people with disabilities.

About 76 per cent of disabled persons live in rural areas. The government introduced, on a pilot basis, a scheme to establish District Rehabilitation Centres (DRC) in the country. They aim to provide rehabilitation services in rural areas, in 11 selected districts of the country. The centres have comprehensive rehabilitation responsibilities to all disabled individuals in the geographical area of the district which has a population ranging between one to two million persons. The main objectives of the scheme are:

(a) To devise suitable delivery systems to reach the entire population in the geographical area of the district;

(b) To promote the most cost-effective technologies;

(c) To restructure the present jobs of rehabilitation professionals, so that the minimum number of specialists could be utilized for the delivery of services.

For the purpose of coordination and administration, there is a Central and Coordination Unit (CACU). Four Regional Rehabilitation Training Centres (RRTCS) – one each at Chennai, Mumbai, Cuttack and Lucknow – have been set up for imparting training to DRC functionaries. A national information centre for disability and rehabilitation has been established at the central level.

State/union territory (UT) governments have rehabilitation schemes, provide various facilities and concessions. Some of the state government give pensions to disabled persons. Old age pensions are given at varying rates by almost all the state/UT governments.

A large number of NGOs have initiated a variety of CBR programmes for the different categories of disabled persons. Most of these programmes have been initiated with the assistance of leading international funding and developmental organizations. India has also developed training facilities at a number of locations for the training of the CBR field functionaries.

The Council for Advancement of People's Action and Rural Technology (CAPART) has taken initiatives to extend its services to people with disabilities. It plans to promote CBR of all categories of people with disabilities through its existing network of thousands of rural development organizations.

10. Assistive devices

The Government of India has implemented a scheme through registered societies, trusts and companies under which assistive devices are provided. They include wheelchairs, crutches, calipers, hearing aids and artificial limbs. Such services costing Rs2,500-3,600 are given free to those having a monthly income of up to Rs1200; and at 50 per cent of the cost to those having a monthly income from Rs1201-2500.

The total allocation under the scheme was Rs550 million under the Eighth Five-year Plan. The proposed allocation of funds during the Ninth Five-year Plan has been projected as Rs1.25 billion. An initiative has been taken to spread the geographical coverage of the scheme so as to make the assistive devices available to the rural disabled population living in far-flung and un-reached areas. The number of organizations assisted under the scheme has increased to 140 during 1996-1997. The district level development agencies are also being encouraged to take up the responsibility of free and subsidized distribution of aids and appliances. There is a proposal to revise the scheme and raise the ceiling of the cost of aids and appliances and the income limit per month.

Individual and group hearing aids are made in the country by half a dozen different companies. A number of tests for assessing intellectual disability have been developed in the country. The National Institute for the Mentally Handicapped has developed an assessment kit for intellectually disabled persons.

The science and technology project in mission mode was launched in 1988 and aims to develop suitable and cost-effective aids and appliances with the application of technology, and also to improve the mobility, employment opportunities and integration of disabled persons into mainstream society.

Suitable research and development projects are identified and funded under the scheme on a 100 per cent basis. So far, 49 projects have been identified for assistance and nine new projects identified for funding in the current year. About 37 of them are at various stages of completion, some have been put to commercial production. Among the important projects are those for the speech synthesizer, computerized Braille embosser, inter-pointing Braille writing frames, close circuit television with magnification facility, multi-functional wheelchair, feeding aids for children with cerebral palsy and safety devices for use in threshers.

The government has set up an Artificial Limbs Manufacturing Corporation (ALIMCO) at Kanpur under the Companies Act with the aim of manufacturing and marketing artificial limbs and, aids and appliances to meet the requirements of people with disabilities. It manufactures a large variety of aids and appliances and artificial limbs in the categories of "orthotic lower", "orthotic upper", "prosthetic lower" and "prosthetic upper". It has 24 regional and peripheral fitting centres in different parts of the country for providing artificial limbs, and aids and appliances to disabled persons. The state-run Indian Drugs and Pharmaceuticals Ltd also manufactures aids and appliances.

The Artificial Limb Centre (Armed Forces) Pune, caters to the needs of servicemen, ex-servicemen and civilians. A few voluntary organizations and institutions also manufacture artificial limbs and, aids and appliances. The Jaipur Foot is manufactured by *Bhagwan Mahavir Viklang Sahayata Samiti*, Jaipur, and is one of the most popular artificial limbs for bare-foot walking. Nevedac at Chandigarh, a private organization, also makes a variety of appliances. Motorized tricycles are being made in private sector. Most of the appliances needed for the education of visually-disabled persons are made within the country. The National Institute for the Visually Handicapped is the main producer.

The Ministry of Finance will be asked to relax the customs duties levied on the import of assistive devices with a view to suggesting further exemption and simplification of the proceedings.

The Government of India is also considering the modalities for establishing a chain of limb fitting centres to increase the availability of assistive devices along with maintenance services at the door steps of disabled people.

11. Self-help organizations

It has been the policy of the government to consult NGOs and self-help organizations, and eminent people with disabilities in formulation of all its policies and programmes for the welfare of disabled persons. In all the committees and advisory bodies, there is adequate representation of NGOs and people with disabilities.

Several self-help organizations have developed in the country. Among them are the National Federation of the Blind, the Handicapped Welfare Federation and Parents Association of Children with Intellectual Disabilities. CAPART has been encouraging formation of self-help organizations by giving them the necessary technical and financial inputs.

Recently the Ministry of Welfare undertook an initiative during 1996-1997, by starting a four-month long training programme for rural disabled volunteers in rehabilitation. The programme aims to impart the necessary inputs on disability and rehabilitation related issues along with knowledge of concessions and facilities provided by the government to disabled persons. These volunteers are also expected to form the self-help organizations of disabled persons.

Furthermore, the Ministry of Rural Areas and Employment has suggested that suitable amendments be made in the integrated rural development programme guidelines and provide an assistance of Rs25,000 to the self-help organizations of disabled persons for taking up suitable economic ventures.

A large number of volunteers are likely to be trained during the Ninth Five-year Plan period from 1997 to 2002. A large number of self-help organizations are expected to be formed during this period.

12. Regional cooperation

The Government of India is a signatory to the Proclamation on the Full Participation and Equality of People with Disabilities in the Asian and Pacific Region. It has contributed US$50,000 to the ESCAP Technical Trust Fund for the Asian and Pacific Decade of Disabled Persons. The above contribution was partly utilized to conduct a technical workshop on the indigenous production and distribution of assistive devices in Chennai, India, in September 1995. Countries such as Bangladesh, Bhutan, Cambodia, China, Fiji, Indonesia, Iran, Malaysia, Maldives, Myanmar, Nepal, Pakistan, Philippines, Sri Lanka, Thailand and Viet Nam participated in the Workshop.

India actively participated in the SAARC Year of Disabled Persons, 1993. India's Ministry of Welfare participated in the Ministerial Conference of SAARC countries held in Islamabad from 16 to 18 December 1993, where a 16-point resolution was adopted. It was decided that a workshop on rehabilitation techniques should be organized in India to exchange information on strategies, programmes and activities undertaken for the identification, treatment, management, special education and rehabilitation of people with disabilities.

Accordingly, a workshop was organized in the premises of the National Institute for the Mentally Handicapped at Secunderabad from 28 November to 2 December 1994. Twelve delegates from SAARC countries attended the meeting. The five-day programme comprised of the scientific-sessions and visits to institutions to enable the participants to observe and obtain first-hand experience about special education and rehabilitation programmes.

A two-point resolution was also adopted. The first concerns the organization of annual workshops to exchange information and review follow-up actions by the SAARC countries on the recommendations made at various meetings. The second relates to requests from the SAARC countries to India to extend its training on disability rehabilitation to professionals working in the field of physiotherapy, occupational therapy, prosthetics and orthotics, speech therapy, audiology, teacher training and rehabilitation to strengthen exchange of information, programmes and skills.

The Joint Secretary, Handicapped Welfare Division and Executive Officer of the National Association for the Blind, Anuradha Mohit, who is visually-impaired, participated in the SAARC workshop titled "The building of linkages among member countries", held from 7 to 9 February 1995 in Kathmandu. Certain useful recommendations have been made in the workshop aimed at building linkages among SAARC member countries.

India has been actively participating in efforts made to develop strategies and plans of action to ensure equal opportunities and full participation for people with disabilities. The Additional Secretary, the Ministry of Welfare and Joint Secretary (IRD) and the Ministry of Rural Areas and Employment jointly participated in the Intercountry Seminar on Multisectoral Collaborative Action for People with Disabilities held in December 1996 in Kuala Lumpur.

As part of its contribution to regional cooperation in the Asian and Pacific Decade of Disabled Persons, India hosted the India-China Seminar on Multisectoral Collaborative Action for People with Disabilities in New Delhi from 25 March to 2 April 1997. The seminar was organized in close cooperation with ESCAP and other members of the Regional Interagency Committee for Asia and the Pacific (RICAP) Subcommittee on Disability-related Concerns.

The purpose of the seminar was to initiate a high-level dialogue between China and India on the means of generating a more conducive policy and programme towards achieving the targets set to help achieve the goals stated in the Asian and Pacific Decade Agenda for Action. Some 78 participants, including senior state and provincial officials, attended the seminar. Leading NGOs were also represented.

Various useful recommendations, both for inter- and multisectoral collaborative actions, emerged from this seminar in all the important sectors such as health, vocational training and employment, communication, access and education, which will promote the inclusion of people with disabilities in the mainstream policies.

The Chinese delegation undertook a field-visit which included observation of subnational and micro-level programmes for the empowerment of people with disabilities.

CHAPTER IX

Indonesia

A. National overview

Indonesia proclaimed its independence on 17 August 1945 after more than three centuries of Dutch rule. The Republic of Indonesia is the world's largest archipelago with more than 17,000 islands, stretching along the equator between the Pacific and India oceans. The country's five main islands are Irian, Java, Kalimantan, Sulawesi and Sumatra. Out of these five, Java is the smallest and the most densely populated with about 814 persons per square kilometre, and some 60 per cent of the country's total population of 200 million live there.

In Java, about 70 per cent of the people live in the rural areas and they are mainly farmers and fishermen. However as industries grow and the country moves from being an agricultural society to an industrialized one, the lifestyle of its people has changed in tandem.

One of the goals of Indonesia's national development programme is to achieve a just and prosperous society, based on *Pancasila,* the five principles of its state ideology.

The country started implementing its national development plan in April 1969. This overall framework covers two aspects; long- and short-term developments. The long-term plans span 25 years while the short-term ones cover five years. Indonesia is now in its sixth short-term development stage while its second long-term developmental stage has just begun.

The national development plan aims to improve the lives and prosperity of Indonesians. When it was implemented in 1969, the country's per capital income was US$100 compared to US$1,000 now. Then about 65 per cent of the total population were living below the poverty line, now the figure has gone down to 11 per cent. The Government of Indonesia hopes to reduce the numbers to zero by the turn of the century.

The welfare of people with disabilities is an important part of the national development plan. Indonesia is committed to implementing the Agenda for Action for the Asian and Pacific Decade of Disabled Persons (hereafter referred to as the Asian and Pacific Decade Agenda for Action), 1993 to 2002. It achieved a milestone when the Indonesian Parliament passed legislation number 4/1997 on People with Disabilities on 28 February 1997.

B. Policy measures

1. National coordination

Under *Pancasila,* people with disabilities are an integral part of society and they enjoy the same rights and obligations as other Indonesians. They are given the same opportunities as their fellow citizens and are also expected to participate actively in and contribute to the development of the country. People with disabilities can also take part in the social and political life in Indonesia.

They have rights to education, social welfare, medical care and rehabilitation, jobs and access to other public facilities and services in the country.

According to the Department of Social Affairs, there are now 6 million people with disabilities, or 3.11 per cent of the total population in Indonesia. There are various kinds of disabilities. As the country industrializes, the figure is expected to increase, thus more needs to be done to help people with disabilities become more independent.

The programmes to promote the welfare and total integration of people with disabilities are implemented both by the government and non-governmental organizations (NGOs). However, NGOs are gradually expected to play more essential roles in carrying out these programmes. The government will continue to develop the basic policies, guide, counsel NGOs and create a more conducive environment for NGOs to carry out their tasks effectively.

The Government of Indonesia also supports, at all levels, organizations for people with disabilities. It promotes coordination and cooperation among NGOs at the national, regional and international levels. Another task is to encourage the business community to cooperate with social development NGOs.

The welfare development programme covers areas such as prevention, rehabilitation, social assistance and care. The government and the NGOs jointly carry out the programme.

A national coordinating body was established in 1983 to oversee the welfare development programmes and to ensure that they are carried out effectively. Its members include various government agencies, NGOs, organization of persons with disabilities as well as representatives from the business community.

2. Legislation

Currently there are 12 statutes which can be used as the basis to advance the welfare of people with disabilities in Indonesia. The most important is the recently enacted law number 4/1997 on people with disabilities. Every government department and institution would use that law to formulate their policies, strategies and programmes to improve and promote the welfare of disabled persons. The implementation of these activities is an integral part of each sector in the overall national development plan.

3. Rehabilitation services

From the rehabilitation centre at Surakarta in Central Java, Professor Soeharso started rehabilitation for people with disabilities in 1950. Since then, the country had witnessed tremendous growth in the development of rehabilitation services for persons with disabilities. The national development plan, and regional and international movements on rehabilitation services helped speed up this growth.

In 1981, the United Nations launched the International Year of Disabled Persons, and two years later, the United Nations Decade of Disabled Persons was proclaimed. In a review of the impact of the United Nations Decade, it was recognized that progress towards improving the situation of disabled persons had been uneven, particularly in the developing and least developed countries. This, together with the concerns raised by governments and NGOs prompted the launch of the Asian and Pacific Decade of Disabled Persons, 1993-2002, in Beijing in 1992.

The national development plan provides the guidelines for rehabilitation works, which are carried out by NGOs and various government agencies, including the Department of Social Affairs, Department of Education and Culture, Department of Health and Department of Manpower.

For the Department of Social Affairs, its aims in rehabilitation are to:

(a) Promote outreach services in rehabilitation;

(b) Promote community participation in rehabilitation;

(c) Develop quality facilities and infrastructure;

(d) Promote partnership between social institutions and corporations.

Social rehabilitation services are provided via two methods: the institutional and non-institutional care systems. Currently, there are 38 institutions for people with disabilities in Indonesia. Non-institutional care systems include sheltered workshops, mobile rehabilitation units, small scheme enterprises vocational learning practices and the re-socialisation and resettlement of former leprosy patients.

The Department of Social Affairs estimates that a total of 50,000 people each year benefit from the two social rehabilitation systems.

The Department of Health and the Office of the Minister for Family Planning had also recorded much success in their programmes to prevent disabilities. Both government agencies have established medical rehabilitation units.

4. Education

Indonesia has special schools for people with disabilities, including schools for visually-impaired persons, intellectually disabled persons, physically disabled persons, hearing-impaired persons and multiply disabled persons. Education for disabled children and youth is also carried out through an integrated system.

5. Training and employment

The Government of Indonesia and the community have been providing vocational training to people with disabilities through institutional care, sheltered and community workshops, and vocational training centres.

The Minister of Social Affairs, Minister of Education and Culture, Minister of Religious Affairs, and Minister of Home Affairs have also pledged to jointly promote the equal opportunity and rights for people with disabilities through the provision of nine years of national elementary education.

In addition, the Minister of Social Affairs, and Minister of Manpower, together with the Indonesia business association, have promised to increase employment opportunities for people with disabilities and also to create better understanding and awareness in society toward disabled persons.

C. Progress made in the first half of the Asian and Pacific Decade of Disabled Persons

1. National coordination

The national coordinating body on the promotion of the welfare of persons with disabilities was strengthened and restructured on 23 August 1997. With the restructuring, the body now consists of 12 working groups: each focusing on one of the 12 areas listed in the Agenda for Action for the Asian and Pacific Decade of Disabled Persons (hereafter referred as the Asian and Pacific Decade Agenda for Action. Such working groups are formed both at the national and provincial levels. To better meet the goals of the Asian and Pacific Decade of Disabled Persons, a national NGO network was established on 16 November 1994. It is the national counterpart of the Regional NGO Network for the Promotion of the Asian and Pacific Decade of Disabled Persons. In addition, five related national organizations have held several conferences on disability.

2. Legislation

A comprehensive law concerning people with disabilities number 04/1997 was enacted on 28 February 1997.

3. Information

Steps have been taken to establish an information system among the Department of Social Affairs, Department of Health, Department of Education and Culture, Department of Manpower, and Department of Information. The national NGOs, including the Indonesian National Council for Social Welfare, the National NGO Network, and the Indonesia Disabled People's Association, also attempted to establish a data centre and an information network.

4. Public awareness

Both government institutions and NGOs carried out nationwide public awareness campaigns through seminars, workshops, discussions, publications, television and radio programmes during the first five years of the Asian and Pacific Decade of Disabled Persons.

5. Accessibility and communication

In May 1997, a team was set up to develop the standards of accessibility in Indonesia. Members of the team include the school of architecture from Gajah Mada University and the institute for research, guidance and development of persons with disability in Yogyakarta.

To break down barriers faced by disabled persons in Indonesia, several organizations have begun to take initial steps to promote accessibility. For people who are visually or hearing impaired, barriers in access to information and communication are gradually removed through the promotion of Braille and talking books, other assistive devices and sign language.

6. Education

The Indonesian Government and NGOs provide educational services for people with disabilities. Currently there are about 240 special schools run by the government and 706 by NGOs. Recently various seminars and workshops were conducted to improve the quality and standard of those schools. Integrated education for children with disabilities started in 1979 and during the Asian and Pacific Decade of Disabled Persons, the system has strengthened and promoted.

7. Training and employment

The Departments of Social Affairs, Defence, and Manpower along with the NGOs conduct various programmes on training and employment for people with disabilities. Some progress has been made through these programmes. The Department of Social Affairs itself employs 200 people with disabilities. One NGO established a Fertrade consortium in December 1996 in Yogyakarta, to encourage people with disabilities to start their own businesses.

8. Prevention of disabilities

Health services in Indonesia have developed steadily, especially during the implementation of the national development plan since 1969. This steady development is due largely to the presence of the comprehensive health care system and services that have been further developed and improved upon during the first half of the Asian and Pacific Decade of Disabled Persons. Increasingly, all over the country, hospitals are building their own rehabilitation units, thus helping to prevent disabilities caused by illnesses and accidents.

Since 1995, the Department of Health has also been implementing a national immunization programme against poliomyelitis. The number of infants and children below five years old receiving immunization in 1995 was 21,745,000, and in 1996, it was 21,870,000. The results for 1997 are still being assessed.

The integrated health services for the villages, which can be found in almost all villages have been used very effectively for early detection and identification of infants with disabilities. In addition, community health centres, or *Puskesmas,* located in every sub-district, have become important links between the community and hospitals. Such referral systems have enhanced the prevention of disabilities.

Community awareness campaigns for the prevention of disabilities were carried out through the print and electronic media as well as through marriage and family planning counselling services

9. Rehabilitation services

Policies and programmes to promote rehabilitation services have been carried out both by government institutions and NGOs. Efforts were made to improve the quality of human resources, equipment, techniques and methods, and managerial skills. Innovative approaches were introduced.

Efforts to widen the coverage of rehabilitation services to reach the rural areas have also been implemented through mobile rehabilitation units, outreach programmes run by rehabilitation institutions, sheltered workshops and community-based rehabilitation. Community participation in the national development plan is stated in the national state guidelines, which include efforts to rehabilitate people with disabilities.

10. Assistive devices

Information on assistive devices has been disseminated through exhibitions, seminars, workshops, mobile rehabilitation units and community-based rehabilitation programmes.

The Government of Indonesia and a few NGOs have provided at low prices assistive devices which are adapted to local conditions. Training for assistive device technicians are carried out at hospitals and rehabilitation centres in collaboration with the United Nations Development Programme (UNDP) and the International Labour Organization (ILO).

11. Self-help organizations

At the national, provincial, and local levels, organizations of people with disabilities were established. Currently there are 752 such groups. However, many still need government assistance as well as empowerment. At the village level there are groups of people with disabilities working together on income generating schemes.

12. Regional cooperation

Through the coordination of ESCAP, relationships among countries in Asia and the Pacific on matters concerning people with disabilities have been continuously improving. Such relationships include cooperation, exchange of experts, fellowships, assistance in technical equipment and devices, and training of rehabilitation personnel from developing countries. Since 1983 the rehabilitation centre in surakarta has been involved in these.

National NGOs for and of people with disabilities have become members of regional as well as international organizations such as Rehabilitation International, Disabled Peoples' International, World Blind Union, and the Regional NGO Network for the Promotion of the Asian and Pacific Decade of Disabled Persons (RNN).

The Centre for Community-Based Rehabilitation Development and Training, an NGO in Indonesia, has been holding various regional and international seminars, workshops, and training on community-based rehabilitation.

D. Activities planned for the second half of the Asian and Pacific Decade of Disabled Persons

From the experiences learned in the first five years, Indonesia is fully aware of the many constraints which lie ahead. Therefore, it is appropriate to formulate a comprehensive programme to overcome those constraints.

These include insufficient funds, shortage of skilled personnel in rehabilitation, uneven distribution of people with disabilities where the majority live in rural areas, cultural barriers and unfavourable social attitudes towards disabled persons, and insufficient facilities and assistive devices.

Despite these constraints, an action plan for the second half of the Asian and Pacific Decade of Disabled Persons should be carried out and to intensify what has already been started. The law number 04/1997 will greatly facilitate such further efforts.

1. National coordination

(a) Promote and empower all organizations involved;

(b) Enhance the coordinating function of national organizations;

(c) Encourage and facilitate effective cooperation among organizations;

(d) Support and guide the implementation of programmes;

(e) Strengthen national and international networks.

2. Legislation

(a) Publicize and undertake a campaign for law number 04/1997 concerning people with disabilities;

(b) Draft rules and regulations to enforce law number 04/1997.

3. Information

(a) Establish a national data and information centre;

(b) Utilize optimally all existing mass media;

(c) Encourage the publication of literature on disability issues.

4. Public awareness

(a) Strengthen public awareness through exhibitions, demonstrations, workshops, seminars and rallies;

(b) The Department of Information should give its full support for campaigns.

5. Accessibility and communication

(a) Formulate special regulations on accessibility and enforce their implementations;

(b) Strengthen public concern for accessibility;

(c) Complete development of the national sign language;

(d) Develop a national network on Braille production and libraries;

(e) Manufacture communication and mobility devices.

6. Education

(a) Promote the inclusion of people with disabilities in compulsory nine-year elementary education;

(b) Improve the quality of training for people with disabilities;

(c) Promote the integrated education of children with disabilities.

7. Training and employment

(a) Develop quality facilities and infrastructure for vocational training of people with disabilities;

(b) Advocate jobs for people with disabilities in the open labour market;

(c) Provide domestic and overseas job opportunities for people with disabilities.

8. Prevention of disabilities

(a) Promote and strengthen early detection programmes for children with disabilities;

(b) Improve the health and nutrition of people with disabilities;

(c) Promote marriage and family planning guidance counselling for people with disabilities;

(d) Strengthen the efforts to enforce traffic regulations;

(e) Advocate job security regulations in industries.

9. Rehabilitation services

(a) Strengthen the quality and quantity of social, medical, educational, and vocational rehabilitation services;

(b)   Strengthen community participation in social rehabilitation services;

(c)   Develop community-based rehabilitation programmes.

10. Assistive devices

(a)   Promote technology for assistive devices for people with disabilities;

(b)   Promote cooperation among government, NGOs, and international agencies in transferring technology at low cost.

11. Self-help organizations

(a)   Empower organizations of persons with disabilities;

(b)   Promote, develop and strengthen self-help organizations of people with disabilities.

12. Regional cooperation

(a)   Develop and further strengthen regional cooperation;

(b)   Participate in regional and international events.

E. Conclusion and recommendations

Indonesia is fully aware that the implementation of the Asian and Pacific Decade Agenda for Action has not been carried out thoroughly.   Nevertheless, there has been a definite trend towards excellent cooperation and better understanding between governments and NGOs.

The Asian and Pacific Decade Agenda for Action has proved to be in line with the national development plan in Indonesia, which emphasizes the alleviation of poverty, and the promotion of social justice.   The Asian and Pacific Decade Agenda for Action has enabled the country to strengthen its unity with regional countries.   Such regional cooperation has given Indonesia the opportunity to share its experiences which, in turn, has helped in social, economic, science and technological, educational and cultural developments in the country.

Thus the Agenda for Action for Asian and Pacific Decade of Disabled Persons should be well supported by the respective governments in the region and there should also be concerted efforts to raise funds to implement programmes.   Finally, it can be stated that the Asian and Pacific Decade Agenda for Action has given all countries the spirit to work earnestly towards the total integration of people with disabilities into society.

CHAPTER X

Islamic Republic of Iran

A. National overview

The Islamic Republic of Iran covers an area of 1,648,000 square kilometres, and is ranked sixteenth in size worldwide. About half of the land is mountainous, one-quarter desert, leaving one-fourth as arable land. Two-thirds of the land is situated on a high plateau with an average altitude of 1,150 metres. The population density is 35 persons per square kilometre with a variation of between 10 and 100. The country is situated in a highly seismic region. Frequent floods threaten some parts of the country.

The country is divided administratively into 27 provinces which are comprised of 236 districts. Districts are subdivided into 578 cities and 630 sub-districts, the latter of which are rural areas further divided into 2,182 townships, constituting some 66,000 villages.

Based on the 1996 census, the population of the Islamic Republic of Iran is currently 60 million, about 40 per cent of whom live in rural and 60 per cent in urban areas. Most of the population is young, with 45 per cent below 15 years of age and 6 per cent over 60 years of age. The average size of a household is five. The population growth rate has decreased in recent years and is about 1.7 per cent in 1997.

Muslims constitute the majority (98.8 per cent) of the population among whom 91 per cent are Shi'a. Other religious groups include Armenians, Assyrians, Jews and Zoroastrians who are officially recognized and who have their own representatives in the Islamic Consultative Assembly.

B. Policy measures

The Government of the Islamic Republic of Iran is preparing a long-term 25-year Socio-economic Development Plan, *Iran in the Year 2020,* which maps out the country's development until the year 2020.

C. Progress made in the first half of the Asian and Pacific Decade of Disabled Persons

1. National coordination

In the Islamic Republic of Iran, the state welfare organization shoulders the task of carrying out the activities and plans to achieve the goals stated in the Agenda for Action for the Asian and Pacific Decade of Disabled Persons, 1993-2002.

The country has achieved the following:

(a) The establishment of the State High Council for Coordination of Disabled Persons Affairs (HCCDPA), presided over by the President of the Islamic Republic of Iran and represented by the Ministers of Health and Medical Education, Labour and Social Affairs, Interior, Housing and Urban Development, Industries, Education, Culture and Higher Education, as well as the authorities of the Organizations of Welfare, Planning and Budget, Administration and Employment, Radio and Television Broadcasting and the Disabled Persons Organization. The Council, as the highest decision-making body in the country, shall be in charge of coordinating state's disabled persons' affairs. Accordingly, in order to speed up decision making, the Minister of Health and Medical Education has been vested with presidential authority;

(b) Cooperation with organizations, institutions and establishments related to disability issues and those providing social services, including Imam Khomeini Aid Committee, Red Crescent, Mostazafan and Janbazan Foundation (Foundation for the Deprived), 15th Khordad Foundation, Social Security Organization, and State Organization for Education of Exceptional Children;

(c) Collaboration with the effective organizations involved in disabled persons' affairs throughout provinces, cities and departments, including the Governor General's Office, Governor's Office, Municipality, Township Administration, Construction Crusade, Disciplinary Forces, Justice Administration, universities, Technical and Vocational Centres, Handicraft Centres and the Traffic Bureau;

(d) The establishment of relations, partnerships and cooperation with associations, non-government charity institutions and charity groups in order to attract necessary support for disabled persons;

(e) Establishing a high council for public participation in the state welfare organization with the membership of the Health Minister, Mayor, heads of trade unions and reliable local people as well as setting up similar councils in different provinces and cities.

2. Legislation

(a) Approval of a Tax Exemption Law for private rehabilitation centres;

(b) Exemption of rehabilitation devices from commercial interest and customs duties;

(c) Exemption of employers from insurance premium payments for their employees with disabilities;

(d) Issuance of orders and regulations by the Cabinet concerning allocation of special privileges for disabled persons in using the transportation system, post and telecommunication services.

3. Public awareness

Promoting public awareness for the purpose of creating positive changes in the people's attitudes towards people with disabilities through execution of plans such as:

(a) Broadcasting radio programmes in a specific local language;

(b) Distributing brochures and tracts on people with disabilities;

(c) Holding various exhibitions of artistic and handicraft activities and innovations of disabled persons;

(d) Holding seminars, conferences and symposiums on disability and rehabilitation in terms of medical, social and vocational rehabilitation as well as job placement aspects;

(e) Participation of disabled artists in different exhibitions;

(f) Distribution of educational brochures on how to deal and communicate with disabled students and civil servants;

(g) Introducing disabled people to society through radio interviews or telling stories of their lives in the media;

(h) Conducting school and university students' visits to disabled people in order for them to get to know better disabled people's special activities and services;

(i) Carrying out consultations with relatives, parents and friends of people with disabilities in order to make them aware of the social status of disabled persons;

(j) Obtaining statistics on the exact number of disabled persons and different types of disabilities, especially in rural areas, for further planning and improvement of services, as well as promotion of education and creation of job opportunities;

(k) Contacting Friday/community prayer leaders and clergymen and seeking their cooperation in creating a positive attitude towards persons with disabilities and transferring such knowledge to the public;

(l) Making efforts, however limited, to release important material in the form of cassettes, Braille and sign language interpretation in television news;

(m) Continuous efforts to bring disabled persons into mainstream society by increasing the awareness of school and university students, civil servants and rural inhabitants;

(n) Producing special radio programmes for blind persons;

(o) Holding film festivals highlighting the capabilities of disabled persons;

(p) The celebration of International Day of Disabled Persons, Welfare Week and special days for each group of persons with disabilities by government and non-governmental organizations with active participation of disabled persons and their self-help organizations to promote public awareness;

(q) Providing plans and preparing preliminary steps for the establishment of the State Rehabilitation Information Centre in order to collect detailed information of the number of persons with disabilities and types and quality of rehabilitation services and to make such information available to experts and authorities in charge of disability issues;

(r) Introducing the concept of self-help to disabled persons in need of rehabilitation;

(s) Providing public information, directly and indirectly, using easy methods to introduce disabled persons, their disabilities and methods for prevention of accidents leading to disability. This will be carried out with the help of assistant teachers, rural health centre officers and religious professors and lecturers;

(t) Starting research projects in universities and institutions of higher learning and research as well as supporting those projects focusing on how to get acquainted with different aspects of disability and rehabilitation.

4. Accessibility and communication

(a) Conducting meetings with bank supervisors, governors, mayors, township administrators and Traffic Bureau officers on preparing public transport facilities for disabled persons;

(b) Conducting seminars on removing environmental barriers for disabled persons;

(c) Establishing special bodies within different Governor Generals' offices for removing environmental barriers for disabled persons in compliance with the High Council of Architecture and Urban Development rules concerning required construction norms and standards for access;

(d) Communicating with various municipalities to ask for non-issuance of permits for those building construction projects in which the removal of architectural barriers has not been considered;

(e) Talking to public transportation authorities in order to prepare facilities for disabled persons to get on and off public transportation vehicles, making necessary changes in city buses, preparing a special place for disabled persons inside the buses and trains as well as manufacturing special buses suitable for wheelchair users;

(f) Taking into consideration the minimum standards and equipment needed for disabled persons in the design of buildings and places to be used by disabled persons;

(g) Releasing books and references in Braille or audiocassettes;

(h) Providing translation services in sign language in public places and departments such as disciplinary forces centres, hospitals, courts and financial and social institutions;

(i) Supplying funding for the purchase of fax machines for deaf persons or mobile phones for other disabled persons;

(j) Removing physical barriers in historical places and buildings, parks and schools;

(k) Supporting research and encouraging scientific and research associations to carry out studies on how to prepare facilities for people with disabilities;

(l) Providing public telephone booths and bathrooms for disabled persons in different places and institutions affiliated with the Welfare Organization and promoting the building of similar facilities in other places;

(m) Identifying major urban architectural barriers and providing necessary facilities for the physical preparation of buildings as well as determining the standard conditions in the reconstruction and renovation of the existing old buildings, in order to achieve barrier-free built environments;

(n) Designing special stairways according to the design criteria for disabled persons, construction of bridges connecting streets and pavements, distribution and attachment of distinctive stickers on disabled persons' cars as well as the installation of elevators in buildings with more than four storeys;

(o) Designing and manufacturing vehicles suitable for disabled persons;

(p) Preparing illustrated reports of cities, provincial albums, printing and distributing brochures on the importance of removing architectural barriers for disabled persons;

(q) Granting interest-free loans or grants to persons with disabilities for the remodelling of their homes;

(r) Contacting the Council of Community Prayer Leaders in order to encourage them to equip religious places with facilities for disabled persons and promoting the same attitude among the public especially during occasions like the Mosque Construction Week;

(s) Transferring the experience of using equipment for disabled persons and other activities to other provinces;

(t) Establishing a call-in transportation service for disabled persons, with proper subsidies by the State Welfare Organization;

(u) Publishing a newspaper in Braille for countrywide circulation in partnership with one of the official government newspapers;

(v) Broadcasting television news in sign language for deaf persons and producing radio programmes for blind persons, which, in addition to promoting public awareness, will facilitate the availability of information to blind persons and deaf persons;

(w) Broadcasting educational television programmes on how families and relatives can take care of disabled persons;

(x) Providing public libraries for disabled persons and making available books in Braille and audiocassettes;

(y) Providing special libraries with audio facilities for blind persons, and preparing and recording books on cassettes with the help of volunteer university students and devoted women.

5. Education

(a) Preparing proper programmes for the teaching of adult disabled persons in conjunction with the literacy campaign;

(b) Conducting pre-school children's disability screening project in cooperation with the State Organization for Education of Exceptional Children;

(c) Preparing pre-school facilities for children with hearing disabilities, through the training of teachers of child care centres for such children;

(d) Coordinating and streamlining educational methods for deaf children under six in cooperation with the State Organization for Education of Exceptional Children;

(e) Encouraging research by experts in order to improve the educational situation for deaf persons;

(f) Collection of national sign language vocabulary and production of a sign language dictionary;

(g) Training teachers to educate persons with disabilities;

(h) Providing audio services for blind students including recording school books on cassettes;

(i) Preparing the required facilities for disabled persons to participate in university entrance examinations;

(j) Granting scholarships to disabled students in universities and school students who are blind, deaf or with motor disabilities, as well as free distribution of Braille materials for people with sight impairments;

(k) Preparing useful school books for partially blind persons and those with sight impairments in cooperation with the State Organization for Education of Exceptional Children;

(l) Preparing special comprehensive educational materials for disabled persons, including private and individual educational programmes and aids;

(m) Conducting educational courses for the trainers of intellectually disabled people;

(n) Using educational and computer technology to advance the welfare of certain groups with disability;

(o) Regular releasing of educational publications, conducting educational seminars and workshops for rehabilitation experts and trainers of persons with disabilities;

(p) Sending the Welfare Organization's experts to other countries in order for them to receive training and to get acquainted with the activities and programmes of other countries;

(q) Conducting courses as well as on-the-job training for disabled persons' trainers and experts throughout the country and different provinces to promote their knowledge and skills and to encourage transference of those skills;

(r)   Benefiting from the educational facilities and programmes of organizations and institutions involved with disabled persons (such as technical and vocational centres of the Red Crescent of the Islamic Republic of Iran, Handicrafts and Metal Industries Organization) for the training of disabled persons and their instructors;

(s)   Cooperating with PTAs to provide facilities for solving the educational problems of disabled persons;

(t)   Distance learning facilities to be provided by open schools and open universities for those students who can not attend regular schools and universities.

6. Training and employment

(a)   Finding proper occupations for persons with certain disabilities throughout urban and rural areas;

(b)   Vocational training of disabled persons in rural areas using existing facilities in the areas;

(c)   Vocational training in those fields in which disabled persons could prove successful, by using the facilities of special training centres;

(d)   Making efforts to conduct vocational training programmes for disabled persons with the cooperation of non-disabled persons;

(e)   Execution of the Disabled Persons Employment Act through implementing the employment quota (3 per cent) for disabled persons required for government organizations;

(f)   Holding various exhibitions on disabled persons' capabilities in producing artistic and other works, including drawing, sewing, embroidery, pottery and handicrafts;

(g)   Encouraging women with disabilities to participate in income-generating occupations and preparing necessary facilities for this purpose;

(h)   Creating job opportunities for some disabled persons through grants, low-interest banking loans and credits, interest-free funds as well as letting them run news stands throughout the cities;

(i)   Supplying financial and assistive devices to those disabled persons involved in training courses offered by the State Welfare Organization's non-affiliated institutions and organizations;

(j)   Establishing, in cooperation with the Ministry of Cooperation, cooperative companies of people with disabilities which are mainly run by disabled persons, as well as providing financial aid, consultation and technical services through the State Welfare Organization;

(k) Granting incentives such as exemption for insurance premium payment to employers for supporting job placement of disabled persons in the open market;

(l) Involving trade unions and guild associations for employment of disabled persons through holding sessions and exchanging views with them to reach basic agreements on the employment of disabled persons in various non-government occupations;

(m) Conducting educational programmes for trade union representatives to introduce to them the needs of disabled persons and their capabilities and strengths;

(n) Concluding agreements between disabled persons and trade union representatives in order to develop areas of cooperation;

(o) Granting loans and other necessary facilities to employers who are employing disabled persons under agreements reached with the Ministry of Commerce and the Ministry of Cooperation.

7. Prevention of the causes of disability

(a) Identifying disabled persons especially in rural and remote tribal areas, in cooperation with health centres;

(b) Studying causes of hearing, visual, physical-motor and intellectual disabilities in order to prevent them in cooperation with health centres and *Behvarzes* (health workers), rural clinics as well as urban hospitals and health care centres;

(c) Conducting prevention programmes of thalassaemia and amblyopia through screening;

(d) Tackling industrial and vocational health issues as well as providing timely medical services and treatments in cases of accident;

(e) Conducting educational and explanatory courses for local clergymen, health corps, pregnant mothers and fourth grade female high school students on the prevention of hereditary and congenital disabilities as well as the dangers of inter-familial marriages;

(f) Providing films and slides for rural and tribal inhabitants on prenatal care and causes of disabilities;

(g) Cooperating with health centres in conducting genetic consultations with young couples;

(h) Identifying students who have scoliosis with the help of the Ministry of Education;

(i) Early detection of infants who have P.K.U.;

(j) Carrying out a hypothyroidism project for infants;

(k) Creating awareness and providing information through placing articles in local and state newspapers and magazines, educational pamphlets, tracts and radio and television programmes on the prevention of disabilities, disability development control and accidents causing disabilities, as well as conducting seminars with the participation of the Welfare Organization experts for disabled persons and other experts in various institutions and organizations in order to promote knowledge of basic measures to prevent disabilities;

(l) Investigation of the high rate of certain disabilities in particular regions by the Welfare Organization's senior directors for the purpose of taking drastic measures to prevent their occurrences;

(m) Vaccinating a high percentage of children against preventable diseases;

(n) Establishing genetic consultation units and broadcasting radio programmes on the issue;

(o) Screening children aged under three for hearing impairment;

(p) Cooperating with the relevant authorities in the poliomyelitis eradication project;

(q) Preparation of the national project for the welfare of older people in order to prevent or decrease disabilities and to promote the quality of their lives;

(r) Making preparations, in cooperation with various organizations, to cover older people with special health care insurance in such a way that people over 60 can benefit from supplementary health care insurance services throughout the country;

(s) Timely identification of disabilities and the provision of services to prevent development and complications of disabilities;

(t) Development of intersectoral cooperation to increase health services and promote the quality of health in cooperation with the Ministries of Education and Construction Crusade.

8. Rehabilitation services

(a) Designing a system for integrating rehabilitation services in the primary health care (PHC) network system and rendering services within the framework of community-based rehabilitation (CBR), while taking into account the needs of disabled persons and their families who require services;

(b) Designing national programmes for providing services to persons with different types of disabilities;

(c) Benefiting from the services of volunteers in the development of rehabilitation services;

(d) Conducting the child-to-child project in order to train school students to introduce the disability issues, thus creating positive attitudes in them and ensuring that equal services are provided by the schools to disabled persons;

(e) Benefiting from the active participation of disabled persons and their associations in making pertinent plans for disabled persons;

(f) Benefiting from charity institutions which provide rehabilitation services;

(g) Determining required education and medical and paramedical specialities concerning disabled persons and preparing the necessary training courses for medical and paramedical staff in rehabilitation centres;

(h) Providing rehabilitation services for more than 30 per cent of people in need of such services through specialized rehabilitation centres;

(i) Establishing mobile rehabilitation clinics to provide services to patients with spinal injuries by periodical examination of such patients to prevent development of subsequent disabilities;

(j) Planning a new style of rehabilitation services based on the potentialities of disabled persons, organizations and the Handicapped Centre to enjoy ordinary social facilities in the areas of health care, education, transportation and occupation;

(k) Holding consultations with charity institutions, self-help organizations of disabled persons, councils and organizations involved in providing services to disabled persons;

(l) Leading the private sector in providing rehabilitation services to disabled persons and supervising their activities;

(m) Giving financial support to rehabilitation services and activities and disability issues as well as rendering financial services to disabled people and their families who cannot benefit from the existing rehabilitation services;

(n) Developing daytime rehabilitation centres;

(o) Making efforts to involve other organizations in disability issues and changing the Welfare Organization's responsibility for disabled persons to a general responsibility involving all other organizations;

(p) Development of a scheduled CBR project.

9. Assistive Devices

(a) Distribution of assistive devices, including wheelchairs, hearing aids and batteries, special motorcycles for persons with mobility impairments, crutches, glasses, tape recorders, Braille equipment, orthosis and prosthesis, for free of charge or at the lowest possible price;

(b) Establishing cooperative companies of disabled persons to produce assistive devices, benefiting from the user's perspective;

(c) Encouraging competition among the manufacturers of assistive devices;

(d) Teaching the proper use of assistive devices to disabled persons and their families;

(e) Studying the effects of the environmental conditions on assistive devices in order to ensure the use of proper materials in the production of such devices;

(f) Procurement and distribution of spare parts for the repair of assistive devices and providing mobile centres to render repair services;

(g) Working with local craftsmen in the production of assistive devices;

(h) Supplying information to rehabilitation staff on assistive devices used throughout the world;

(i) Training special individuals for assessment, fitting and adjustment, and repair of assistive devices;

(j) Establish close cooperation with industrial university centres in the designing and production of proper assistive devices for disabled persons.

10. Self-help organizations

(a) Establishment of an umbrella association of persons with disabilities which comprises organizations of different types of disability;

(b) Establishment of an association for blind persons;

(c) Establishment of an association for deaf persons;

(d) Establishment of an association for the families of intellectually disabled persons;

(e) Representation of self-help organizations at legal bodies to defend the rights of persons with disabilities;

(f) Transferring vocational establishments of working places and facilities to disabled persons' self-help organizations and providing educational facilities for their members;

(g) Development of disability-specific associations for disabilities at the provincial and city levels throughout the country;

(h) Supporting the NGOs' role in promoting awareness of disability issues;

(i) Providing certain services required by disabled persons through associations of disabled persons.

C. Activities planned for the second half of the Asian and Pacific Decade of Disabled Persons

1. National coordination

(a) Development of activities determined for the High Council for Coordination of the Disabled Persons' Affairs (HCCDPA), taking into account the different requirements of disabled people;

(b) Promotion of HCCDPA's activities in provincial areas through establishing committees under the supervision of governor-generals to pursue the council's resolutions and adopt methods appropriate to each province's cultural and social structure;

(c) Execution of plans for helping disabled persons in rural and remote areas;

(d) Promotion of CBR programmes through local councils throughout the country;

(e) Further advancement and promotion of measures taken during the years 1993-97 for establishing national cooperation on disability issues;

(f) Encouraging public participation and cooperation as well as rendering voluntary services to disabled persons, especially those living in rural and tribal areas;

(g) In order to enjoy financial facilities in society and with regard to the disabled persons' interests and requirements in planning and decision making, all ministries and institutions shall elect a person from among their employees to oversee disability issues in the pertinent organizations and make every effort to involve the disabled persons in social activities.

2. Legislation

(a) Presentation of plans and legal bills by the Cabinet and representatives of the Islamic Republic of Iranian Parliament and the approval of necessary acts concerning employment of persons with disabilities;

(b) Pursuing the issue of supplementary health insurance coverage for disabled persons in urban and rural areas;

(c) Presenting legal plans aimed at officially recognizing "the rights of disabled persons" to enjoy education, employment, health care, family raising, participation in social and cultural activities, and removal of discrimination based on disabilities;

(d) Approval of laws and regulations concerning the support of disabled women and children with no families or guardians;

(e) Establishment of the Handicapped Employment Fund;

(f) Approval of comprehensive laws to fully cover issues including central and regional cooperation on disability issues, promotion of education and employment, prohibiting discrimination against disabled persons, issuance of permits for social security centres, appointment of a special representative for disabled persons in judicial bodies and departments as well as providing legal assistance for disabled persons.

3. Public awareness

(a) Carrying out applied research on better understanding of disabled persons, types of disabilities, rehabilitation structure and new rehabilitation methods;

(b) Promotion of the Rehabilitation Information Association;

(c) Conducting various programmes to promote public education through distance education, including special radio and television programmes for inhabitants of rural and remote areas;

(d) Making short films and video and television movies on the capabilities of disabled persons, causes of disabilities and the rehabilitation of disabled persons;

(e) Promotion of special radio and television programmes for deaf persons and blind persons;

(f) Holding art and sport competitions among disabled persons which will be publicized widely;

(g) Using art as a means of promoting public awareness, in conjunction with technical and art cooperation among ESCAP member countries.

4. Accessibility and communication

(a) Promotion and development of plans which were begun during the first five years of the Asian and Pacific Decade of Disabled Persons;

(b) Preparation of the Tehran subway for accessibility for disabled persons which will be commissioned during the second half of the Asian and Pacific Decade of Disabled Persons;

(c) Qualitative improvement of accessibility to public roads and passageways.

5. Education

(a) Integrating children and adults with disabilities into ordinary education programmes;

(b) Paying special attention to the education of young girls and women with disabilities especially in rural areas;

(c) Providing learning facilities and mobile services for those disabled persons who are not able to attend regular classes.

6. Training and employment

(a) Promotion and enhancement of programmes undertaken in the first five years;

(b) Using computers in the vocational education of persons with disabilities;

(c) Further involvement of guild associations and trade unions in the employment of disabled persons.

7. Prevention of the causes of disabilities

(a) Pursuing the activities and measures of the first five-year period concerning prevention of causes of disabilities, with emphasis on certain aspects;

(b) Dissemination of information to rural families on the prevention of causes of disabilities in cooperation with rural health centres and rural welfare assemblies;

(c) Execution of timely disability identification programmes through screening of different age groups.

8. Rehabilitation services

(a) Continuously implementing the measures of rehabilitative services undertaken in the first half of the Asian and Pacific Decade of Disabled Persons;

(b) Development of CBR services throughout the country;

(c) Development of daytime rehabilitation centres;

(d) Involving other state organizations in providing rehabilitation services for persons with disabilities and their families.

9. Assistive devices

(a) Promotion of the activities being carried out in the first five years of the Asian and Pacific Decade of Disabled Persons;

(b) Development of cooperative companies for the production assistive devices;

(c) Benefiting from experiences of other countries in Asian and Pacific in the utilization of local facilities to produce indigenous assistive devices.

10. Self-help organizations

(a) Encouraging the effective participation of organizations and councils of disabled persons in planning of programmes that concern them;

(b) Educating disabled persons and members of self-help organizations to become involved in issues important to them;

(c) Supporting the activities of self-help orgnizations in promoting public awareness and knowledge toward disability issues.

CHAPTER XI

Japan

A. Progress made in the first half of the Asian and Pacific Decade of Disabled Persons

1. National coordination

In accordance with the Disabled Persons Fundamental Law, Japan's Central Council for the Promotion of Measures for Disabled Persons was established in June 1994 to survey and consider the establishment of basic and comprehensive measures for disabled persons. Members of the council comprise academics, persons with disabilities, representatives of groups involved with disabled persons, and government officials.

2. Legislation

In November 1993, the Disabled Persons Fundamental Law was revised to include in its basic philosophy that "all persons with disabilities are to be given the opportunity as members of society to participate in social, economic and cultural activities in all spheres". It was also made clear that the purpose of the law is to achieve "full participation and equality" of persons with disabilities. The types of disabilities included under the law are distinguished as physical disabilities,[1] intellectual disabilities and mental disabilities.

The revision encompasses the following concerns:

(a) Measures to reduce economic hardships on enterprise owners hiring disabled persons;

(b) Measures to improve the ease of use of electronic communication and broadcast services by disabled persons;

(c) Measures needed for the improvement of public transportation and other public facilities so that they are accessible to disabled persons.

In addition to the revision of the Disabled Persons Fundamental Law, related laws were also enacted or revised in various policy areas.

---

[1] In Japan, physical disability includes visual impairment, hearing impairment and orthopaedic disability.

To meet the requirements of the Disabled Persons Fundamental Law, the new long-term programme for government measures concerning disabled persons, formulated in March 1993 by the Headquarters for Promoting the Welfare of Disabled Persons, was approved.

In December 1995, the Headquarters for Promoting the Welfare of Disabled Persons formulated the Government Action Plan for Persons with Disabilities, setting numerical goals regarding what should be implemented by 2002 in the various policy areas.

Concrete Goals for the Government Action Plan for Persons with Disabilities

Target measure	1995	1996	1997	–	2002
Securing places for living, work and activities				–	
* Group homes and welfare homes (number of people)	5,347	7,422	9,173	–	20,000
* Sheltered workshops and welfare factories (number of people)	41,783	45,874	50,795	–	68,000
Regional support for self-sufficiency				–	
* Day care projects for children (persons) with extensive motor and intellectual disabilities (number of facilities)	307	368	460	–	1,300
Promotion of social reintegration for persons with mental disabilities				–	
* Facilities for training in daily living for persons with mental disabilities, i.e., care homes (number of people)	1,660	2,060	2,840	–	6,000
* Social rehabilitation training for persons with mental disabilities (number of people)	3,770	3,984	4,198	–	5,000
* Psychiatric day care facilities (number of facilities)	372	471	549	–	1,000
Comprehensive care services					
(1) Home-based services					
* Home helpers (number of people)	92,482	8,000*	15,500	–	45,000
** additional people			**	–	**

Target measure	1995	1996	1997	–	2002
* Short-term stays (number of people)	1,082	1,454	1,836	–	4,500
* Day care service (number of facilities)	501	559	627	–	1,000
(2) Residential services					
* Nursing home for physically disabled persons (number of people)	17,169	18,069	19,169	–	25,000
* Rehabilitation facilities for persons with mental disabilities (number of people)	84,490	86,393	88,296	–	95,000

Japan also amended Mental Health Law in 1993. The following amendments were made:

(a) The definition of persons with mental disabilities was revised from persons with psychosis, intellectual disability and personality disorders to "persons with schizophrenia, psychotic disorders due to psychoactive substance use, intellectual disability, personality disorders and other mental disorders";

(b) The setting up of a centre for promoting social reintegration of persons with mental disabilities to conduct research and development of assistive techniques at rehabilitation facilities as well as for the raising of public awareness;

(c) Absolute disqualification of the persons with mental disabilities to be dieticians, cooks, radiographers was changed to non-absolute disqualification.

The Mental Health Law was renamed the Law concerning Mental Health and Welfare for Mentally Disabled Persons in 1995 to improve the welfare services for persons with mental disabilities.

The purpose of the new law is to provide medical care, protection, promotion of social reintegration, and enhancement of mental health of the people. A new measure supporting independence and social participation was added in the amendment.

As for the social reintegration facilities, four types of facilities, namely rehabilitation facilities, sheltered workshops, welfare homes and welfare factories are regulated under the law. The mentally disabled person's certificate was introduced to certify that a person has a mental disability. The persons issued with the certificate are entitled to various welfare service provisions, including tax deductions and waiver of medical fees.

The Law concerning the Promotion of Research, Development and Distribution of Assistive Devices was enacted in 1993. Through this law, research and development of assistive devices was promoted and the distribution system improved upon.

The Law for Employment Promotion of Disabled Persons, 1960, which regulates the promotion of employment and vocational training based on the obligations for employment of persons with physical disabilities, was amended in 1997. In it, the term "the obligations for employment of persons with physical disabilities" was changed to "the obligations for employment of persons with physical disabilities and/or intellectual disabilities".

To promote the construction of buildings that can be used easily by older persons and physically disabled persons, in June 1994, the Act on Buildings Accessible to and Usable for Older Persons and Physically Disabled Persons was enacted. It provides guidelines to make specified buildings barrier-free through advice or instructions to owners of buildings, and the use of supportive measures such as subsidies, tax exemptions, and public funding for buildings approved by the prefectural governor as having met the directive's standards.

In November 1993, road construction ordinances were revised to make sidewalks and other pedestrian avenues safe for wheelchair users, defining these as "wide" sidewalks, with a width of three metres or more. In May 1996, the Public Housing Law was revised, relaxing the conditions on the number of households in public housing rebuilding and other projects where these are jointly-built social welfare facilities. The revision allows social welfare bodies that are carrying out certain social welfare projects to use public housing for residential purposes.

The Law for Promoting Businesses that Facilitate the Use of Communications and Broadcast Services by the Physically Disabled was established in 1993. Based on this law, in April 1994, the Telecommunication Advancement Organization of Japan began to offer information on communication and broadcast services for blind and deaf persons. Under this law grants are now available to create captioned television programmes for hearing impaired persons as well as commentatory television programmes for visually disabled persons.

Japan's main plan for disaster measures, the Basic Plan for Disaster Prevention, which was revised on 18 July 1995, clearly states the need for detailed measures that take into consideration those most vulnerable in a disaster, including disabled persons. Based on this philosophy, local public entities are being given guidelines, including paying attention to information dissemination, providing evacuation guidelines and making provisions for people living as evacuees, and cooperating with residents in regional areas and groups such as volunteer disaster prevention organizations.

In the Disaster Measures Basic Law, revised on 8 December 1995, there were articles clearly stating the measures required to prevent disasters for older persons, disabled persons, babies and others who require special attention. These are efforts that must be carried out by national and local governments to prevent disasters or to prevent disasters from escalating. Efforts are being made to promote the measures across the board, including getting local governments to promote the reformulation of regional disaster prevention plans with attention to measures for those most vulnerable in disasters and local financial measures to assist with the projects aimed at improving disaster infrastructure.

All prefectures, municipal governments, towns and villages have been required to formulate a basic policy plan for disabled persons under the Disabled Persons Fundamental Law. Many local governments are in the process of formulating such plans.

Administratively, disability concerns are under three bureaus: bureau on physical disability, intellectual disability and mental disability. For promoting comprehensive health and welfare services for persons with all types of disability, the Department of Health and Welfare for Persons with Disabilities was created on 1 July 1996 under the Ministry of Health and Welfare. The new department is facilitating the formulation of a comprehensive plan and municipal plans for all types of disability.

Based on the Law for Employment Promotion of the Disabled, the basic policy on measures of employment for disabled persons was established in 1992, and implemented from 1993.

Many persons with mental disability are institutionalized in Japan. To facilitate reintegration of persons with mental disabilities into the community, social workers with professional knowledge and skills in dealing with mental disability are urgently needed. To meet that need, Japan is legislating qualification system for psychiatric social workers.

3. Information

The Headquarters for Promoting the Welfare of Disabled Persons has, since 1994, been publishing an annual White Paper on Persons with Disabilities, which it submits to the Diet. The white paper covers the general state of measures being taken concerning disabled persons. In the effort to educate the public and deepen understanding of the measures being taken in this regard, the white paper has also been distributed to relevant organizations and individuals.

To facilitate the independence and social participation of persons with disabilities, an information network system *Normanet* was set up. Other information dissemination systems concerning volunteer activities, facilities for persons with disabilities, assistive devices and coping with emergencies were also established.

To promote the prevention of disabilities, rehabilitation and equalization of opportunities, an Information system for research on health and welfare of persons with disabilities was established. Domestic and overseas research results can thus be collected and stored in database. The information is then disseminated through the Internet.

A basic survey of adults and children with intellectual disabilities was conducted in September 1995 to collect data on the living conditions and needs of adults and children with intellectual disabilities. The data can be used for planning and implementation of welfare services for them.

The survey on physically disabled persons was also conducted in November 1996 to obtain information on the types, degrees, causes of disabilities, the possession of assistive devices, pension coverage and housing. The information will be used as basic data for planning and promoting welfare measures for persons with physical disabilities.

A survey on employment of persons with physical disabilities was conducted in 1993 to gauge the situations of employment of persons with physical disabilities and/or intellectual disabilities as well as their attitudes toward getting work and their working life. Annual reports on the employment situation of persons with disabilities are also collected from each employer.

In 1994, a study group was set up to draft measures to help workers who became physically disabled due to traffic accidents or labour accidents and have returned to their former workplace. That same year, a report was published detailing the problems of persons with extensive disabilities who work from home.

In 1996, Japan implemented the dietary improvement project for older persons and persons with visual impairments, targeting persons with visual problems, because the number of such persons are expected to rise as the population ages. In order to contribute to the improvement of their diet, information is provided in the form of Braille books and cassette tapes. Research and development on support systems for shopping and eating out of those people have been carried out and a work is being undertaken to develop a technique for food identification via non-visual recognition.

The Braille and English versions of the white paper on persons with disabilities have also been released, with the Government of Japan working to educate the public of the measures being taken.

Japan is also publishing books in Braille and producing videotapes with subtitles to boost the distribution of information on disability issues. Various government bulletins are published in Braille or produced on audiotapes. In addition, other books in Braille and recorded tapes have been produced and lent out.

In 1993, Japan established a subsidy scheme for the production of closed-captioned television programmes. In 1997, it expanded and enhanced the system with a new subsidy scheme of some 130 million yen. To make the production of closed-captioned programmes more efficient, the country also begun research and development on an automatic production system for captioned programmes and other broadcasting software production technology for persons with visual and hearing impairments.

With the revision of the Broadcast Law in May 1997, the licensing system related to closed-captioned programmes was revised. Close-captioned broadcasting is now allowed without a multiplex broadcasting license. The law also stipulates that television broadcasting businesses must strive to produce as many close-captioned programmes as possible.

4. Public awareness

Under the disabled persons fundamental law, 9 December was designated Disabled Persons' Day in Japan to encourage disabled persons to participate in society and to generate greater public interest and understanding toward disabled persons.

In addition, the Government of Japan and local governments would carry out activities suitable for Disabled Persons' Day. Every year the Government of Japan holds a conference to commemorate Disabled Persons' Day and carries out various projects to educate the public.

In 1995, the week between 3 December, which is the International Day of Disabled Persons and 9 December, was designated as the Disabled Persons' Week. During this period, campaigns are organized to promote the participation of disabled persons in society and to encourage their self-sufficiency, and to further raise the level of public awareness and understanding of issues involving disabled persons. The Government of Japan promotes disability issues via the media during the period while local governments and groups related to disabled persons hold various commemorative activities.

September is designated the Promotion of Employment of Persons with Disabilities Month to encourage persons with disability to find jobs and be independent. The aim is also to further generate national interest and under-standing about employment issues of persons with disability through promotional campaigns. Activities of the month include holding a national conference on the promotion of employment of persons with disabilities. The Ministry of Labour recognizes employers who hire persons with disabilities and excellent employees with disabilities by presenting them awards.

Except for 1995, the national skill competition of persons with disabilities (Abilympic) is held every year to promote the development of vocational skills of persons with disabilities. The event helps them build their confidence and pride in being able to participate in society as a skilled worker. It also increases social understanding and awareness and encourages the promotion of their employment and improvement of their social status.

The year 1997 marks the mid-point of the Decade, and from 12 to 15 November, the Government of Japan plans to hold an international culture and arts festival for disabled persons. The festival will feature an exhibition of paintings, sculptures and other art works by disabled persons, stage art performances, as well as an international forum and other events. The active participation of all countries of the ESCAP region is welcome.

An opinion survey on disabled persons was conducted over the summer of 1997. The survey which is the third in a series aims to gauge the public's ideas about disabled persons, knowledge about Japan's disability policies, changes in attitudes towards interacting with disabled persons, requests to national and local governments. The survey was previously carried out in 1987 and 1992.

The Ministry of Education organizes a number of programmes in social education, including those that provide an opportunity to meet and interact with children and adults with disabilities. In addition, sponsored events for disabled children and students have been held at youth education facilities under the jurisdiction of the ministry.

5. Accessibility and communication

Guidelines for school building facilities were devised from 1992 to 1996. The guidelines set out the creation of building plans and design of special education schools and special classes in elementary and lower secondary schools, paying close attention to the type and degree of disabilities, so that young students with disabilities would be able to lead barrier-free school lives.

At public schools, ramps, elevators, handrails, toilets for disabled persons and other amenities were planned to make it possible for disabled persons to receive a proper education. In addition, efforts were made to build school facilities and equipment accessible to disabled persons. The same measures were applied to the equipment of other public school facilities. The Government of Japan subsidizes these efforts.

At government facilities, efforts were made toward removing barriers for disabled persons. Efforts to make equipment at police stations and police boxes accessible to persons with disabilities are being carried out. Some of the measures included the building of a ramp at the entrance of the police boxes, making low counters, the provision of an inter-phone with Braille symbols, and installing accessible toilets at public facilities.

In November 1993, road construction ordinances were revised to make sidewalks and other pedestrian walkways safe for wheelchair users, requiring so-called "wide" sidewalks with a width of three meters or more. Barrier-free of existing sidewalks was improved through the elimination of steps and making ramps, and installing the electricity lines underground. Creating parking space for bicycles which tend to block walkways and installing Braille tiles for persons with visual impairments were also implemented to make sidewalks barrier-free. The building of accessible pedestrian bridges was promoted through the installation of ramps and elevators, creation of pedestrian decks, and links to adjacent buildings.

In recent years, along with an ageing society and technological advancement of information processing machines and tools, municipal governments and security companies have started providing security services where guards are present at the time of emergencies. A "patrol visit guard" makes a home visit for older persons living alone and persons with disabilities. Such services provided by security companies are given guidelines and inspected by the authorities. Currently research has been undertaken to develop and disseminate a security system that could help meet the needs of persons with disabilities in the area of crime and fire prevention.

Japan also promotes traffic safety facilities that help meet the needs of disabled persons. These include audio traffic signals for persons with visual impairments, and traffic signals that respond to the persons who cannot move quickly by automatically extending the time for them to cross the road. In addition, Japan also promotes the creation of a community zone in which humps were constructed in residential areas. Traffic regulations such as zone regulations were designed in 1996.

In order to make it more convenient for people with physical disabilities to take a driver's license, attempts have been made to make accessible a driver's license examination centre at each prefectural police headquarters by installing ramps and elevators. Advisory services can be received at the driving aptitude counter from examiners who are knowledgeable about the driving aptitude of persons with physical disability. There is also a consultation centre for those with disability who want to enrol in an authorized driving school.

In a residential district, to restrain through-traffic coming into a district, community zone formation projects were established in 1996. The projects includes the following measures: road surface changes for community roads and roads for both pedestrian and vehicular traffic; speed bumps and narrow sections set up by road administrators with the help of zoning regulations and other measures created by the national public safety commission.

Measures to help drivers, including securing road structures that offer space and improve the visual environment and prevent fatigue from driving, the construction of additional lanes (passing lanes), more street lights, toilets for disabled persons, and simple parking areas and parking lots for use by disabled persons were promoted.

To upgrade the information and communications infrastructure, road information systems were improved. This included having large signs and other easy-to-read road signs, devices providing traffic information, road information boards and information terminals, as well as a fibre optic network and other supporting infrastructure.

The Government of Japan allows local governments to issue bonds to fund their emergency disaster prevention infrastructure projects. It has also set up a local allocation tax to offset repayment of the principal and interest for repair work to improve the earthquake resistance of public facilities. These include social welfare, public and government facilities used as evacuation sites for those most vulnerable in times of disaster, as well as the building of emergency radio and other disaster prevention infrastructure.

Financial support measures have been in place since 1991 for independent local projects such as the systematic, comprehensive elimination of steps in pedestrian walkways, the installation of ramps at entrances of public facilities, the installation of accessible toilets, as well as town-building projects aimed at being user-friendly to disabled persons and older persons. These measures are carried out by local governments with a view to improving the health and welfare of disabled persons and older persons, making use of the community's creativity and ingenuity.

The provision of an amiable environment with such basics as wide sidewalks and sites for social service facilities has been promoted since 1996 at agricultural districts in mountainside and fishing villages. These are based on the following plans: the vision for the older persons at the agricultural districts in a mountainside and fishing villages; the physical improvement plan (amenity plan for older persons and persons with disabilities); and the health and welfare plan for older persons at the municipalities.

In 1997, architectural design standards for government facilities that incorporate the concept of normalisation were established.

The housing design guidelines for the society of longevity also set forth housing design considerations that make it possible for a person to continue living in a residence even if some of their physical functions deteriorate. In addition, public housing in Japan also offers access features to disabled persons through design and various furnishings. Preferential loan measures were set up by the government Housing Loan Corporation for housing that conforms to the standards which are in accordance with the housing design guidelines for the society of longevity.

In 1993, the former guidelines on the construction of facilities for disabled persons at transportation terminals were revised into the guidelines on the construction of facilities for older persons and disabled persons at transportation terminals. In drafting the new guidelines, the target was expanded from railroad stations to bus terminals, passenger boat terminals and airport terminals, and also reflected the most recent technological developments.

The drafted and revised guidelines for the installation of escalators and elevators in railroad stations require that new stations and stations which will undergo major renovations be installed with escalator and elevators. Existing stations which have the vertical difference of five meters or more between hallways and platforms as well as more than 5,000 passengers per day will be given priority in installing escalators and elevators.

With the enactment of the Act on Buildings Accessible and Usable by Older and Physically Disabled Persons, the standards of post-office building design were revised.

Training was carried out for architects using architectural design standards catering to the needs of older persons and disabled persons and for construction companies using the housing renovation manual for an ageing society.

In studies carried out in 1994 and 1995, actual cases of efforts being made to assist those most vulnerable to disasters, including disabled persons, were introduced. A category dealing with those most vulnerable to disasters was established and included in a leaflet on independent disaster prevention organizations under the editorial supervision of the Fire Defence Agency. In addition, there were television programmes introducing the activities of independent disaster prevention organizations put out by the Fire Defence Agency. Other educational efforts are also being made to further the efforts of these independent disaster prevention organizations.

Since 1991, as a rule, the construction or upgrade of urban parks and similar projects must consider the accessibility of people with physical disabilities. The aim is to make the facilities more user-friendly.

In 1996, the Ministry of Health and Welfare established the sea and greenery health zone construction (healthy seaside projects) to carry out construction that would enable disabled persons to use seaside areas with greater ease. These projects are carried out with the cooperation of "health and culture towns" (so designated by the Ministry of Health and Welfare) and they include the building of gently-sloped embankments and slopes.

Work is now being carried out to create spaces where water can be enjoyed through environmental construction to control rivers and erosion, securing spaces with water and greenery that are accessible to disabled persons. Such places include rivers, seaside areas and waterfalls where a balance with natural space is maintained.

Japan is also actively promoting the dissemination of information about rainfall and river water to help ensure the safety of people with visual and hearing impairments. It is also building information systems that can communicate emergency information, for example, through a teletext display or a warning buzzer when rainfall exceeds a certain level.

In 1994, model city projects for disabled persons was reorganized and expanded to promote people-oriented towns where facilities are built to ensure accessibility for disabled persons.

Various meetings were held to inform concerned parties that the building of elevators, ramps, accessible toilets for disabled persons, Braille information boards would be encouraged in community centres, libraries and other social education facilities. Subsidies for local public entities to build these facilities were given to offset construction costs. The construction of public educational facilities for youth which are accessible to disabled persons is also being encouraged.

For persons with disabilities who have difficulty communicating on the phone, FAX 100, which accepts emergency reports by fax, was introduced nationwide. Research was conducted on information and communication devices which persons with disabilities could use with ease. New guidelines to improve the efficiency of information and communication devices were formulated following the research.

Surface mail containing Braille materials, recordings for persons with visual impairments and selected Braille paper can be posted free of charge. In addition, mailing charges were reduced for periodicals issued by organizations of persons with physical and mental disabilities, large books in Braille, selected videotapes for persons with hearing disabilities and postal packages of books sent and received between libraries and persons with extensive physical and mental disabilities.

To allow disabled persons, older persons, and persons who serve as their caretakers to use telecommunications with equal ease, funds have been provided for financing easier-to-use telecommunications systems or for equipment required to develop communications and broadcast services.

Starting in 1997, through the Telecommunication Advancement Organization of Japan, assistance was given to companies that conduct research in the area of communications and broadcast technology to develop services that are easier to use for disabled persons and older persons.

By establishing an information network using a fax machine at police boxes, organizations of disabled persons, and at private homes of persons with disability, information about crimes, accidents and crime prevention is readily provided.

Since 1992, training workshops on sign language for post office personnel working at the counters have been conducted so that they can communicate with customers with hearing impairments. Similarly workshops on Braille have been organized for post office personnel so that they can read addresses written in Braille.

Sign language interpretation services were provided at the major public employment security offices in order to give effectively vocational guidance to persons with hearing impairments.

Police officers who are able to use sign language wear a sign language badge created in cooperation with the Japanese Federation of the Deaf. These officers are stationed at police boxes in order to make it more convenient for persons with hearing impairment to report lost property and to ask for help if they are in trouble.

Since 1995, sign language interpretation was provided for live television programmes for election candidates prior to the election for the House of Councillors. Furthermore, since 1996, political parties are able to add sign language interpretation in their video broadcast for elections of the House of Representatives.

In order to allow people with visual impairments who write on standard post office postcards using Braille word processors to easily distinguish the top from bottom and front from back, Japan started selling in 1990, postcards that have a depression in the front lower left corner.

A service is also being offered that allows a person with a visual impairment (or their representative) to phone the nearest post office if they want to purchase the postcards and have them delivered to their doors on the following day.

6. Education

The national curriculum standards were revised in 1989 to take into account the change in the social environment surrounding persons with disabilities, and the severity, multiplicity and diversity of disabilities of children. It was implemented gradually from 1990 to 1996. To achieve the national curriculum standards, publication of various manuals and professional training for teachers are being carried out.

Since April 1993, instructions through the "resource room" system *(Tsu-kyu)* have been provided as a new form of education for children with disabilities. It could respond closely to the needs of each child and student with disability.

A study group was set up to look into how vocational education could be further improved, especially in promoting the occupational independence of disabled students, after they have graduated from upper secondary studies. Based on the group's report, the Ministry of Education, Science, Sports and Culture in 1996, sent a notice to all prefectures advising them to further improve and enhance vocational education and career counselling. It is also conducting a practical study on the improvement and enhancement of vocational education and career counselling jointly with private companies and labour organizations.

A group was set up to study the education of children with learning disabilities, and an interim report was collated in 1995. However, since not all areas of learning disabilities are clearly understood at this stage, the research is continuing. Along with the research, projects for enhancing teacher training on children with learning disabilities are being conducted.

Responding to the severity, multiplicity, and diversity of disabilities of children and students, a study group discussed the need to improve and enhance education in this area. Based on the group's report, Japan introduced on a trial basis, a teacher training programme for upper secondary level students at schools for blind persons, deaf persons, and persons with orthopaedic disabilities in February 1997.

To enhance the education of children with disabilities, attempts are being made to use multimedia as a complimentary tool. The country is also studying the provision of educational counselling for infants under the age of three, and measures to encourage interaction between children at special schools and children at ordinary classes, and the community.

Since 1993, enhancement of the quality of teaching staff is being conducted annually at public schools including schools for blind persons, deaf persons and persons with orthopaedic disabilities.

The hardware and equipment are in place at all schools to ensure that disabled students are able to take their university entrance examinations and go to universities or other institutes of higher education. Many universities are equipping themselves to help their disabled students.

The Government of Japan has also raised its national subsidies for private universities, junior colleges, and technical colleges, providing funding to help them equip themselves to be disabled user-friendly as the number of disabled students have increased.

The Tsukuba College of Technology was established in October 1987 as a national three-year junior college to provide an opportunity for persons with visual and hearing impairments to obtain a higher education. Enrolment of students started in 1990 and since then the Government of Japan has continued to support its upgrade of educational equipment and facilities for persons with disabilities.

The law concerning special cases with regard to the educational personnel certification law as pertains to the award of a regular certificate to elementary and junior high school teachers was formulated in June 1997. To enhance understanding of the philosophy of individual dignity and social solidarity, it is now made compulsory for anyone who intends to receive an elementary or junior high school teaching license to acquire experience in caring for, and engaging in personal contact with, persons with disabilities.

Various extra-curricular activities are being implemented by the Ministry of Education. Those offering the experiencing and interacting with nature were carried out for disabled children. A programme involving children and students with disabilities was carried out at a national youth education facility.

7. Training and employment

In 1992, the International Labour Organization Convention Number 159 (Convention Concerning Vocational Rehabilitation and Employment of Disabled Persons) was ratified.

According to the Standard Labour Law, except in cases of limited employment in specified occupations, there is no discrimination towards women and girls with disabilities with regards to gaining entry into public vocational skills development facilities. Japan is reviewing the training courses of vocational ability development schools for persons with disabilities.

Since 1992, the actual enterprises in the community, where persons with disabilities live, have been utilized as venues for vocational rehabilitation where "supportive programmes for on-the-job adjustment training" is carried out to provide support that ranges from advice to the teaching of skills for occupational independence.

The total model programme for promotion of employment of persons with disabilities in the community has been implemented since 1993 to build a support system, which conducts counselling and provides support until the person is settled at the work place, by connecting welfare and employment departments at the municipality level.

The project plan for promotion of employment of persons with extensive disabilities has been implemented since 1991. Under this project, cases of employment of persons with extensive disabilities in various fields were documented and their results distributed among the owners of enterprises.

In order to increase the employment of persons with extensive disabilities, the promotion of establishing enterprises that employ persons with extensive disabilities is carried out by the third sector scheme. Since 1993, 17 enterprises have been set up, and the total is 34 so far. To ensure the occupational independence of persons with disabilities, employment support centres for disabled persons were set up in 1994 as an organization to provide a support mechanism by connecting the welfare and employment departments at the municipality level. Nine centres have been set up.

A report about how vocational rehabilitation should be responding to the increasing severity and diversity of disability was published in 1996.

Sheltered workshops and welfare factories for those disabled persons who find it difficult to get employment in the open market have increased in number. Improvement of work productivity was promoted. The mutual use of sheltered workshops for persons with physical disabilities and for persons with intellectual disability was started in 1993 for the user's convenience. Welfare factories were opened for persons with mental disabilities from 1993. Non-residential facilities for persons with mental disabilities were introduced as a branch of residential facility for them from 1995.

From 1994, telework centres construction projects have been promoted. Japan is offering assistance to offset costs of building joint-use offices (telework centres) in municipalities where telework could be done. The hardship of commuting will be reduced when employees work at locations separate from managers, at satellite offices, at home using telecommunications and working a full day according to the company's in-house system. This is particularly true for people with extensive disabilities. Feasibility of telework for persons with disabilities would be further studied.

At the vocational schools for persons with disabilities, training courses and curriculum have been reviewed in addition to renewing equipment to better meet the need of employers as well as disabled trainees. Those disabled persons who may be able to take vocational training in mainstream vocational skills development facilities have been encouraged to do so, on condition that the facilities and equipment are made fully accessible for them.

8. Prevention of the causes of disability

In accordance with the basic plan for traffic safety, measures are being promoted to secure safety in the construction of transportation facilities infrastructure and transport equipment on land, sea and air. At the same time, measures are being aggressively promoted to set up a rescue system for victims of accidents.

To prevent the causes of disability and to establish fundamental treatment methods, research on physical, mental and neurotic disorders was promoted. In particular research in the fields of mental disorders and incurable chronic diseases which is less developed in Japan was promoted.

Research and development concerning causes of disability, early detection and an early treatment system were also conducted. Based on the results of the research, medical examinations of 18 month-old infants and those with congenital metabolic disorders and prenatal medical care were strengthened.

With the amendment of the Mental Health Law of 1993, parents or guardians of persons with mental disability who are discharged from mental hospitals are also covered under public health nurse services.

Under the Community Health Law of 1994, the functions of health centres and mental health and welfare centres for persons with mental disability were strengthened. These centres are basic technical agencies for mental health in the community, and counselling services were promoted to address psychological and mental needs, as well as pubescent mental health, and alcoholic-related problems.

Periodic medical examinations are carried out on all pupils at primary and secondary schools for early detection and treatment of disabilities. From 1995, the medical examination at school was reviewed based on recent changes in health problems of pupils and on the recent developments in medical technology.

9. Rehabilitation services

The number of the persons with disabilities who are in need of periodic medical care is increasing. To this end, outreach medical services for the persons with extensive disabilities who are restricted at home have been provided. This service is aimed to meet needs of those who have difficulty going to hospitals because of the extensiveness of their disabilities. In addition to medical services, advice, guidance and counselling on issues concerning daily living have been provided.

The numbers of the rehabilitation facilities for persons with physical disabilities and the rehabilitation facilities for persons with intellectual disabilities are increasing. Through full use of these facilities, rehabilitation services have been strengthened.

The care service delivery system and care management system, including community-based rehabilitation (CBR) have been studied and developed as trial projects for persons with extensive and multiple disabilities to support their living in the community.

The National Care Insurance System was drafted and will be ready for its operation from early 2000 to meet the total care needs of older persons over 65 years old and for the persons over 40 years old with specific impairments such as one due to stroke.

Rehabilitation professionals, such as doctors, nurses, social workers, physiotherapist, occupational therapists, speech therapists, prosthesis and orthosis technicians, care workers and other staff, have been regularly trained and their skills have been upgraded through numerous training programmes.

In Japan, the Tokyo Paralympics of 1964 spurred enthusiasm in sports activities for persons with disabilities. The National Sports Games for Physically Disabled Persons has been annually held since 1965. The National Sports Games for Intellectually Disabled Persons was started in 1992. At present, there are many kinds of sports that disabled persons can engage in to improve their independence and social participation. Sports activities by disabled persons also enhance public understanding of the abilities and aspirations of persons with disabilities. The Winter Paralympics Games in Nagano, Japan, held in March 1998, was the first winter Paralympics games in Asia. It is expected to promote the welfare for persons with disabilities and the mutual understanding and international cooperation among participating countries.

10. Assistive devices

Research and development of assistive devices have been enhanced with the opening of the laboratory for assistive devices for older persons with disabilities, and the laboratory for evaluation of assistive devices at the research institute within the National Rehabilitation Centre for Disabled Persons. Research on the standardization of evaluation method on the strength of prostheses, orthoses and walking aids was conducted.

Since 1995, research and development has been carried out on sign language cognition and formation technologies, second-generation data transmission technologies and other basic and more widely used technology related to telecommunications equipment and systems for disabled persons and older persons.

Since 1996, research and development has been carried out on basic telecommunications technologies that are user-friendly and that enable disabled persons and older persons as well as ordinary people to collect and disseminate information freely and at any time through a multimedia network.

To promote the standardization of assistive devices, a basic research project has been initiated to establish evaluation and measurement methods, systematic data collection and accumulation. This research was started in 1996 by the Ministry of International Trade and Industry Products Evaluation Technique Centre.

11. Self-help organizations

To promote the New long-term programme for government measures for disabled persons and the goals of the Asian and Pacific Decade of Disabled Persons, 1993-2002, the Council for Promoting the New Decade of Disabled Persons was set up in April 1994. It serves as a coordinating body for NGO activities in the field of disabilities. It comprises four leading organizations: the Japanese Federation of Organizations of Disabled Persons, the Japan Council on Disability, the National Council of Social Welfare and the Japanese Society for Rehabilitation of Persons with Disabilities.

The main activities of the Council include research, advocacy to promote the rights of persons with disability, policy recommendations to the government, organizing conferences and seminars on current issues faced by disabled persons, supporting the Regional NGO Network for the Promotion of the Asian and Pacific Decade of Disabled Persons.

To promote the activities of self-help organizations, the fund for community care services for older persons and disabled persons has been set up. The social welfare and medical service corporation started the welfare fund in anticipation for longevity society, totalling 70 billion yen, to provide grants to projects. Another 50 billion yen was added in 1997 to further promote these services. Grants are provided for projects that help establish a network of community care services and personal care assistance services, and promote the social participation of older and disabled persons. Self-help organizations of disabled persons and other NGOs are encouraged to apply for the grants.

Representatives of self-help organizations of persons with disabilities are appointed as members of the Central Council for the Promotion of Measures for Disabled Persons, as well as the local councils. This encourages effective participation of self-help organizations of disabled persons in the policy formulation and programme implementation concerning disability at the national and subnational levels.

To strengthen the activities of self-help organizations and to increase their grass-roots membership, the Central Centre for Promotion of Social Participation of Persons with Disabilities and prefectural centres for the same purpose were established with government grants. Self-help organizations comprise members of these centres and actively participate in their operation.

Normanet, the nationwide information network system for persons with disabilities, was established in 1996 to facilitate the information exchange among various self-help organizations, and thus to promote social participation of persons with disabilities. This electronic network is sponsored by the Ministry of

Health and Welfare and managed by the Japanese Society for Rehabilitation of Persons with Disabilities.

Community living support service for persons with disabilities started from 1996. The services can be entrusted to self-help organizations of disabled persons as a service provider. Peer counselling by disabled persons has been introduced as one of the essential service menu in this new service.

With the grants by the Government of Japan, the development and promotion of sign language has been pursued by Japanese Federation of the Deaf. The Japanese Federation of the Blind has been active in production and dissemination of Braille books and audiotapes.

12. Regional cooperation

Japan has been promoting international cooperation in the field of disability in the Asian and Pacific region through various means, including despatch of youth volunteers, experts, providing training opportunities in rehabilitation and leadership development of persons with disabilities, as well as building training facilities and supplying necessary equipment. One important area is training. (See Table 1-1. Technical cooperation by type).

Japan International Cooperation Agency (JICA) under the Ministry of Foreign Affairs provides various types of training courses, including courses for rehabilitation professionals, leaders with disabilities, technicians in prosthesis and orthosis, professionals in welfare for intellectually disabled persons, sports instructors for people with disabilities and leaders in mental health and care.

Japan International Cooperation of Welfare Services (JICWELS) under the Ministry of Health and Welfare provide long-term training in Japan for government officials as well as NGO personnel who are in charge of social welfare programmes in developing countries.

At the mid-point of the Decade in 1997, several commemorative events are been planned in Japan. Through participation of people with disabilities and professionals in the Asian and Pacific region, Japan wishes to evaluate national rehabilitation services, as well as to host a forum for information exchange and discussions, with a view to developing strategies for further international cooperation activities. The main events include:

(a) The 20th National Rehabilitation Conference, Rehabilitation of Japan – What have we achieved? What should we do?, 10-12 November 1997, Tokyo;

(b) WHO Seminar Commemorating the Mid-point of the Asian and Pacific Decade of Disabled Persons, 10-14 November 1997, Tokyo;

(c) International Forum in Prosthetics and Orthotics, 31 January – 5 February 1998, Tokyo.

In cooperation with the Asia and the Pacific Programme of Educational Innovation for Development (APEID) of UNESCO, the following activities were carried out:

(a) Seminars for specialists on special education in countries of Asia and the Pacific have been held annually by the National Institute of Special Education;

(b) Experts of National Institute of Special Education were sent as resource persons to training seminars on special education held in Laos (1993) and Mongolia (1995);

(c) Specialists on special education from Mongolia (1994) and Uzbekistan (1996) were trained at the National Institute of Special Education.

To enhance cooperation in Asia and the Pacific, specialists on employment of persons with disabilities were sent to countries in the region since 1992 for the employment promotion of persons with disabilities. Japan held international seminars on public awareness to which vocational rehabilitation specialists from Asian countries were invited. Assistance on vocational rehabilitation skills development to Indonesia has been provided since 1989.

Furthermore, cooperation is taking place through the United Nations and other international organizations. Since 1988, continuous contributions to the United Nations Voluntary Fund for Disabled Persons have been made. In 1996, a sum of US$100,000 was contributed.

Japan is fulfilling an important role to promote regional cooperation through supporting a number of ESCAP activities which assist ESCAP member and associate member governments in implementing the Decade Agenda for Action.

As cooperative measures toward the Asian and Pacific region, Japan has been supporting ESCAP projects concerning the development of persons with disabilities through the Japan-ESCAP Cooperation Fund (JECF) since 1986. After the declaration by ESCAP countries and areas of the Asian and Pacific Decade of Disabled Persons in 1992, active support has been given to ESCAP for its project implementation, including "Assistance in development and strengthening of self-help organizations of disabled persons and the "Promotion of non-handicapping environments for disabled and elderly persons in the Asia-Pacific region".

The total amount of support given to ESCAP projects related to disabled persons since 1990 is approximately US$1.46 million (See Table 1-1. Technical cooperation by type and Table 1-2. Project-style technical cooperation).

Table 1-1. Technical cooperation by type

Type / Year	Trainees accepted (only related to group training)					Specialists and JICA Members Despatched		Equipment Supplied		
	Welfare course for people with intellectual disability Period: 6 months	Technical course on making assistive devices Period: 3.5 months	Disability rehabilitation instructors course (specialists' course) Period: 1 month	Disability rehabilitation instructors course (for the physically disabled) Period: 1 month	Sports Instructors course for the physically disabled Period: 1.6 months	Despatch of specialist (destination)	Despatch of JICA members (occupational therapists, physical therapists, etc.)	Recipient country	Amount (thousand of yen)	Project name
1992	People 5	People 4	People 9	People 8	People 9	People	People 24	Indonesia	8,668	Vocational training equipment for the physically disabled
1995	7	4	10	10	8	5 (Indonesia, Sri Lanka, Uruguay)	35	Sri Lanka	9,083	Hearing Examination equipment for schools for the deaf
1996	7	4	9	10	9	6 (Indonesia, Thailand, Uruguay)	37	Zambia	10,000	Equipment to make prosthetic assistive devices
1997	8	5	10	11	10	8 (Thailand, Indonesia, Philippines, Uruguay, China)	38	Paraguay	13,986	Development of rehabilitation for people with mental and physical disabilities
1998	8	4	11	10	12	4 (Indonesia, Thailand, Sri Lanka)	32	Indonesia Bolivia	2,000 2,000	Vocational training equipment for the physically disabled and equipment for elocution and speech training

Courtesy of the Ministry of Foreign Affairs.

Table 1-2. Project-style technical cooperation

Project name / Year	Thai Rehabilitation Centre			China Rehabilitation Centre for Limb Disabilities			Indonesian Rehabilitation Centre for Limb Disabilities		
	Specialists despatched	Trainees accepted	Equipment supplied	Specialists despatched	Trainees accepted	Equipment supplied	Specialists despatched	Trainees accepted	Equipment supplied
1984	8	5	11						
1985	13	3	12						
1986	17	3	24	10	5	22			
1987	18	6	55	52	5	55			
1988	12	0	74	14	5	45			
1989	6	7	45	21	5	54			
1990	10	5	57	19	5	55			
1991	5	3	7	30	5	48			
1992				12	3	20			
1993				19	3	20			
1994							7	3	25
1995							10	3	19
1996							10	3	2

Note: Equipment supplied (unit): 1 million yen.
Courtesy of the Ministry of Foreign Affairs.

Through funding the above-mentioned projects and in addition to them, Japan's support for ESCAP includes:

(a) Despatch of a Japanese project expert on disability who assists in implementation of ESCAP projects, in particular on issues pertaining to support for self-help organizations of disabled persons.

(b) Despatch of a JICA expert on accessible environments to assist in the implementation of guidelines on the promotion of non-handicapping physical environments for disabled and older persons in the Asian and Pacific region, through pilot projects in Bangkok, Beijing and New Delhi;

(c) The issuance of Asian and Pacific Decade-related publications.

(See Table 2-1. General grants-in-aid cooperation, Table 2-2. Grassroots grants-in-aid cooperation, and Table 3. Government support for NGOs)

(See Overview of projects in cooperation with ESCAP)

Table 2-1. General grants-in-aid cooperation

Year	Recipient	Amount (thousands of yen)	Project description
1980-1991	Peru	2,200,000	Building of local mental health centres
1983	Thailand	1,090,000	Building of rehabilitation centres
1985-1986	China	3,380,000	Building of rehabilitation research centres for people with lost limbs rehabilitation equipment
1989	Indonesia	220,000	Building of vocational rehabilitation centres for disabled persons
1995-1997	Indonesia	1,655,000	Equipment for centres for people with physical disabilities
1996	El Salvador	344,000	Centre for Physically Disabled Persons (Development of materials)

Table 2-2. Grassroots grants-in-aid cooperation

Recipient	Amount (thousands of yen)	1993 Recipient	Amount (thousands of yen)	1994 Recipient	Amount (thousands of yen)	1995 Recipient	Amount (thousands of yen)	1996 Recipient	Amount (thousands of yen)
Ecuador	7,164	China (3 cases)	15,818	India (3 cases)	14,417	Peru (2 cases)	19,157	Jordan (4 cases)	28,748
Tonga	6,909	Palestinian Nat. Authority	11,824	South Africa (4 cases)	10,864	Morocco (2 cases)	11,563	Tunisia (5 cases)	23,399
Cambodia	6,306	Sri Lanka (2 cases)	9,788	Ghana (2 cases)	8,371	Cambodia (2 cases)	9,158	India (5 cases)	21,465
Yemen	5,560	Pakistan	7,539	Jordan	8,006	Uzbekistan (2 cases)	8,614	Thailand (2 cases)	19,216
Mongolia	4,879	Thailand	5,074	Thailand	5,512	China	7,640	China (3 cases)	17,785
Fiji (2 cases)	4,495	Uganda	4,714	Ecuador	4,982	Jordan	6,939	Zaire (2 cases)	17,541
Paraguay	4,457	Ecuador	4,551	Egypt	4,496	Zaire	5,757	Palestine (Israel) (3 cases)	17,190
China	4,327	Fiji	4,209	Fiji	4,215	Indonesia	5,477	South Africa (3 cases)	11,682
Papua New Guinea (2 cases)	4,205	Morocco	3,052	Guatemala	3,895	Pakistan (2 cases)	5,382	Uzbekistan (3 cases)	11,442
India (2 cases)	3,819	Nepal	2,903	El Salvador	3,476	Thailand	5,121	Egypt (3 cases)	10,826
Central Africa	3,413	Honduras	2,832	Cambodia	1,708	Philippines (2 cases)	5,093	Indonesia (5 cases)	10,123
Honduras	3,288	South Africa	2,689	Honduras	1,671	Fiji	5,085	Fiji	8,171
Ethiopia	2,649	Philippines	2,359			Israel (2 cases)	4,075	Malaysia (2 cases)	8,123
Uganda	824	Dominican Republic	1,749			Myanmar	2,806	Bangladesh	8,093
						Egypt	2,459	Macedonia (2 cases)	7,410
						South Africa	2,032	Madagascar	7,375
						India	1,975	Ecuador	7,188
						Yemen	1,960		
						Mauritania	1,337		
						Bolivia	472		

(continued)

Table 2-2 *(continued)*

	1993		1994		1995		1996	
	Recipient	Amount (thousands of yen)	Recipient	Amount (thousands of yen)	Recipient	Amount (thousands of yen)	Recipient	Amount (thousands of yen)
							Morocco	7,097
							Panama	6,435
							Nicaragua	6,194
							Pakistan (2 cases)	5,811
							Western Samoa	4,895
							Costa Rica	4,802
							Colombia	3,903
							Paraguay	3,647
							Papua New Guinea	3,478
							Haiti	2,829
							Sri Lanka (2 cases)	1,928
							Malawi	1,901
							Solomon Islands	1,734
							Swaziland	1,691
							Lesoto	1,541
							Tonga	1,540
							Syria	1,028

Note: As grassroots grants-in-aid cooperation, assistance was given for rehabilitation facilities for people with disabilities, training facilities, vocational training facilities, etc.

Courtesy of the Ministry of Foreign Affairs.

Table 3. Government support for NGOs (unit: thousands of yen)

Year	Amount of subsidy	Country	Content
1992	4,000	Cambodia	Medical aid for landmine victims. Despatch of prosthesis specialists, establishment of facilities for supplying prostheses.
1993	12,000	Cambodia	Medical aid for landmine victims. Despatch of prosthesis specialists, establishment of facilities for supplying prostheses.
1994	2,600	Viet Nam	Job training (handicrafts, tailoring, etc.) for young orphans with hearing and speech disabilities.
	3,000	Cambodia	Construction work for the expansion of the leatherworks school at the Centre for Victims of Gangrene.
1995	2,000	Viet Nam	Job training (handicrafts, tailoring, dressmaking etc.) at an orphanage for children with hearing or speech disabilities.
	2,000	Viet Nam	Job training for young disabled persons. Supply of sewing machines, tools, machinery, and materials.
	8,000	Cambodia	Increasing the number of courses in tinsmithing and radio/television repair.
	1,500	Thailand	Instruction in Japanese massage techniques for persons with visual impairments (lectures and practical).
	1,298	Thailand	Instruction in rehabilitation techniques, especially techniques feasible in the home. Promotion of social reintegration.
	3,000	Palestine	Early detection and treatment of hearing disabilities. Fitting of hearing aids. Training in hearing aid repair.
1996	3,000	India	Plastic surgery for victims scarred by earthquakes. Examination of mentally disabled children. Medical treatment and social reintegration in line with individual cases.
	700	Indonesia	Training in oesophageal speech for persons whose vocal chords have been removed due to throat cancer.
	1,700	Indonesia	Instruction in Japanese massage techniques for persons with visual impairments (lectures and practical).

(continued)

Table 3 *(continued)*

Year	Amount of subsidy	Country	Content
	4,480	Indonesia	Fitting of hearing aids for children with hearing disabilities. Speech rehabilitation by speech therapists.
	5,000	Cambodia	For persons with lower limbs damaged by landmines or polio, instruction in reading, wheelchair making, and radio, television and motorcycle repairs.
	3,300	Thailand	Mobile dental service and instruction for sufferers of Hansen's Disease, the effects of which make it difficult to main oral hygiene.
	1,000	Thailand	Clinical care and rehabilitation for children with disabilities. Job training (sewing, bicycle repair, etc.) for adults with disabilities. Publicity campaign to promote understanding and prevention of disabilities.
	7,750	Thailand	Provide a vocational aid centre where disabled persons can work, training them in printing and bookbinding.
	3,000	China	Construction of medical facilities for disabled children. Medical treatment and training to assist reintegration into mainstream society.
	600	Philippines	Training in oesophageal speech for persons whose vocal chords have been remove due to throat cancer.
	2,600	Philippines	Psychiatric treatment of persons who have returned to the Philippines after experiencing psychological problems in Japan.
	900	Peru	Psychiatric treatment of persons who have returned to Peru after experiencing psychological problems in Japan.
	4,200	Serbia	Expansion of the only facility for the blind in the former Yugoslavia. Provision of nutritional food for the blind. Treatment for senior citizens suffering from senility.
	1,800	Angola Djibouti	Provision of clothing, wheelchairs, canes, and other such items to victims of conflict, including internal refugees and incoming international refugees.

Note: These programmes for physically disabled persons are carried out using subsidies provided to NGOs in connection with various international development cooperation programmes.

Data: Courtesy of the Ministry of Foreign Affairs.

B. Overview of projects in cooperation with ESCAP

1. Assistance in the development of
self-help organizations of disabled persons (Phases I and II)

This project to assist in the development of self-help organizations of disabled persons, which began in 1990, was carried out in two phases over a period of six years. The project made it possible to despatch to ESCAP a Japanese expert on disability who was himself disabled. The project objectives were two-fold. The first was to spur increased mutual support among disabled persons and to empower members through peer support and group solidarity. The second was to create a national mechanism in which disabled persons themselves were able to participate in the formulation of national policies and programmes that affect disabled persons.

Under this project, guidelines on the development and strengthening of self-help organizations of disabled persons were developed and by using the guidelines, national and regional training workshops for leaders with disabilities were conducted. Under this project, the Meeting to Launch the Asian and Pacific Decade of Disabled Persons was convened in Beijing in December 1992. The first regional meeting (held in 1995 in Bangkok) to review the progress of the Decade was also organized under this project. Thus, this project played an important role in promoting the Asian and Pacific Decade for Disabled Persons, 1993-2002.

2. Promotion of non-handicapping environments
for disabled persons and older persons in the Asia-Pacific region
(Phase I and Phase II)

In the first half of the Decade, the Asian and the Pacific region was undergoing a period of remarkable economic development. As a result, many high-rise buildings were erected in cities throughout the region. However, the access needs of disabled persons and older persons were rarely taken into consideration by architects and building contractors. In response to the situation, the project was formulated with the following two objectives:

(a) To raise awareness in the developing countries of the Asia-Pacific region about the need for access, and to promote the adoption of relevant standards;

(b) To develop and disseminate guidelines on the promotion of barrier-free environments for disabled persons and older persons.

The Ministry of Construction and the Governments of Hyogo Prefecture and Yokohama City contributed to the development of the guidelines by despatching experts and representatives to participate in an expert group meeting and a regional meeting.

Phase II involved pilot projects in Beijing, Bangkok, and New Delhi. In each of these three cities, a one-square kilometre area was designated as a demonstration access site. The current three-year phase II project calls for an access specialist from the Ministry of Construction to be despatched under the auspices of JICA to support ESCAP in carrying out this project.

The pilot project in Bangkok, which is being carried out jointly by Bangkok Metropolitan Administration (BMA) and the ESCAP secretariat, entails the upgrading of sidewalks suited to the needs of wheelchair users and persons with visual impairments. This project is a landmark in infrastructure development for Bangkok's disabled persons and older persons. Once the project is on its way, Bangkok is expected to become the first city in Thailand with an environment friendly to disabled persons and older persons.

3. Other support from Japan

Japanese NGOs, Takarazuka city and a Japanese coalition of labour unions, have donated funds to support the activities involved in the Asian and Pacific Decade of Disabled Persons. In addition, the Honda Motor Company Labour Union has donated funds to the Technical Cooperation Trust Fund for the Asian and Pacific Decade of Disabled Persons.

C. Activities planned for the second half of the Asian and Pacific Decade of Disabled Persons

1. Legislation

The social misconception and prejudice concerning persons with mental disabilities are hindering their independence, employment and construction of facilities for their social reintegration in community. Therefore, greater public awareness and social exchanges among people with mental disabilities and those without must be promoted.

There are also plans to review the system of classifying the levels of mental disability. Plans are also underway to develop the guardianship system for persons with intellectual disabilities and older persons to protect their rights, including property right. The Japanese expression for intellectual disability, *seishin-hakujyaku* will be reviewed with input from people with intellectual disabilities, their parents groups and other relevant representatives.

Domestic disaster prevention programmes will be revised in accordance with the spirit of the amendments to the basic plan for disaster prevention and the revisions to the disaster measures basic law. The revisions are aimed at dealing with disaster victims, including physically disabled persons, through, improved dissemination of information, guidance out of the stricken area, organization of daily activities in temporary shelters and cooperation with local residents and autonomous disaster prevention organizations. The Government of Japan also strives to promote the adoption of comprehensive measures to enable local governments to develop a disaster prevention infrastructure that is suited to meet the needs of people with disabilities.

Japan will regularly review the progress that has been made in implementation of the New Long-term Programme for Government Measures for Disabled Persons, to ensure that it is smoothly completed by 2002. In addition, it will also carry out regular follow-up reviews of the government action plan for persons with disabilities to ensure that it is smoothly completed by that same year.

Japan will continue to provide guidance to prefectural and local governments throughout the country to ensure the prompt formulation and implementation of municipal plans for disabled persons. It will also announce the contents of amendments of Law for Employment Promotion of the Disabled in 1997 to employers and people with disability. It will amend the basic policy of measures of employment for disabled persons in 1997, and implement it from 1998.

2. Information

The Headquarters for Promoting the Welfare of Disabled Persons will prepare a white paper on persons with disabilities every year and deliver a report to the Diet. The white paper on persons with disabilities will be prepared in Braille and English. It will be distributed to concerned parties in order to promote greater understanding of the measures related to disabled persons.

Japan will also conduct a survey on the employment situations of persons with physical disabilities in 1998 and continue assessing the situations in each enterprise. It will continue to implement the dietary life improvement project for elderly and persons with visual impairments till 2000. The country will also continue to contribute to the realization of their independent dietary life, promote the creation of the dietary life environment for older persons and persons with visual impairments, through providing information concerning dietary life in Braille and cassette tapes and other means. It will work to promote the use of closed-captioned television programmes throughout the nation, and to increase the amount of time allotted to closed-captioned television programmes.

3. Public awareness

Japan will examine ways to make systematic use of the mass media and also work on further promoting public awareness through such activities as Disabled Persons Day and Disabled Persons Week.

The country will also continue its campaign on promotion of employment of persons with disability. Abilympics will continue to promote the development of the vocational abilities of people with disabilities, and to help them develop confidence and pride to participate in society as skilled workers. Abilympics will also help increase the understanding and awareness of society about the abilities and aspirations of people with disabilities, and encourage the promotion of their employment and improvement of their social status.

Japan intends to continue the programmes carried out during the previous five years. These include activities that enhance interaction between disabled children and disabled adults. It will continue to use national education facilities for youths to carry out events for children and students with disabilities.

4. Accessibility and communication

The Government of Japan will provide guidance, in accordance with the school facility construction guidelines, to those involved in the building of schools. The guidance will enable the building constructors to formulate detailed plans to accommodate the needs of children and students with different types and degrees of disabilities. To ensure that disabled persons can receive the fullest education possible given the degree of their disabilities, it will ascertain that state-run schools are fully equipped with ramps, elevators, hand railings and accessible toilet stalls for disabled persons.

When a local government builds ramps, elevators, handrails, and toilet stalls for persons with disabilities with considerations for their learning and use, part of its building expenses can be subsidized by the government.

More meetings and other such activities will be held to make the general public more aware of the needs of disabled persons and to consider their requirements in the design and construction of civic halls and other public educational facilities. The country will work to ensure that national education facilities for young people are fully equipped to accommodate the needs of disabled young people.

It is Japan's goal to ensure that all government facilities which provide direct services to the public are remodelled in accordance with the guidelines on the architectural design standards for government facilities to accommodate the needs of disabled persons. This will be completed by the beginning of the 21st Century.

More police stations and police boxes will be made accessible to people with disabilities. The officers will also give guidance to security companies on the types of services for older persons and people with physical disabilities. The aim is to provide appropriate and effective services.

Japan will also ensure an environment in which people with disabilities are able to walk with a sense of security by promoting the formation of a community zone. It will also actively promote the further installation of traffic safety facilities to accommodate people with disabilities.

The country will promote measures to help people with physical disabilities obtain their drivers' licences by providing adequate training at driving schools, improving accessibility at the examination rooms of each prefectural police headquarters and further promoting technical driving skills tests.

The Government of Japan will continue to support the efforts of local governments which, out of a commitment to improve the health and social services for disabled persons and older persons, seek to tap the creativity and ingenuity of local residents to create urban environments that meet their needs. This can be achieved through the systematic and comprehensive execution of various projects, including the levelling of sidewalks and the installation of ramps and toilets for wheelchair users at public buildings.

It will continue to allow bonds to be issued by local governments to fund social welfare facilities, measures for dealing with disaster victims and disaster prevention infrastructure, including repairs and making earthquake-resistant facilities that can serve as evacuation sites and emergency radio equipment. These bonds will have tax-sharing measures on part of the principal and interest until 2000.

Japan will also actively provide facilities such as wider sidewalks and sites for social service facilities. It will also ensure that older and disabled persons are able to live comfortably with a sense of relief. We will further examine architectural design standards for government facilities.

To allow disabled persons to walk the streets safely, comfortably, and without encountering inconvenience, Japan will promote the building of wider sidewalks, the lowering of steps, the use of Braille blocks for guiding persons with visual impairments, and the construction of pedestrian bridges with ramps or lifts. Along with these projects, the country will support other efforts to build a pleasant pedestrian environment including construction of bicycle parking facilities, of common utility tunnels, burying power and utility lines underground, construction of public squares outside bus and train terminals and the building of community zones.

In order to improve the aesthetic appeal of cities and make driving a less exhausting experience, extra car lanes will be built, more street lighting added, larger signage and automatic-switch equipped traffic lights put in place. Easy parking areas such as "road stations" will also be put in place.

Japan will continue to improve access for disabled persons using public transportation facilities. Concerned parties will also be provided the following guidelines:

(a) Construction of facilities for older persons and disabled persons at transportation terminals;

(b) Installation of elevators;

(c) Installation of escalators at the railroad station.

It will also upgrade devices used by people with disabilities. It plans to introduce nationwide, FAX 110, which accepts emergency reports by fax from persons with disabilities who are unable to communicate on the phone.

In the next five years, Japan also aims to facilitate the social participation of persons with disabilities and improve on accessibility by providing accessible transport, sign language interpreters and publishing public bulletins in Braille. Such facilities will be introduced in the local municipalities. Social welfare facilities in city centres will also be introduced systematically.

To guide security companies and manufacturers of crime prevention tools, Japan will further encourage the study, development and dissemination of a security system that takes into account the characteristics of persons with disabilities.

It will continue to award the prize for disaster prevention excellence in community development as a means of recognizing local governments which have shown particular ingenuity and imagination in carrying out community development emphasizing themes such as social services, volunteerism and disaster prevention. Videocassettes and pamphlets which describe the work of prize winners will be distributed to local governments and concerned organizations throughout the nation so that readers and viewers can learn what has worked well elsewhere.

It will continue to provide guidance to local governments and urge them to keep in mind the need to obtain the cooperation of local residents and other related organizations when formulating disaster prevention measures. These measures should take into account the needs of disabled persons and others who are especially vulnerable in times of disaster. The Government of Japan will survey and study what local governments are doing and discuss the feasibility of various concrete measures.

The country will continue to support the construction of public squares outside bus and train terminals and bicycle parking facilities in accordance with the provisions of the new street plan, 1998 to 2002. Japan will also facilitate the construction of urban parks that accommodate the needs of disabled persons.

Needed changes at existing post offices will be made, including the addition of Braille guide blocks, hand railings, and parking lots for wheelchair users. These will be in accordance with the five-year plan. Postage rate reductions and exemptions shall continue to be offered to disabled persons.

Japan will make efforts to further construct the information network by using faxes at the police boxes, at the disabled persons' organizations and at private homes of persons with disabilities, and to provide information more actively.

It will keep sign language interpreters at the examination rooms for drivers' license, as well as include videos with captions for such training courses on traffic safety for persons with hearing impairments at each prefectural police headquarters.

To allow disabled persons to enjoy waterside locations in a safe and pleasant environment, Japan continues to promote the construction of rest facilities and gently sloping levees and ramps along rivers and marine coastlines.

In order to ensure swift and adequate access to information after floods, typhoons, landslides, and other disasters, Japan will continue to promote the construction of disaster prevention information systems that accommodate the needs of disabled persons. It will encourage expansion of a project to promote people-oriented towns in an effort to make community development more respon-sive to the needs of disabled persons.

The training and securing of volunteers is to be promoted for Braille transcription and tape recording, and sign language interpreters and other staff with professional knowledge and skills are to be trained.

Japan will continue to educate postal employees to ensure that persons with visual or hearing impairments who go to the post office will be able to receive adequate service. Sign language interpreters will also be available at major public employment security offices.

It will continue to train police officers on the use of sign language and enhance the means for persons with hearing impairment to report the loss of their property at police boxes.

Japan will continue to publish and distribute a mini public information paper in Braille and a patrol card in Braille. Also, the functions of Braille Libraries will be improved along with the development of information processing technology. Postcards for persons with visual impairments will continue to be issued.

Japan will continue to provide appropriate sign language interpretation for television programmes in which political viewpoints are presented to the public. The number of the information centres for persons with hearing disability will be increased where videotapes with caption or with sign language are produced and lent out.

5. Education

Improvement and enrichment of curricula will be planned for schools for blind persons, deaf persons, and persons with orthopaedic disabilities in order to cope with the change of social environment surrounding persons with disabilities and to the diversity of realities of each child, and to encourage their zest for living.

In order to deal with the variables connected with the conditions surrounding education of children with disabilities such as the severity, compound nature and diversity of the disabilities of each student, Japan will work to provide special education teachers with training, thereby improving the educational quality. It will also work to improve the overall quality of teachers throughout the school system, from elementary through to lower and upper secondary schools by ensuring that all teachers receive basic training in education of children with disabilities. It will work towards further expanding an early counselling system.

Exchange activities, in which children at schools for blind persons, deaf persons, and persons with orthopaedic disabilities participate with children at regular elementary or high school and people of the community, are extremely meaningful for all participants. Therefore there should be more such exchange activities.

In order to make it possible for students with disabilities to participate independently in society, a further expansion and preparation of an upper secondary division for schools for blind persons, deaf persons and persons with orthopaedic disabilities will be made.

Japan will continue to support the constant improvement of educational equipment at Tsukuba College of Technology which was established by the national college for the education of persons with visual and hearing impairments. For disabled persons pursuing studies at private universities, junior colleges, and colleges of technology, the Government of Japan will increase subsidies to the institutions based on the number of disabled students that are accepted and the number of students that take examination in Braille.

A law concerning regular certificate to elementary and junior high school teachers will go into effect on 1 April 1998. Accordingly, anyone who enters university during or subsequent to the 1998 school year with the intention of receiving an elementary or junior high school teacher certificate will be required to acquire experience in caring for, and to have personal contact with, people with disabilities.

Following the first five years, projects sponsored by the national youth educational facility on outside school activities in the community, targeting children with disabilities, will be conducted.

6. Training and employment

Reviews will be made on the training courses that look at the vocational ability of persons with disability particularly the considerations for employment of women and girls with disabilities.

A supportive programme for on-the-job adjustment training will continue as would the total model programme of promotion of employment of persons with disabilities in the community, and the project plan for promotion of employment of persons with extensive disability will be implemented.

The promotion companies that employ persons with extensive disabilities conducted by the third sector system will be continued, as would the employment support centres for disabled Persons.

There are also aims to establish measures which can be a guideline for building and organizing a community network that covers general employment support for persons with extensive disabilities, and to conduct research.

Japan will review the training courses and curriculum, renew the equipment corresponding to the needs of enterprise owners, as well as characteristics and degree of vocational skills of each disability group. It will also improve the provision of facilities and make equipment accessible for persons with disabilities, and promote their acceptance by general vocational skills development facilities. It will also try to enrich the study sessions for trainers who provide vocational training to persons with disabilities at the vocational ability development colleges.

Accommodation in sheltered workshops and welfare factories will be increased up to 68,000 persons by 2002. The non-authorized small-scale workshops will be changed to the authorized facilities by introducing a branch system of authorized sheltered workshops or by enlarging the functions of day-care services. Financial assistance will be increased for their stable management.

Furthermore, in considering the personality traits of persons with mental disabilities, the rehabilitation programmes will be improved upon to promote their social independence and gainful employment, in cooperation with employment measures by the Ministry of Labour. The number of facilities for the social reintegration of people with mental disabilities will be increased, and the functions of these facilities strengthened.

7. Prevention of the causes of disability

Japan will continue to work in accordance with the provisions of the basic traffic safety plan to formulate concrete safety projects each year, and shall carry out comprehensive measures for land-based, sea-based and air-based transportation.

To prevent the causes of disability and to establish fundamental treatment methods, research on physical, mental and neurotic disorders will be further promoted. This is especially so in the fields of mental disorders and incurable chronic diseases, which are less developed in Japan. Research and development concerning disability causes, and the early detection and early treatment system will be continued. Based on these results, the medical examination of 18 month-old children and studies of congenital metabolic disorders and prenatal medical care will be further strengthened.

Based on the Community Health Law of 1994, the functions of health centres and mental health and welfare centres for persons with mental disabilities will be further strengthened. As these centres are basic technical agencies for mental health in the community, and counselling services will be provided to address psychological and mental needs, pubescent mental health, and alcohol-related problems.

8. Rehabilitation services

Based on the Government Action Plan for Persons with Disabilities, the service delivery systems of health and welfare services will be improved upon by setting specific and concrete numerical targets to be attained by the end of 2002. Proper medical care, including dental care, will be secured along with the expansion of medicinal rehabilitation services at local medical facilities. The comprehensive rehabilitation service system will be established with the coordination of various functions of counselling and evaluation at rehabilitation centres and medical facilities.

The home helper (personal assistant), staff at various facilities and other professional staff working in community will be systematically-trained and maintained, along with the qualitative and quantitative expansion of allied medical staff such as physical therapists and occupational therapists.

The training programmes of home-helper (personal assistant) will be improved upon and expanded to respond to specific needs of persons with various disabilities.

The community health and welfare programmes for people with mental disabilities will be expanded through improvement of counselling and guidance services by mental health and welfare centres for persons with mental disabilities and health centres. Assistance to self-help or family groups, and service improvements by social reintegration centres for persons with mental disabilities and for persons who are issued mentally disabled person certificates will be improved.

The systems for care and other services will be developed to meet the individual needs of various types and degrees of disabilities to enable extensively disabled persons to live in the community.

Two centres for persons with physical disability, two centres for persons with intellectual disabilities and two centres for persons with mental disability are to be established per 300,000 population as coordination centres for counselling, guidance, support and information services.

The service delivery system at the municipal level will be established for persons who are in need of personal assistance and other services such as home help service, including guide help, day-care service and short-term stay (respite) service.

The sports activities of people with disabilities will be promoted by holding events such as the Winter Paralympic Games, Nagano, March 1998, other sports games, sports courses and recreational events, as well as by constructing sports facilities for them.

The training programmes for sports instructors for persons with disabilities will be improved upon and the active participation of volunteers in sports events will be promoted to enhance public awareness concerning sports activities of persons with disabilities.

Japan will continue to financially support the efforts of local governments which, out of a commitment to the improvement of health and social services for disabled persons and older persons, seek to tap the creativity and ingenuity of local residents to create urban environments suited to their needs. This can be achieved through the systematic and comprehensive execution of various local projects, including the construction of rehabilitation facilities for disabled persons and others.

9. Assistive devices

To provide proper assistive devices based on the needs of persons with disabilities, guidance and supply systems will be diversified and follow-up systems improved upon. The training of professionals who engage in guidance, evaluation and fitting of assistive devices will be improved, and more appropriate usage and distribution system will be promoted.

Through the development of evaluation systems on assistive devices, the adaptability and safety of the assistive devices will be promoted. It will continue to carry out research and development (R and D) on basic and more widely-used technology related to telecommunications equipment and systems for disabled persons and older persons. It will also continue to conduct R and D related to basic telecommunications technology that is suited to the needs of disabled persons and older persons. In conjunction with the 1998 Winter Paralympic Games in Nagano, there will a demonstration to showcase the country's R and D work.

Japan will continue to study the development of total support skills for expanding the work place for persons with extensive disabilities.

A project on medical and social service assistive devises, the study, development and utilization of assistive devises and their developmental promotion will likely be registered, to promote the study and development of assistive devises and their utilization.

10. Self-help organizations

The representatives of various self-help organizations will be appointed as members of the Central Council for the Promotion of Measures for Disabled Persons and the Local Councils for the Promotion of Measures for Disabled Persons. This will secure more effective participation in national or local policy and to increase their role in decision-making on disability matters. More representatives of various self-help organizations and parents associations will also be appointed as members of the Advisory Council on Welfare of Physically Disabled Persons.

Normanet will be strengthened with more participation of individuals with disabilities and with more numbers of self-help organizations.

The Leadership Training Programme for Persons with Disabilities, which was started in 1995 as part of JICA training schemes, will be continued to encourage the leadership potentials and promote the activities of self-help organizations.

The number of the Community Living Support Centres for Persons with Disabilities, which began in 1996, will be increased with the participation of self-help organizations. Peer counselling services are expected to be further promoted.

The advocate centres for persons with disabilities, called 110 for Human Rights of Persons with Disabilities, will be opened in all prefectures possibly from 1998.

11. Regional cooperation

Japan is actively promoting projects that invite trainees from overseas and despatching experts and volunteers through the Japan International Cooperation Agency (JICA) and Japan Overseas Cooperation Volunteers (JOCV). It is investigating the possibilities of persons with disabilities participating directly in international cooperation projects as trainers or service providers.

To meet the diverse needs in measures for persons with disabilities overseas, international cooperation through grassroots projects grants and subsidies for NGO projects will be promoted.

The linkage with Asian and Pacific countries is expected to be strengthened through training programmes for rehabilitation professionals which are planned by the National Rehabilitation Centre for Disabled Persons and other agencies, and also through exchange programmes among NGOs.

Japan will cooperate with the Asia and the Pacific Programme of Educational Innovation for Development (APEID), an UNESCO programme, to further promote regional cooperation in special education. It will also continue international cooperation with Asian and Pacific countries and the work on the transfer of vocational rehabilitation skills to Indonesia.

In the second half of the Asian and Pacific Decade, it is Japan's intention to build on the achievements of the first five years. It will work to eliminate all barriers to disabled persons throughout the ESCAP region and the world. It will also make an effort commensurate with its international status and resources to cooperate in the effort to achieve the full participation and equality of persons with disabilities.

In particular, Japan will actively support the efforts of the Japan-ESCAP Cooperation Fund (JECF) and cooperate with all relevant private organizations to carry out various ESCAP projects related to persons with disabilities.

CHAPTER XII

Lao People's Democratic Republic

A. National overview

The Government of the Lao People's Democratic Republic has tried, since the launch of the Asian and Pacific Decade of Disabled Persons, 1993-2002, to adhere to the agreements and recommendations made in the Agenda for Action for the Asian and Pacific Decade of Disabled persons (hereafter referred to as the Asian and Pacific Decade Agenda for Action) by implementing various policies and activities for people with disabilities in the country.

B. Progress made in the first half of the Asian and Pacific Decade of Disabled Persons

1. National coordination

The Government of the Lao People's Democratic Republic has set up a National Committee for Disabled Persons headed by the Minister of Labour Social Welfare. Its committee board members include the Vice Ministers of Health, Education and Foreign Affairs, and other staff from the related ministries.

The national committee pursues measures similar to the government policy for the country's disabled persons, including prevention of causes of disabilities, free medical care and medical rehabilitation, as well as free professional, social and educational rehabilitation services.

All government ministries and concerned organizations implement these measures according to their respective authority and responsibilities. They also coordinate and work with each other to implement the measures (see Diagram 1, Annex).

2. Legislation

The Government of The Lao People's Democratic Republic has no specific legislation as yet to protect the rights of people with disabilities. However, the country's laws and constitution ensure democracy for the entire Lao population. Disabled persons have equal rights as others.

3. Information and public awareness

A report, detailing the meeting in Bangkok from 26 to 30 June 1995 to review the progress that Asian and Pacific countries have made two years into the Asian and Pacific Decade of Disabled Persons, was translated into Lao, and published and distributed to all government ministries, organizations and all provincial offices in early 1996. This has helped change some attitudes of the Lao people towards disabled persons.

In April 1996, the country held a medical conference aimed at establishing measures to strengthen the provision of medical rehabilitation services and improve the system of providing such services at the provincial and district levels. Some 56 participants attended the conference and they were mainly representatives from provincial health service providers and various hospital board directors.

Another such meeting, the Conference on Cooperation for Disabled Persons, was held in September 1996. Some 24 representatives from the Department of Social Welfare and provincial health services and rehabilitation units attended the conference.

From 1995, a course on medical rehabilitation was included in the medical studies curriculum at the local university. Medical students in their fifth year have to attend 60 hours of both theoretical and practical training on medical rehabilitation. They also have to assist doctors and nurses in providing care for people with disabilities.

In early 1996, with the cooperation of the Health Ministry, Prosthetic and Orthotic Worldwide Education and Relief (POWER) conducted a survey to investigate the number of individuals with specific disabilities in the Lao People's Democratic Republic. The national survey of disabled persons was carried out nationwide, reaching almost every town and village in the country. Its aim was to determine the number of amputees (arm or leg), the number of people with foot deformities, leg deformities, blind persons and deaf persons

The results after surveying some 11,778 villages are as follows:

Types of disability	Number of persons
Arm knee amputees	1,241
Below knee amputees	965
Above knee amputees	479
Foot deformities	5,074
Leg deformities	2,613
Deaf persons	12,977
Blind persons	5,278

However, the above survey did not cover all people with disabilities as the aim was to find information that would help determine the provision of artificial limbs and orthopaedic aids and educational service for only four categories of disabilities.

A publicity campaign covering information on the prevention of the causes of disability, rehabilitation and promotion of equalization of disabled persons was carried out.

The campaign covered four aspects:

(a) A television advertisement titled *Lives are Valuable* was broadcast twice a week and is still being shown now, at least once a week;

(b) Distribution of manuals and posters of accidents prevention from explosives from the previous civil war, the prevention of traffic accidents, the prevention of diseases and the rehabilitation of disabled persons;

(c) Conducting seminar and training on community-based rehabilitation (CBR) and primary health care (PHC) in 649 villages around the country;

(d) Holding charity concerts and musical dance evenings to raise funds, as well as to demonstrate the artistic talents of people with disabilities. Their performances received enthusiastic responses from all levels of society, clearly demonstrating the positive attitudes of the Lao people towards disabled persons.

4. Accessibility and communication

Currently, the Lao People's Democratic Republic still lacks regulation on design, construction, renovation and expansion of buildings to facilitate the movement of disabled persons. There are only design codes and guidelines for general construction and maintenance works. As such, disabled persons could not easily access public buildings, state buildings, hospitals, schools and roads which are deemed difficult and dangerous to persons on wheelchairs and crutches.

As more people with disabilities assimilate into the mainstream society through higher enrolment of disabled students in regular schools, this shift would help teachers understand more the need to provide accessible classrooms, toilets and other facilities. In addition, courses on designing accessible building are being conducted at the university's architecture faculty. Similarly, issues on accessibility, CBR and integrated education were raised and discussed with the provincial authorities, village leaders and teachers.

5. Education

In 1995, primary education was made compulsory in the country. All schools must now also accept disabled students. Since then, parents have been encouraged to send their disabled children to school and the enrolment of students with disabilities have steadily increased each year.

For deaf and blind children, since 1993, the government has organized special learning and teaching programmes for them. The programmes are very popular and many parents want to send their children to these special education schools. However, as school capacities are limited, not all who applied are enrolled. Dormitories for special education schools located in more remote areas are also inadequate.

The country's integrated education programme started as a pilot project at a primary school in Vientiane. Started in 1993, the project was supported by Save the Children Fund UK (SCF/UK), the United Nations Education, Science and Cultural Organization (UNESCO) and the United Nations Children's Fund (UNICEF). Under the programme, mildly and moderately intellectually-disabled children study in the same classes with non-disabled children. Proven to be successful, the project has expanded to four provinces involving 21 primary schools and 18 kindergartens (refer to Annex, Table 2).

The Government of the Lao People's Democratic Republic has designed a teacher-training course curriculum for disabled children and adults in an attempt to gradually improve education services for people with disabilities.

6. Training and employment

The country currently does not provide professional training and job placement services for people with disabilities as it is a very difficult task and there are not many jobs available in the market. However, the government does, occasionally try to provide some CBR-training programmes using funds provided by international organization and non-governmental organizations (NGOs) (refer to Annex, Table 1).

7. Prevention of the causes of disability

The Government of the Lao People's Democratic Republic, together with international organizations and NGOs, has undertaken many steps to prevent the causes of disability. They include the following projects:

(a) National immunization programme;

(b) Mother and child healthcare and protection programme;

(c) Prevention of blindness and the treatment of eye diseases programme;

(d) Demining programme;

(e) CBR and PHC programme.

In addition, a programme aimed at preventing traffic accidents is already in place, as well as narcotics and alcohol abuse prevention projects (refer to Annex, Table 3).

8. Rehabilitation services and assistive devices

The Lao People's Democratic Republic is still undeveloped, and having recently recovered from war, there are a large number of disabled persons in the country, whose conditions resulted from disease, mines, weapons and accidents. Besides that, natural calamities, such as floods and droughts occurring almost yearly, cause starvation among the villagers.

The Government of the Lao People's Democratic Republic is now trying to solve these problems by training technical staff and extending the rehabilitation network to 16 provinces and six districts throughout the country. However, these projects are not viable and the government is facing some difficulties in implementing them.

The provision of assistive devices is supported by USAID (prostheses and rehabilitation), World Vision and Power. In all, the amputees were provided with some 2,533 artificial limbs (refer to Annex, Table 8).

9. Self-help organizations

The National Rehabilitation Centre and the National Community for Disabled Persons have met five times to try to draft an action plan covering regulation and organization of self-help groups of disabled persons. The action plan is now pending government approval.

10. Regional cooperation

The Government of the Lao People's Democratic Republic has continued to receive support and cooperation from various international organizations and NGOs, especially those concerned with the prevention, rehabilitation and education of disabled persons. These organizations include the United Nations Development Programme, the World Health Organization, the Food and Agricultural Organization, Economic and Social Commission for Asia and the Pacific, UNICEF, UNESCO, United Nations High Commissioner for Refugees (UNHCR), USAID, Japan International Cooperation Agency (JICA), World Vision, World Concern, SCF/UK, DED, POWER and Handicap International. The country is grateful for the support in helping it implement its programmes and is confident of receiving their continuous support.

C. Activities planned for the second half of the Asian and Pacific Decade of Disabled Persons

To achieve the targets set out in the Agenda for Action for the Asian and Pacific Decade of Disabled Persons, the Government of the Lao People's Democratic Republic has listed out the following plans for the second half of the Asian and Pacific Decade of Disabled Persons.

1. Strengthen the National Committee for Disabled Persons by seeking representatives of disabled persons, as well as women and youth groups and trade unions.

2. Organize and build an executive secretariat to implement the work of the National Committee for Disabled Persons.

3. Set up committees for disabled persons at the provincial and district levels.

4. Complete drafting laws covering the following aspects:

    (a) Human rights for disabled persons;

    (b) Quotas for disabled persons in the job market;

    (c) Job placement services for disabled persons in the public and private sectors;

    (d) Design and construct buildings and streets to make them accessible.

5. Improve the public communication system to disseminate more the prevention of causes of disabilities and rehabilitation; this could be implemented with the cooperation of the Ministry of Information and Culture.

6. Expand the integrated education system and delegate provincial officials to implement it at primary schools and kindergartens in the provinces and districts.

7. Request support from neighbouring countries, international organizations and NGOs to help develop schools for deaf and blind children, as well as skills training institutions for disabled persons. This would help improve and make available, rehabilitative services at the provincial and district levels. Staff training and skills improvement programmes could also be provided at the same time.

8. Accelerate efforts to set up officially a committee for people with disabilities.

9. Enhance regional and international cooperation with organizations and NGOs to provide support for meeting the needs of people with disabilities in the country.

ANNEX

Activities carried out according to the National Plan of Action from January 1993 to 1997.

Diagram 1. Establishment of national committee for disabled persons for national coordination: 27/1/1995 N. 18/PMA

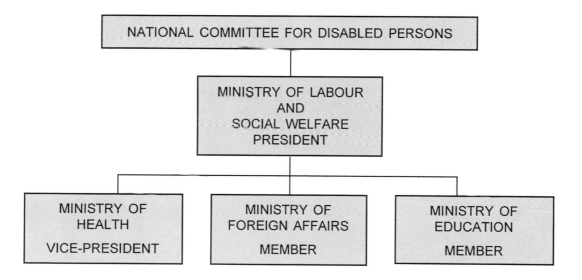

Diagram 2. Plan to establish by the end of 1997

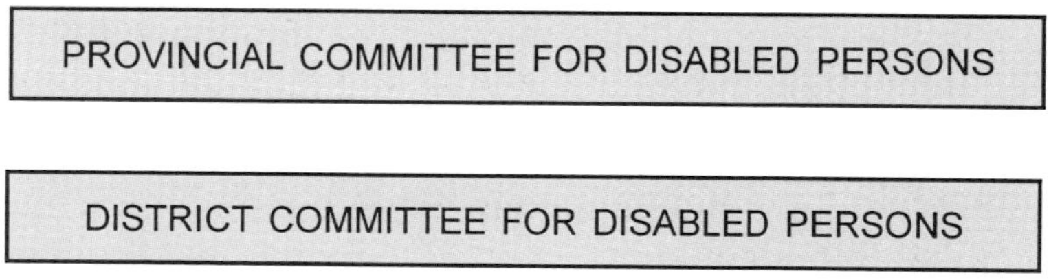

PROVINCIAL COMMITTEE FOR DISABLED PERSONS

DISTRICT COMMITTEE FOR DISABLED PERSONS

Table 1. Vocational training and employment for disabled persons

N	Description of training	Number of trainees			Remarks
		1993-1994	1995-1996	1997	
1	Hair styling	3	7	5	Self-employed and generating incomes of US$50-US$100
2	Beauty treatment	6	0	0	
3	Tailoring	12	7	2	
4	Fish breeding	12	1	0	"
5	Poultry breeding	164	105	160	"
6	Cow breeding	295	12	20	"
7	Buffalo breeding	7	1	10	"
8	Pig breeding	21	3	10	"
9	Goat breeding	1	6	10	"
10	Vegetable growing	5	105	120	"
11	Bicycle repairs	4	2	3	"
12	Blacksmith trainees	0	3	–	"
13	Radio and television repairs	3	5	6	"
14	Traditional massage	4	4	8	"
15	School teachers	9	2	1	Government salary
16	Public sector workmen	13	15	18	"
17	Government office staff	7	9	15	"
	Total	**566**	**287**	**388**	**1,241**

Table 2. Education

Description	Year began	Number of pupils	Remarks
1. Normal Schools			
a. Physical handicap	1992-1997	350	Compulsory education.
b. Intellectual disability	1993-1997	252	Integrated education
(Mild and moderate)			programme started
			from 1993
2. Special Schools			
a. School for blind persons			(started from the
– Preparatory Class	1993-1997	16	school year 1993-94
– Primary 1st year		2	till 1997)
– Primary 2nd year		3	
– Primary 3rd year		2	
– Primary 4th year		3	
– Primary 5th year		8	
b. School for the deaf persons			(started from the
– Preparatory Class	1993-1997	34	school year 1992-93
– Primary 1st year		12	till 1997)
– Primary 2nd year		17	
– Primary 3rd year		9	
– Primary 4th year		7	
– Primary 5th year		6	
Total		**721**	

Table 3. Prevention of causes of disabilities: coverage of vaccination in the country (in percentage terms)

Type of vaccination	1993	1994	1995	1996
BCG	42	69	59	61
DPT3	25	48	54	58
OPV3 (Polio)	26	57	65	68
Measles	46	73	68	73

Table 4. Rehabilitation services in the country

Location	Activities	Unit	Number in year				
			1993	1994	1995	1996	1997
Vientiane capital (NCMR)	Kinesitherap	Patients	1,785	1,915	3,844	4,302	2,950
Provinces 16	Kinesitherapy	Patients	6,975	9,825	9,720	9,830	5,760
Rehabilitation service in 4 central hospitals	Kinesitherapy	Patients	1,275	1,595	1,605	1,625	1,405
Total			10,035	13,335	15,169	15,757	10,115

Table 5. Staff training: training and further skills upgrading

Description	Type of training	Number of staff trained in year					Total
		1993	1994	1995	1996	1997	
Physician	Rehabilitation	2	2	3	2	0	9
Surgeon	Restoring deformity	8	2	0	0	0	10
Orthopaedic technicians	For limb fitting BK. AK. and arm fitting	25	15	16	24	1	81
Physiotherapist		16	12	20	49	5	102
Orthopaedic technicians	Metal wheelchair and aluminium crutch	0	2	0	0	2	4
Teachers	Special education	16	0	9	5	6	36
Teachers	Integrated education	43	47	40	108	119	357

Table 6. CBR integrated into PHC programme in two provinces 1993-1997

Districts:	8
Villages:	649
Persons with disabilities	2,598
Hazard awareness concerning the prevention of the causes of disabilities to local authorities (Under a five-day seminar)	3,918
CBR training at sub-district level and villages	649
Traditional birth attendant (TBA) training	61
Training for water pump maintenance technicians	127
Water-well drilling	127

Table 7. Artificial limbs workshop

Description of location	Number of workshop	Observation
NCMR* Vientiane	1	Production and fitting
Vientiane Province	1	Fitting only
Luang Phrabang Province	1	Fitting only
Xieng Khouang Province	1	Fitting only
Khammouane Province	1	Fitting only
Savannakhet Province	1	Fitting only
Champassak Province	1	Fitting only
Saravanne Province	1	Fitting only
Houaphanh Province	1	Fitting only
Total	**9**	

*   National Centre for Medical Rehabilitation.

Table 8. Production of components and fitting of artificial limbs

Description	Number in year					Total
	1993	1994	1995	1996	1997	
Production						
Artificial feet	300	200	0	300	157	957
Artificial knees	35	17	45	30	35	162
Wooden elbow crutches	130	105	160	139	141	675
Metallic Canadian crutches	0	0	0	2	2	4
Wooden canes	6	15	2	0	0	23
Wheelchairs	3	1	8	14	41	67
Braces (short & long)	9	9	8	16	9	51
Orthopaedic shoes	28	18	21	49	14	130
Corset	16	13	5	7	9	50
Fittings						
Limb fitting below-knee (BK)	164	597	877	286	234	2,158
Limb fitting above-knee (AK)	30	36	86	62	80	294
Arm fitting	7	12	26	30	6	81

CHAPTER XIII

Macau

A. National overview

Macau is a Chinese territory under Portuguese administration until 1999 when it will revert back to China. Macau comprises a peninsula city and two islands, with a total area of 21 square kilometres. According to the population census of 1981, the resident population is 124,430. So far no survey has been conducted to determine the number of people with disabilities. However, the estimates are about 42,000 people with various forms of disability.

The Government of Macau has long recognized the importance of disability issues and has enacted several laws protecting the rights of disabled persons. These include the Law on the Suppression of Physical Barriers, Law on the Access to Health Care, Law on the Education System which includes special education for disabled children. The government has also established that the Social Security Department and the Labour Department must give special attention to people with disabilities. The territory has made considerable progress towards achieving the goals set out in the Agenda for Action for the Asian and Pacific Decade of Disabled Persons during the first half of the Decade.

B. Progress made in the first half of the Asian and Pacific Decade of Disabled Persons

1. National coordination

The Government of Macau has developed close cooperation and good coordination with the non-government organizations (NGOs) and both sides have jointly organized various activities, including commemoration of the International Day of Disabled Persons.

Although Macau is short in human resources, including professional and technical staff, it is still able to conduct research on selected subjects. The Government of Macau also supports and helps NGOs raise funds, to which the people of Macau have always responded positively.

Training courses have been organized regularly for NGO staff, families and clients. The first course, offering training for all NGOs concerned with people with disabilities and related issues, was held a few years ago. The second such course is expected to be held in 1998.

2. Legislation

Macau has enacted various laws protecting the rights of people with disabilities. They enjoy various forms of tax relief (for example, 35 per cent off on private cars) and are entitled to subsidies, medical welfare and social security funds. The government also provides social housing to people with disabilities and some public social services, including handicapped housing, day-care centres, workshops, vocational training and free special education and parking. The territory has also provided accessible public facilities such as parking lots, escalators and special road surfaces for blind and other disabled persons.

3. Information and public awareness

Information on disability and people with disabilities has regularly been broadcast on radio and television and published in the newspapers and other journals. These have proved effective in transmitting information to the people. The government and NGOs have also produced various printed materials on the subject. The Macau Education Department is planning to establish a central computer information system for disabled persons.

The Government of Macau and NGOs have also jointly organized various activities to raise public awareness, particularly on the International Day of Disabled Persons. Through seminars, conferences, sports and games, people's attitudes and beliefs have changed and will continue to change as they overcome their deep-rooted superstitions about disability and people with disabilities.

4. Accessibility and communication

To meet the needs of people with disabilities, Macau is trying to improve accessibility for people with disabilities in some institutions and centres. Under the law, these institutions and centres must be accessible and are effectively barrier-free in design.

However, more could be improved upon in the area of sign language development. Most people with hearing impairments face many difficulties when communicating with staff at hospitals, banks, the Police Department and even in the job market. There are only two organizations, Escola Concordia and Associacao de Surdos, which are dedicated to the promotion and use of sign language.

For visually-impaired persons, there are still not enough support services and facilities. These include the absence of Braille reading material in some public libraries and the university. The government and NGOs are in the process of establishing a training centre for visually-impaired persons.

5. Education

Special education has been developed as a formal education programme; there is one for children and another for adults. The government's budget for supporting these programmes has been increasing every year.

The Education Department has begun evening classes for less educated or non-educated adults. Some disabled persons are also enrolled in these classes.

Macau's special education programme has been rather lop-sided in its focus. It is mainly targeted at those who are intellectually-disabled. It also focuses more on children with disabilities under 16 rather than on adults. Most adults with disabilities still cannot receive further education and additional training. Special education organizations have tried their best to provide enough support services such as transportation and accommodation, to facilitate the participation of persons with disabilities in education programmes. Furthermore, the special education programme is encouraging parent and teacher consultative groups. Many schools are now incorporating the programme to try to meet their educational goals for people with disabilities.

6. Training and employment

People with disabilities are still unable to participate actively in the local job market due mainly to the absence of policy and the necessary legislation to support an employment programme. As people with disabilities can not find jobs, some NGOs have begun providing vocational training for disabled persons to better prepare and help them integrate into the community.

Unfortunately, most have never received any, or have had little, formal education. As a result, it is sometimes difficult for them to attend the training courses and acquire the necessary skills. Most want to learn but do not have enough abilities to do well.

The Government of Macau and NGOs are trying to arrange and implement a job skills training scheme to help disabled persons meet the needs of the job market. Some NGOs have taken the initiative to provide advice and skills training to them.

The Government of Macau also provides financial support, in the form of seed money, to help disabled persons start their own businesses. However, not all are capable of doing so. NGOs also encourage disabled persons to start their own businesses and operations.

The task of providing skills training and jobs for people with disabilities is hindered by various difficulties and barriers, including the following:

(a) Educational institutions cannot accommodate special education in their curricula;

(b) Insufficient training schemes exist;

(c) Many NGOs and staff are unable to fully understand the concept of an employment programme for people with disabilities. Most just know it as "that the employer must accept people with disabilities and employ them". They do not understand that an employment programme is integrated with many different areas such as assessment, education, training, evaluation, economics (supply and demand) of the labour market and other goods;

(d) Lack of professional staff such as social workers, occupational therapists, psychologists and marketing managers providing support services for disabled persons.

7. Prevention of the causes of disability

The NGOs are usually dedicated to helping raise public awareness of the causes of disability, including the dangers of drug abuse, neglect, accidents and violence.

Over the years, many improvements have been made in the provision of ante- and neo-natal care as more hospital staff are well-trained. Technological advancements and the use of new technology in hospitals have also played major roles in preventing the causes of disabilities. In addition, hospital staff and personnel undergo continuous training to upgrade their skills and knowledge.

The Macau Urban Council and the Macau Health Services Department both actively promote community cleanliness and personal hygiene. They also cooperate with other agencies to tackle the issues of pollution and toxicity in the food chain. The Health Services Department has stringent regulations and measures, especially on food products and consumption.

Similarly, the Macau governmental hospital also has a system to assess and manage children who are at high risk of becoming disabled due to pre- and post-natal causes.

The government is now paying more attention to health care and is continuously enhancing the provision of good health care services. However, as a result of a lack of well-trained service providers, Macau still faces difficulties in developing high quality services to people with disabilities.

8. Rehabilitation services

Macau does not have current statistical data on people with disabilities. Its Social Welfare Institute is planning to conduct a survey to collect the information. Preparatory work, involving the participation of various government agencies and NGOs, is currently underway.

Prior to 1993, nine centres and institutions for people with disabilities were entitled to subsidies from the Social Welfare Institute. The number has now increased to 16 centres and institutions for people with mental and physical disabilities. From 1993 to 1997, the Institute subsidized seven more such centres.

Out of the 16, 11 were set up to provide services to people with intellectual disabilities, two for persons with mental illness, one unit for deaf and physically-disabled children, one workshop for blind persons and one for those with mental and physical disabilities. Moreover, such services are provided free to disabled persons and they are also given an allowance.

According to the administrative policy for 1997, the Government of Macau is currently drafting a mental health policy, which outlines the measures for the care of people with mental disabilities. Another policy that is being drawn up covers rehabilitation and it includes the push for the development of organizations for people with disabilities, and to set up a special authoritative body, in cooperation with the Health Ministry, to coordinate and provide care for disabled persons.

Currently consultations for disabled persons at government hospitals or clinics affiliated with the Health Ministry are provided free. However the Government of Macau could do more to expand and strengthen the quality of the services provided and upgrade the skills of the disabled persons. Some NGOs are actively developing vocational training programmes for people with disabilities and to help them find jobs.

The community as a whole is beginning to accept people with disabilities as citizens and they are less discriminated against. Parents are no longer ashamed of their disabled children. Certain practices of locking their disabled children at home all day and sometimes, all their lives, are fast disappearing.

Prior to 1993, the Social Welfare Institute gave financial and technical assistance to organizations that provide rehabilitation services. Now, besides funding and technical assistance, the institute also helps locate rehabilitation facilities which are operated by the NGOs.

Previously the public knew little about the type of rehabilitative services that are provided by the government nor how and where to get them. However, through greater publicity and community activities, more people are beginning to find out about the community resources available.

The Social Welfare Institute has organized a few short-term courses to enhance the quality of services provided and raise the skill levels of employees from the centres and institutions. Another new course is being prepared and will be launched in 1998. The Health Department also holds on-the-job training for nurses, including mental illness and rehabilitative service courses. The courses also include site visits to some relevant organizations.

It is useful to tap on local cultural resources to enhance the quality of the rehabilitative services provided. In the Chinese tradition, the role of the family is of primary importance. In line with this tradition, the Social Welfare Institute and the NGOs organize activities, focusing on the relationship between the family and people with disabilities.

Moreover, through these activities, they meet people who share the same experiences and eventually form self-help groups. The NGOs also hold talks with the family members to better understand their needs and fine-tune the teaching curricula to meet demand.

9. Assistive devices

People with disabilities acquire the assistive devices they need from private companies which import them from Hong Kong, China, or elsewhere. These imported products are more expensive. The only cheaper device is the hearing aid which is made locally. Depending on the circumstances, some of the assistive devices are provided free. More could be done to further improve the services provided.

10. Self-help organizations

There are few self-help organizations here that provide services. The government provides financial and technical assistance to help these organizations although some do lack professionals to establish the services.

11. Regional cooperation

Macau is a small territory with limited technical resources. It is hoped that some assistance could come from neighbouring areas such as China, Hong Kong, China, and Singapore. Mutual visits and regular meetings should be encouraged to exchange information and experiences.

CHAPTER XIV

Malaysia

A. National overview

The Government of Malaysia is committed to the welfare and well-being of people with disabilities. Over the years, the Government has introduced various policies and programmes to ensure disabled Malaysians enjoy truly meaningful lives. The fostering of a caring Malaysian society is one of nine challenges mapped out by Vision 2020. This is significant to the Asian and Pacific Decade of Disabled Persons, 1993-2002, as Vision 2020 has paved the way for services to be provided to persons with disabilities, and for them to be integrated into the Malaysian community. As a result, there is great potential for action and change to benefit disabled persons. Currently in Malaysia, about 65,000 disabled persons are registered with the Department of Social Welfare.

B. Policy measures

Currently Malaysia is moving towards industrialized country status as reflected in the Seventh Malaysia Plan (1996-2000), which also emphasizes social development, particularly in creating a civil society that stresses shared responsibility among its multi-ethnic population. All parties, including individuals, families, existing social institutions and relevant government ministries as well as the private sector and non-governmental organizations (NGOs) are partners. They are all given equal responsibility to effectively deliver services to the disabled population.

The International Year of Disabled Persons followed, by the United Nations Decade of Disabled Persons, with its World Programme of Action concerning Disabled Persons saw Malaysia move ahead with various policies and programmes to improve the quality of life of persons with disabilities.

One milestone in the development of social welfare in Malaysia is the proclamation of the National Welfare Policy, 1990. The policy aims to:

(a) Create a society that upholds the spirit of self-reliance;

(b) Equalize opportunities for the less fortunate;

(c) Foster a caring culture.

Disabled persons have been identified as a special target group to be given due attention. Under this policy, early detection and the necessary facilities are to be made available for the treatment, rehabilitation, education and training of persons with disabilities. Efforts must also be made to help them reintegrate into the community.

The strong and structured government administration at the national, state and district level ensured that all policies, programmes and activities planned could be implemented at all levels. However, ad hoc projects and the lack of coordination was a stumbling block to effective implementation of well-planned policies and programmes.

To overcome this major problem, in 1990, the Government of Malaysia set up an Advisory Panel on Disabled Persons. The Panel comprises of representatives from key government agencies, NGOs and disabled persons themselves. It would mainly look into the problems and needs of disabled persons, review existing facilities and programmes in both the public and the private sectors, identify issues that require immediate attention, and recommend short- and long-term programmes to meet the needs of disabled persons.

C. Progress made in the first half of the Asian and Pacific Decade of Disabled Persons

Malaysia's commitment to improving the quality of life of its disabled citizens was further enhanced by its signing of the Proclamation on the Full Participation and Equality of People with Disabilities in the Asian and Pacific Region on 16 May 1994. The move providing fresh impetus to meeting the goals of the Agenda for Action for the Asian and Pacific Decade of Disabled Persons, 1993-2002, covering the 12 policy areas discussed below.

1. National coordination

Having established its national commitment to its disabled citizens, the Government of Malaysia, through the Ministry of National Unity and Social Development, set up an Inter-Ministerial Coordinating Committee on 30 August 1990.

Chaired by the Secretary-General of the Ministry of National Unity and Social Development, this Committee aims to secure close cooperation and coordination with relevant government agencies in the planning and implementation of programmes for the well-being of people with disabilities.

The Committee comprises representatives from relevant ministries and departments and other related NGOs. With the inclusion of the membership of NGOs through the participation of the Malaysian Council for Rehabilitation (MCR), the committee serves as the national focal point on disability matters and facilitates a continuous national coordination and collaborative approach to implementing the World Programme of Action concerning Disabled Persons. Accordingly, steps are being taken to strengthen the MCR as a national coordinating body for the NGOs and as a permanent body with sufficient infrastructural support and fair representation of self-help organizations of persons with disabilities.

Recently, a proposal was submitted to the Cabinet, to upgrade the existing committee to the status of a council, which will be known as the National Coordinating Council for Disabled Persons. The Council will be chaired by the Minister of National Unity and Social Development with the Secretaries-General from relevant ministries as members. The function of the Council, though advisory in nature, will constitute a platform for collaboration and coordination between and among the various ministries, departments and NGOs. Several technical working groups (TWGS) have been formed to draw up plans of action:

(a) TWG 1 deals with health matters, especially in the areas of early intervention and prevention of causes of disability, it is headed by the Secretary-General, Ministry of Health;

(b) TWG 2 deals with social service matters, especially in the areas of prevention, rehabilitation, institutional care and development; the Director-General, Department of Social Welfare, heads this TWG;

(c) TWG 3 deals with the education, training and employment of people with disabilities; the Secretary-General, Ministry of Education, heads it;

(d) TWG 4 deals with public awareness matters in the form of advocacy and community mobilization; the Secretary-General, Ministry of Information, heads this TWG;

(e) TWG 5 deals with public amenities and transportation; it is headed by the Secretary-General, Ministry of Housing and Local Government;

(f) TWG 6 deals with the formulation of legislation and the Attorney-General, Prime Minister's Department, is in charge;

(g) TWG 7 deals with sports and cultural matters; it is headed by the Secretary-General, Ministry of Culture, Arts and Tourism.

The TWGs are given the task of preparing reports on the existing situation on the well-being of people with disabilities in their respective fields of interests. The reports will eventually help the Council develop a national plan of action for disabled persons covering the 12 policy objectives as outlined in the Asian and Pacific Decade Agenda for Action.

Networking support at the district levels is crucial to ensure wider coverage by the programmes implemented. Furthermore, programmes and activities for persons with disabilities can also be referred to and discussed in the National Consultative Council on Social Development, which is composed of ministers from the relevant ministries and departments, as well as the state executive officials dealing with social development and welfare matters.

2. Legislation

There is no specific legislation concerning disabled persons in Malaysia, but there are piece-meal laws in areas like tax exemption. However, efforts are being made to formulate legislation to protect the rights of persons with disabilities. The laws will seek to prohibit abuse, neglect and discrimination against disabled persons. The Attorney-General's Office has been assigned to deal with the formulation of the legislation. A technical working group has been established to draft this legislation.

Constitutionally, a disabled person may claim his rights based on Article 8 of the Federal Constitution that guarantees equality to all persons unless under conditions expressly authorized by the Constitution.

3. Information

The Department of Social Welfare, as a focal point, has developed its own mechanism to collect and analyze data. It carried out a major nationwide voluntary registration campaign on 8 May 1996 with the help of CELCOM Malaysia, which provided a toll-free line to facilitate and expedite registration. To date, the number of disabled persons registered with the department stands at 63,517. The department also provides information to various agencies on matters relating to disability.

4. Public awareness

Public awareness programmes are undertaken by the Government of Malaysia, NGOs and the mass media from time to time, to create awareness on issues regarding people with disabilities. Awareness-raising exercises like seminars, workshops and campaigns will continue to sensitize service providers and the general public. Normally, these programmes are carried out in conjunction with celebrations for the National Day of Disabled Persons.

In December 1996, a telephone hot-line, *TeleKU,* was launched with the cooperation of CELCOM Technology Sdn Bhd. With this special facility, it is expected that more disabled persons will come forward to register them-selves.

5. Accessibility and communication

The major breakthrough in overcoming environmental and structural barriers was the gazetting of the amendments to the Uniform Building By-Laws 1984 under the Street, Drainage and Building Act 1974. The Malaysian standard code of practice for access for disabled people outside buildings has been accepted by the government and incorporated into the uniform building by-laws 1984, making it mandatory for all new buildings to have facilities and amenities as contained in the code of practice.

The implementation of these codes of practice will greatly enhance the mobility of disabled persons and improve their quality of life. The country has also established minimum standards for public toilets. All new public toilets must now have ramps and special toilet cubicles for disabled persons.

From 3 December 1995 onwards, sign language interpretation of prime-time news over national television has been introduced.

Malaysian Airlines, Malaysian Railways, and a few major bus companies offer concession fares for people with disabilities. The operators of the Light Rail Transit system in Kuala Lumpur have fitted lifts at the elevated stations.

Bus operators are also required to provide three rows of front seats to disabled persons and older persons, and are encouraged to use buses with low floor for the convenience of disabled persons.

6. Education

Although there is no specific legislation to ensure and protect the rights of disabled persons in the area of education, Section 25 of the Education Act 1961 states that the Ministry may establish and maintain special schools which provide special education for students with disabilities.

Subsequent to the new provisions of the Education Act, the Ministry has expanded special schools and integrated classes to include schools for visually-impaired persons, hearing-impaired persons, children with learning disabilities and for autistic children. In October 1995, the Department of Special Education was formed to focus on the education of children with special needs. The Department also provides training in special education for teachers involved in integrated programmes.

Existing facilities such as classrooms and teaching aids are also being upgraded, taking into account new facilities that meet the needs of disabled children. The same also applies to facilities for higher institutions.

Specific awareness campaigns for parents are conducted regularly, with emphasis on developing the potential of children with disabilities. In addition, information regarding facilities and opportunities provided for children with disabilities is also disseminated.

7. Training and employment

There are a number of vocational training centres to cater to the training needs of persons with disabilities. These vocational training centres are either run by government agencies or by NGOs. A comprehensive industrial training centre for physically disabled persons has been built at the cost of M$3 million. The centre is designed to provide training and rehabilitation for physically disabled persons and is expected to be fully operational in early 1998. This centre is also designed to serve as a resource centre for other agencies.

There are also financial schemes and incentives for disabled persons in the form of a monthly allowance for disabled workers and launching grants to start small businesses.

The United Nations Decade of Disabled Persons has seen some positive social policy initiatives in favour of disabled persons, especially in respect of employment. In the public sector, the government issued a circular in 1989, directing that at least 1 per cent of employment opportunities should be allocated to persons with disabilities.

To facilitate the employment of disabled persons in the private sector, a National Committee for the Encouragement of Employment of Disabled Persons in the Private Sector was established in 1990. This Committee has launched activities and campaigns for the promotion of employment of disabled persons in the private sector. Employers are also encouraged to provide user-friendly environments to their disabled workers as well as to provide hostels and transport for those needing such facilities.

8. Prevention of the causes of disability

The Ministry of Health has initiated a number of comprehensive programmes providing ante-natal and pre-natal care and disability prevention programmes, such as the National Programme for the Prevention of Blindness and the National Iodine Deficiency Prevention Programme. The Ministry also implemented early intervention programmes for children with disabilities providing for the active involvement of families in both rural and urban areas.

9. Rehabilitation services

In line with the global trend, community-based rehabilitation (CBR) is being given greater emphasis in Malaysia. There are rehabilitation facilities within local communities and less dependence on traditional institutionalized rehabilitation.

The Government of Malaysia is fully committed to increasing and improving CBR programmes that are expected to cover the entire country in time to come. There are now 167 centres providing CBR services for 3,000 children and this figure is expected to increase manifold.

The Government of Malaysia has also provided adequate financial assistance for the training of CBR workers. Apart from CBR programmes, other alternatives to institutional care, such as group homes, home help and fostering, have also been considered.

10. Assistive devices

The Department of Social Welfare has a programme to provide assistive devices, such as orthopaedic appliances, hearing aids and wheelchairs, for those who need the devices. Besides this, the National Welfare Foundation also assists individuals in obtaining motorized tricycles and other equipment.

11. Self-help organizations

The importance of the voluntary sector can hardly be overemphasized in the area of the rehabilitation of persons with disabilities. Voluntary welfare organizations constitute an important component of the welfare system in Malaysia.

Concerned citizens, motivated by a strong sense of community service, have initiated and maintained a variety of services for disabled persons. Such services supplement and complement those of the Government.

These organizations have been able to tap substantial community goodwill and resources, thereby relieving, to some extent, the burden of the state. In return, the government provides grants to enable them to maintain their services. Up to 1997, there were 64 organizations catering to the needs of various categories and age groups of disabled persons and receiving grants of more than M$2 million annually.

12. Regional cooperation

By hosting the Consultative Experts' Meeting on National Disability Legislation for the Asian and Pacific Region from 6 to 8 December 1993, Malaysia established her commitment to regional cooperation. Malaysia's latest contribution is through funding and organizing the Intercountry Seminar on Multisectoral Collaborative Action for People with Disabilities from 2 to 6 December 1996. Malaysia is also represented at international meetings hosted by ESCAP, regional governments and NGOs on matters pertaining to disabled persons.

Malaysia's NGOs for disabled persons also play an equally active role, such as when the Kuala Lumpur Society for the Deaf hosted the Fifth Asia and Pacific Games for the Deaf in March 1996. Malaysian disabled athletes also participate in international games, such as the Paralympic Games and the Abilympic Games.

The Government of Malaysia, through her various ministries, departments and NGOs, will continue to play a prominent role in achieving the targets of the Asian and Pacific Decade of Disabled Persons, 1993 to 2002.

Having established that the country is fully committed to issues pertaining to people with disabilities, it is recommended that programmes and activities for persons with disabilities be jointly addressed and the principle of collaborative action be effectively executed, transcending the inherent inter-agency differences and barriers.

There is no doubt that Malaysia's disabled people enjoy improved living conditions now as compared to some three decades ago. Today, there exist institutions of higher learning which employ disabled persons and many disabled persons are also outstanding academicians. The fact that disabled Malaysian athletes participate and compete in high performance sports at the national, regional and international levels is testimony to the effectiveness of existing linkages. Strong regional and international linkages among government officials and NGOs and other self-help organizations have helped make successful the Intercountry Seminar on Multisectoral Collaborative Action for People with Disabilities held in December 1996.

To this end, it is recommended that the 12 policy areas outlined in the Asian and Pacific Decade Agenda for Action should always be used as guidelines in policy formulation and planning practice in both the national and subnational development strategies of a country.

D. Activities planned for the second half of the Asian and Pacific Decade of Disabled Persons

1. Short-term strategies 1998 to 1999

(a) Translate and disseminate the Agenda for Action into the national language, Bahasa Malaysia, and other relevant languages;

(b) Review present legislation to identify whether provisions given are sufficient; if not, new legislation will be introduced. Enforcement components will also be strengthened;

(c) All ministries and departments, especially those for transport, housing, local government, public works, health, education and social welfare will review their existing facilities to ensure that they are accessible, barrier-free and allow freedom of movement for people with disabilities;

(d) The one per cent employment policy for people with disabilities will be fully implemented by the private and public sectors;

(e) Provide an additional allocation in the current budget of individual ministries; review existing policies on the allocation of resources accordingly, to enhance the benefits for persons with disabilities, in the light of the new awareness for the inclusion of people with disabilities in mainstream society;

(f) Encourage and assist self-help groups of disabled persons by providing more funds through the various ministries;

(g) Channel United Nations Development Programme funding into training programmes of personnel involved in providing care for people with disabilities;

(h) Establish a centre for the performing arts for disabled persons to encourage their greater participation in various cultural activities;

(i) Review policies regarding tax relief for disabled persons as well as for their dependents;

(j) Raise public awareness of the people's role and responsibilities towards the well-being of children with special needs.

2. Long-term strategies for 2000 and beyond

(a) Set up medical rehabilitation units in government hospitals;

(b) Build, towards the end of the Seventh Malaysian Plan, 11 special schools for children with disabilities;

(c) Support implementation of the one per cent employment policy decision for people with disabilities through the provision of skills training programmes;

(d) Develop a comprehensive database for inter-ministry collaboration with the secretariat based at the Department of Social Welfare;

(e) Complete national registration of people with disabilities and conduct a national survey in collaboration with the Statistics Department;

(f) Develop a centre of excellence for research and a resources centre concerning people with disabilities;

(g) Formulate and develop indicators for the purpose of monitoring and evaluation;

(h) Follow up with the Malaysian Sports Council for Disabled Persons concerning its review of the development of sports for disabled persons;

(i) Increase annual grants given to NGOs running programmes and activities for persons with disabilities.

CHAPTER XV

Maldives

A. National overview

Maldives accords high priority to the development of its human resources, focusing mainly on the provision of greater health, education and social services to its citizens. To better formulate and implement the various concerns of people with disabilities, the country has set up the National Committee for the Welfare of Disabled Persons.

A survey in 1981 showed that there were 1,390 disabled persons in the country, comprising 0.8 per cent of the total population. The categories of disabilities are mental, physical, intellectual, visual, and speech and hearing impairment.

The main causes of physical and other disabilities include leprosy, accidents and cerebral vascular accidents (strokes). Cataract was the main cause of visual impairment and blindness.

The national committee conducted a second survey in January 1990 and gathered a random sample of 3,117 persons from 704 households. The survey found that 130 had speech impairment, 97 with visual impairment, 71 with intellectual disabilities and 122 had physical disabilities.

Currently, there are 99 persons receiving government aid at Guraidhoo Centre and another 450 persons in the islands. A nationwide survey is being conducted to determine the magnitude of disability.

B. Progress made in the first half of the Asian and Pacific Decade of Disabled Persons

1. National Coordination

In 1995, the National Committee for the Welfare of Disabled Persons was reorganized. Committee members now include disabled persons, representatives from non-governmental organizations (NGOs) and other experts.

The Committee made the following recommendations that are being considered by the government:

(a) Create equal opportunities for disabled persons in the job market;

(b) Ensure that all buildings are accessible by disabled persons;

(c) Enforce regulations to facilitate and help disabled persons cross roads and streets safely; and set up on every street corner special crossing points and pathways for use by disabled persons;

(d) Draft legislation that recognizes and protects the rights, interests and needs of disabled persons;

(e) Develop a sound mechanism to use welfare funds efficiently and to help nurture a sense of self-reliance and worth among people with disabilities;

(f) Ensure the participation of disabled persons in the planning, implementation and evaluation of community-based rehabilitation (CBR) programmes;

(g) Develop terms that will eliminate negative attitudes towards disabled persons;

(h) Revise the school curriculum to include rehabilitation issues;

(i) Develop curricula for teacher-training and for health workers-training that include issues on rehabilitation;

(j) Require traditional birth attendants to identify and report the presence of disabilities at birth; and consider making mandatory for health workers to report and register people with disabilities;

(k) Integrate disabled students in regular classes;

(l) Maintain a registry of disabled persons at the community level.

2. Information and public awareness

Since 1990, nationwide activities and campaigns to disseminate information on people with disabilities and the prevention of causes of disability have been carried out regularly through the mass media.

3. Rehabilitation services

The Government of Maldives, through the Ministry of Women's Affairs and Social Welfare, takes responsibility for providing welfare and rehabilitation services to disabled persons.

Physiotherapy and other medical services are provided to disabled persons upon recommendation by a medical doctor. Wheelchairs, prostheses, crutches and other assistive devices are provided to physically disabled persons. Those with visual problems are provided with glasses and, in some cases, are sent abroad for medical treatment. Persons who are totally blind are paid an allowance of Rf150 per month. Mental health facilities are provided at the Indira Gandhi Memorial Hospital. A rehabilitation centre for the needy was established at Guraidhoo.

4. Accessibility and communication

With a new building code coming into effect shortly, all new buildings in the country will have to be accessible by disabled persons.

5. Education

Based on the 1981 survey, the Government of Maldives provided educational facilities for children with speech and hearing impairment at Jamaaluddeen Primary School. After the 1990 survey, all teaching institutions and school curricula have been revised to include rehabilitation issues. Disabled children are encouraged to attend the same schools as other children. In April 1997, a workshop was held for teachers on the early detection of children with special needs.

C. Activities planned for the second half of the Asian and Pacific Decade of Disabled Persons

Although clear priorities for disabled persons have yet to be set out, the following are the major concerns for both the government and the private sector:

1. The policies on people with disabilities, over the next five years, will be reflected in the National Development Plan, which encourages disabled persons to be self-reliant. The family, the community and the private sector will be encouraged to be more involved in the prevention and solving of social problems.

2. In view of the limited resources available, disability prevention programmes will focus mainly on the prevention of accidents, spread of communicable and non-communicable diseases, and safe deliveries.

3. One of the main aims is to strengthen the management capabilities at the Guraidhoo Centre, to improve its skills training and rehabilitation programmes, thus enabling disabled persons to participate actively in the socio-economic development of the country. The centre will develop programmes to initiate community-based rehabilitation, integrate disabled persons into the mainstream education system, as well as vocational training and employment.

CHAPTER XVI

Mongolia

A. National overview

Mongolia is situated in central Asia. Its climate is sharp continental, with four seasons in a year. Mongolia is 1,580 metres above sea level and covers an area of 1,565,000 square kilometres. This area consists of mountainous and hill plains covered with highland plants, marshy coniferous forests, as well as grasslands, deserts and semi-deserts. To the north it is bordered by the Russian Federation and to the south, east and west by China.

The population of Mongolia is 2.3 million. The way of life, traditional culture and customs are suited to the specific living conditions of a nomadic culture and civilization. The majority of the population is Khalkh Mongol. Most are Buddhists, but people have the right to exercise any faith.

The basic economic activity of the Mongols is traditional animal husbandry. Mongolia has over 32 million heads of livestock. By virtue of its state structure, Mongolia is a unitary state and its territory is administratively divided into a capital city and 21 *aimags* or provinces. The Mongolian people's highest state and legislative power is represented, exercised by and vested in the State Ikh Khural elected by and for the people themselves. The country has a multiparty and parliamentary system.

The capital city is Ulaanbaatar. It has over 600,000 inhabitants, which represents more than one quarter of the entire population.

People with disabilities in Mongolia are particularly vulnerable to the changes which have taken place in the transition from a centrally planned to a market economy. They find it very difficult to meet their basic needs and have been designated as one of the "six vulnerable groups" to be targeted in the National Poverty Alleviation Programme. A range of special measures is needed to promote their integration into training and employ-ment schemes, so that they, like other citizens, will be able to acquire vocational skills and engage in gainful employment in the same way as other people.

B. Progress made in the first half of the Asian and Pacific Decade of Disabled Persons

1. National coordination

In 1993, the Prime Minister of Mongolia signed the Proclamation on the Full Participation and Equality of People with Disabilities in the Asian and Pacific Region. The national committee in charge of implementation of Decade activities at the national level was set up under the Ministry of Health and Social Welfare and has been operating for five years. To assist the committee, the review group responsible for disabled persons' related issues was established in 1997.

Within the last five years, the committee has organized activities such as setting up its constituents in provinces and cities, and is assisting and providing them with guidance.

In line with the above, several seminars have been organized, including an international seminar on equal rights and opportunities for disabled persons, a national seminar on the social situation of disabled persons, and a workshop for the working group in charge of issues related to disabled persons, which reviewed and evaluated the achievements and hardships encountered in previous years and adopted declarations and recommendations to be followed for the next decade with regard to disabled persons.

In line with the recommendations, certain activities have been undertaken and some adequate results have been achieved at the provincial, city and district levels, which focused on ensuring social security for disabled persons. These include safeguarding their normal working and living conditions and assisting in the operation of organizations representing the rights of disabled persons.

Eight security centres, one special kindergarten for disabled children, 11 integrated kindergartens and state rehabilitation centres for deaf and speech-impaired children have been set up. A prosthesis and orthopaedic device factory has started independently and is financed from the state budget. Approximately Tug 80 million from the state budget and donor investment have been spent for security centres established in 21 *aimags*. Along with the above, 3,163 persons were provided grant aid of about Tug 17.1 million, international and national charity organizations granted assistance to about 32,000 disabled persons by providing them with flour, rice, medicine, clothing and other essential items.

Financial matters such as pensions, allowances, reliefs, benefits and any other assistance provided by the state for disabled persons are regulated and implemented within the framework of the government's policy on population and its Law on Reliefs and Services for Disabled Persons.

A project proposal was made to the International Labour Organization (ILO) on improving opportunities for people with disabilities in Mongolia and some activities are under way. In the framework of the above, the ILO supported a project in which four persons from the working group in charge of issues concerning disabled persons were sent on study tours to China, India and Thailand in June 1997.

The study tours were aimed at enabling the working group to formulate and develop a policy regarding persons with disabilities in Mongolia. The reports of the participants of the study tour were presented at the Seminar of Social Assistance in Mongolia, which involved the officials and directors of social security centres at the provincial and local levels.

Some follow-up activities are being undertaken. Among these is the integration of the activities of 13 non-governmental organizations (NGOs), dealing with disabled persons and the setting up of the National Association of Disabled Persons' Organizations of Mongolia, with the unanimous election of a member of parliament as the president of the association. This means that the NGOs dealing with disabled persons has a place in parliament. In addition, the date for the association's establishment was designated as the Mongolian Disabled Persons' Day.

2. Legislation

In the first five years of the Asian and Pacific Decade of Disabled Persons, the Government of Mongolia enacted a Social Insurance Package Law. This piece of legislation included provisions for pension allowances and payments through the social insurance fund for disabled people who became disabled due to industrial accidents and occupational diseases.

According to this law, the organization and employer will be responsible for the medical expenses of disabled workers whose disabilities were due to industrial accidents and occupational diseases.

In February 1996, the legislation on social protection and discounts for disabled persons came into force. The specific articles of this legislation include:

(a) Charity and special credit for disabled students and children;

(b) Supply of specific equipment such as acoustic apparatus and wheelchairs;

(c) Employment opportunities and rights;

(d) Part-time jobs and household work;

(e) Tax relief for disabled persons;

(f) Training for disabled persons.

3. Information and public awareness

With a view to ensuring the equal participation of disabled persons in society, two local newspapers, *Amidralyn Toirog* and *Unuudur* are publishing articles highlighting the fact that disabled persons are capable of studying, working and living full lives in the same way as people who are not disabled. The editor of the *Amidratyn Toirog* is herself disabled.

However, there is much less media coverage of disabled persons in national and mainstream publications, and on radio and television.

4. Accessibility and communication

In order to involve deaf and speech-impaired persons in society, television programmes and films have been broadcast with special explanations. Since May 1997, some parts of television programmes have also been broadcast in sign language. It is also necessary to improve conditions of their physical environments and new housing for persons with disabilities as reflected in the 1994 plan of action to implement the Agenda for Action for the Asian and Pacific Decade of Disabled Persons.

However, currently, there are inadequate provisions for accommodation, roads and squares for disabled persons due to the socio-economic situation of the country. The physical environment in Mongolian cities, including buildings and streets, are generally inaccessible to people whose mobility is impaired. Public transport is also inaccessible, making it difficult for people with physical disabilities to travel. This lack of accessibility makes it difficult for them to attend training courses, hold employment or generally participate in their communities.

5. Education

Before 1991, the provision of food, clothes and financial assistance was predominant among the social welfare measures for people with disabilities. However, the provision of education for disabled children is limited, and only about 10 to 15 per cent of people with disabilities receive some education. Moreover, special education is mostly given in segregated schools and classes and is concentrated in the few big cities and *aimag* centres.

There are more than 30 special schools for children with disabilities in Mongolia. Five of these are located in Ulaanbaatar. There are four schools for mentally handicapped children and only one for deaf and blind children in Mongolia. The children are generally taught to the eighth grade over a 10- or 12-year period.

An estimated 70 to 80 per cent of children who are blind, deaf and/or otherwise physically disabled become unemployed on leaving school. A few may find relatively low-skilled manual jobs at the Blind Production Centre or elsewhere, or they go on to a vocational training course. Some of them study at the vocational training centre. One of the main obstacles to training disabled persons is the lack of training materials, particularly Braille materials for blind persons.

6. Training and employment

To provide jobs and assist people born with disabilities and people with disabilities due to disease and injury is one of the most important aspects of the government's policy towards persons with disabilities. Therefore, the government has established vocational training and production centres for youth with disabilities.

The Vocational Specialization Training Centre annually trains youth from over 200 poor households in the following areas: tailoring of western and Mongolian clothes, shoe-making, rug-making, carpentry, typing, knitting, baking, straw and felt art and craft, and massage.

The training lasts from three to nine months and covers 120 people with disabilities in one session. Some 40 per cent of the youth with disabilities, who completed the training, work in the public and private sectors.

There is also a production and training centre for blind persons. There are 120 workers at this centre, the majority being blind people and some people with other sensory disabilities. They make articles of the Mongolian ger (inside and outside cover of the ger) and children's clothes.

7. Prevention of the causes of disabilities

Mongolia will implement the following measures from 1993 to 2002 in stages:

(a) Study the main diseases which lead to disability in Mongolia, especially iodine deficiency;

(b) Improve the quality of diagnosis;

(c) Detect cardiac diseases earlier;

(d) Improve the health monitoring of pregnant women.

Following the recommendation of the national meeting on iodine deficiency diseases (IDD), the Mongolian government adopted in January 1996 a National Programme for the Eradication of IDD.

The main objective of this programme is to prevent the Mongolian population from acquiring IDD. The programme also aims to set up a national system to supply iodized salt, to define ways to alleviate IDD and to mobilize public resources on this matter. The National Coordination Committee on IDD Programme was established.

8. Rehabilitative services

From 1992 to 1997, the Ministry of Health and Social Welfare, with the support of the Italian NGO, Association Italian Amici di Raoul Follereau (AIFO), and the Rehabilitation Unit of WHO, initiated a community-based rehabilitation (CBR) project in 1992 and the United Nations Children's Fund (UNICEF) will support the setting up of a regulation programme with disabled children.

The projects are to be implemented in 11 *aimags,* and eight districts of Ulaanbaatar. Their objectives are to:

(a) Improve the living conditions of at least 50 per cent of the disabled people living in the area covered by the project;

(b) Improve the national orthopaedic workshop and create two regional workshops;

(c) Promote the integration of disabled children in existing ordinary schools;

(d) Support the vocational training activities for disabled young adults;

(e) Promote the facility for special education for children with extensive disabilities;

(f) Promote the integration of disabled persons in community life;

(g) Further stabilize and strengthen the Rehabilitation Centre in Ulaanbaatar.

C. Activities planned for the second half of the Asian and Pacific Decade of Disabled Persons

1. National coordination

For the second half of the Asian and Pacific Decade of Disabled Persons, the integrated policy of Mongolia with respect to disabled persons will be implemented by the Ministry of Health and Social Welfare, which will collaborate closely with other ministries. It is expected to adopt the government resolution on the step-by-step implementation of the policy towards disabled persons. The policy will be carried out with the assistance of international and national organizations and charity institutions.

2. Legislation

Over the next five years, Mongolia plans to develop a national programme to ensure the equality of disabled persons so that they can participate fully in society. It also plans to enact the Quota Law on Employment by the Ikh Kbural, or parliament, in order to expand employment opportunities for disabled persons.

3. Information and public awareness

To increase media coverage of disabled persons in the national mainstream publications, and on radio and television, activities shall be undertaken over the next five years which will focus on raising public awareness. The Minister for Health and Social Welfare and the Director of the Radio and Television Cabinet of Mongolia will collaborate in this area.

4. Accessibility and communication

During the next five years, there are plans to improve provisions for accommodation, roads and squares for disabled persons by undertaking certain projects. Funding from external and internal donors is currently being sought.

5. Education

In the field of education, Mongolia plans to achieve the following in the next five years:

(a) Implement a project on the education of blind persons under a Danish-sponsored project in 1998;

(b) Start regional integration training among disabled children in four *aimags;*

(c) Improve the professional skills of teachers, particularly in sign language.

6. Training and employment

The country is planning to implement the following measures in the next five years:

(a) Expand the activity and re-equip the production and training centre for blind persons and people with other disabilities;

(b) Provide jobs and create income-generation opportunities for people with disabilities.

For the second half of the Asian and Pacific Decade of Disabled Persons, there is a need for companies to expand employment possibilities for disabled persons covered under the country's labour employment practices.

7. Self-help organizations

For the second half of the Asian and Pacific Decade of Disabled Persons there are plans to help disabled persons who are capable of working by establishing self-help working places within the framework of the Poverty Alleviation Programme or with the assistance of international funding.

CHAPTER XVII

Myanmar

A. National overview

During the first half of the Asian and Pacific Decade of Disabled Persons, Myanmar has taken efforts towards achieving the targets for the implementation of the Agenda for Action for the Asian and Pacific Decade of Disabled Persons (hereafter referred to as the Asian and Pacific Decade Agenda for Action). The country also recognizes the need for future efforts to be made during the second half of the Asian and Pacific Decade of Disabled Persons. Considering the resources available, the constraints and opportunities, and the economic condition, Myanmar has made some practical recommendations, which are in line with the targets set in the Asian and Pacific Decade Agenda for Action.

B. Progress made in the first half of the Asian and Pacific Decade of Disabled Persons

1. National coordination

Although a National Coordination Committee on Disability Matters could not be formed as yet, a steering committee consisting of representatives from various related ministries has been set up for children in especially difficult circumstances (CEDC). Issues discussed include children with disabilities, workshops for persons with visual impairments conducted by the Ministry of Social Welfare, Relief and Resettlement, and the formation of a national coordinating body.

2. Legislation

Prior to the proclamation of the Asian and Pacific Decade of Disabled Persons, 1993-2002, the Central Law Scrutinizing Committee was reviewing the disabled persons law in Myanmar. It is now in the last stages of technical finalization and it is hoped that the law will be enacted in the near future.

The newly-drafted law ensures broader rights for people with disabilities, including the right to health, education and work opportunities. A new child law ensures education and protection for all children with disabilities.

3. Information

In this area, the Ministry of Health and the Ministry of Social Welfare, Relief and Resettlement have made much effort to meet the target. Information on preventive measures such as community-based rehabilitation (CBR) services and other disability issues are disseminated through booklets, pamphlets, journals and newspapers. The World Health Organization training manual provided people with disabilities, their families and the community, especially in remote areas, with information regarding the management of disability and the services available.

4. Public awareness

Public awareness, considered to be the focal starting point for the success-ful implementation of the programme, has been carried out on a much larger scale. Relevant ministries concerned with the issues of disability, especially the Ministry of Health and the Ministry of Social Welfare, Relief and Resettlement, together with the non-governmental organizations (NGOs), have worked towards creating more awareness through various activities, special programmes, adver-tisements and showing the daily activities of special schools on television. There is also televised coverage of special occasions such as the celebration of the International Day of Disabled Persons, annual disabled sports events and blind persons' football matches.

To create greater awareness of the different talents and abilities of the various groups of people with disabilities, stage shows by schools for blind persons, and talent shows jointly performed by blind persons, persons with physical disabilities and intellectually disabled persons have been produced. Deaf people also performed in a Christmas concert.

To commemorate the annual International Day of Disabled Persons on 3 December, skill contests in art, singing, dancing, and cane weaving are held. People with different disabilities take part enthusiastically in these events. Blind persons' football matches attract a lot of interest and attention. These aware-ness-raising activities, focusing on the skills demonstrated by the differently-able persons, have been very effective.

The Ministry of Health also held an awareness workshop and advocacy meeting in 1996 for health workers. In Myanmar, most NGOs have included public awareness-raising in their short training programmes.

5. Accessibility and communication

The creation of a "barrier free environment" is still an area that has to be planned and implemented. In rehabilitation centres, hospitals and special schools, these facilities exist. It is hoped that with further economic development, the target here could be met.

To facilitate communication between people with hearing impairments and hearing people, a course was conducted to teach international sign language. Steps are being taken to further develop Myanmar sign language, which is envisaged to help the whole hearing-impaired population.

In comparison with services provided to people in other disability groups, those for persons with visual impairments are considered to be progressive. Public awareness here is quite high and the support given by the government, NGOs, international NGOs and private individuals is much higher.

Braille computer equipment and audio cassettes are used. There is, however, still a great need to further develop these services. The reason why the visually impaired-groups have made progress in recent years is due to the efforts of a few visually-impaired persons themselves taking the initiative to promote their cause to the public through musical performances. The government is very supportive, helps promote this awareness campaign and hopes to solicit more backing from the private sector.

6. Education

Special schools under the Ministry of Social Welfare, Relief and Resettlement are open for persons with different types of disability, but there remains a need to open more such schools to act as training grounds to prepare the children for integration into regular schools.

According to the New Child Law, enacted recently, a child with a disability is entitled to education. Although special schools have been integrating their students into regular schools, integration is still a new process in Myanmar. It hopes to implement the system fully in the near future. World Vision has helped in the process of integrating 40 disabled children into regular state schools.

7. Training and employment

The country recognizes the importance of having qualified personnel in the implementation of programmes. To fulfil the required target, short courses on rehabilitation issues have been conducted. Training courses have also been conducted to equip the teachers in various social welfare schools with specialized knowledge in caring for disabled children. They are also sent overseas to widen their knowledge and gain more expertise and experience. It is envisaged that the knowledge gained will help in the implementation process.

Concerning training and employment for people with disabilities, efforts have been made to create more such opportunities. Apart from government services for vocational training, various NGOs are now trying to find ways and means for training and employment. The United Nations Development Programme, World Vision, and the private sector have now implemented income-generation projects for people with disabilities. These will eventually lead to proper and suitable placement.

Currently, placement is done through three levels: open employment, self-employment and cooperative societies. Sheltered employment could not be carried out as yet due to financial constraints. The country hopes, of course, for future improvement in this area as the economy of the country continues to develop and with increasing awareness of this issue. This past half Decade has seen increasing public support both in financial and voluntary terms.

8. Prevention of the causes of disability

Preventive measures are largely being carried out by the Ministry of Health, the Myanmar Mother and Child Welfare Association and the United Nations Children's Fund. An anti-polio campaign, followed by national immunization, has been carried out throughout the country.

An accident prevention workshop and education on the prevention of deformities from leprosy are part of the preventive programme. A breast-feeding campaign has been launched to educate mothers in the benefits of breast-feeding in the rearing of healthy, strong and well-adjusted children. There is however more work to be done in the area of making the public more aware of the virtues of some of the natural old-fashioned and traditional ways of doing things, especially in nutrition and baby care.

9. Rehabilitation services

Considerable progress has been made through a variety of rehabilitation services, hospital-base rehabilitation services, community-based rehabilitation (CBR) and production of low-cost technical aids.

However, the services rendered are centred mostly on people with physical disabilities in urban areas. There is still much to be done for intellectually disabled persons. The extension of CBR programmes is aimed at reaching out to more people with disabilities and to include all forms of disabilities. Currently, the Government of Myanmar, United Nations agencies, international NGOs and NGOs are collaborating and coordinating their efforts to render a more effective rehabilitation service.

On medical care, disabled persons are entitled to free general health care services.

10. Assistive devices

Prosthetic and orthotic devices are provided free, except in cases where the person is deemed to come from the higher income bracket and is able to contribute to the services provided.

Although basic assistive devices are being supplied to people with disabilities, there is still a need for more modern and sophisticated devices, to enable people with disabilities to be independent, to have equal rights, and to participate fully in the community.

11. Self-help organizations and regional cooperation

There has been greater coordination and collaboration in the first half of the Asian and Pacific Decade of Disabled Persons among concerned governmental and non-governmental agencies, including the organizations of and for people with disabilities and United Nations agencies.

Although United Nations agencies, international NGOs, NGOs and private individuals have been helping in the funding and implementation of rehabilitation services and income generating projects, there is still a need to intensify technical cooperation in terms of the sharing and exchange of information.

The country could strengthen the implementation of these programmes if it is able to generate more income by tapping both local and international sources to fund its special projects.

C. Activities planned for the second half of the Asian and Pacific Decade of Disabled Persons

The activities and progress already mentioned will act as a foundation for future activities to achieve the targets set in the Asian and Pacific Decade Agenda for Action.

CHAPTER XVIII

Nepal

A. National overview

Nepal is a developing country located on the southern lap of the Himalayas, bordered by China in the north and flanked by India in the south, east and west. Nepal spans an area of 147,181 square kilometres, stretching 885 kilometres from east to west and 193 kilometres from north to south. There are also great changes in altitude from north to south. The southern territories are less than 100 metres above sea level whereas the northern tips are more than 8,000 metres above sea level.

Currently, Nepal has a population of about 21 million people, with an annual growth rate of 2.1 per cent per year between 1981 and 1991. The number of disabled is estimated at 2.6 million assuming that they form 12 per cent of the population.

B. Policy measures

The Government of Nepal has always been committed to preventing disability. The country supported the International Year of Disabled Persons (IYDP) 1981, the United Nations Decade of Disabled Persons, 1983-1992; the Asian and Pacific Decade of Disabled Persons, 1993-2002; and the SAARC Year of Disabled Persons, 1993. Every year, Nepal marks the International Day of Disabled Person on 3 December, and makes it a point to attend regional and global conferences on disability.

The Government of Nepal has put serious thought into the disability issue and has developed policies and strategies to address it under the Ministry of Women and Social Welfare. With the assistance of the Danish International Development Agency (DANIDA), the Ministry of Education has done a good job with special education.

C. Progress made in the first half of the Asian and Pacific Decade of Disabled Persons

1. National coordination

Since many ministries and non-government organizations (NGOs) are involved in helping people with disabilities, coordination on a national level is quite essential. In Nepal, the Ministry of Women and Social Welfare is the focal point of efforts in disability affairs, but other ministries also have programmes for disabled persons.

The first and most important initiative in Nepal to help disabled persons was the setting up of the Social Services National Coordination Council in 1977. In 1992, it was renamed the Social Welfare Council. Though the name has been changed, there is no major shift in working style.

The Ministry of Women and Social Welfare plays the biggest role in protecting the welfare of disabled persons. It plans policies, enacts the necessary legislation, and implements and coordinates programmes to provide equal opportunities for disabled persons. It has developed two landmark policies: the National Disabled Policy Plan of Action of 1996 and disabled persons Service National Policy of 1996. It faces a challenging job ahead as quite a few changes in legislation are necessary before the policies can be implemented and considerable coordination with other ministries will also be required.

Significant investment is needed for the implementation of the programmes mentioned in the Plan of Action. The Government of Nepal has to plan carefully so as to implement these programmes to the fullest extent possible. The programmes are divided into three phases:

(a)   First phase: 1996 to 1998

The first phase stretches over two years from 1996 to 1998. During this period, the necessary infrastructure to protect the rights and the welfare of disabled persons will be put in place. Existing laws, rules and regulation related to disabled will be brought in line with that objective. The necessary organizational structure will be set up and human resource requirements will be met. The conceptual framework defining what constitutes disability will be established and disabled persons will be issued with identity cards.

(b)   Second phase: 1998 to 2000

An assessment will be made on whether the programmes have been implemented well and if adequate services have been rendered to disabled persons. The evaluation will be conducted through research surveys.

(c)   Third phase: 2001 to 2002

Phase three will see an increase of activities championing the rights, interest, and welfare of people with disabilities. Evaluation undertaken in the preceding years will form the basis for any reforms in the laws and any refinement of the policies and the programmes in the Plan of Action.

2. Legislation

Judicial attention to address issues concerning person with disabilities started only a few years ago. The first major legislation was put in place in 1982. The Disabled Persons' Protection and Welfare Act focused on protecting and developing the rights of person with disabilities. The underlying principle of the Act was that if person with disabilities were provided with the right education, proper health care, and equal opportunities in employment, they would be capable members of society and dynamic, productive citizens.

The areas which the Disabled Persons' Protection and Welfare Act of 1982 focused on were the conceptual framework of disability, protection of disabled rights, equality, education and training, health services, employment, and crime against person with disabilities. Although a lot of changes have taken place within the government, the Act has not kept pace with the times.

So in 1990, the Constitution of Nepal made special provisions for person with disabilities. After re-establishing the multi-party system, the government introduced the Protection and Welfare of the Disabled Rules and Regulations in 1992.

Under the new laws, a committee was formed to define what constituted disability. Identity cards were given to person with disabilities, and homes were set up to house them. These homes were run by management committees and given government assistance and private sector donations. Person with disabilities were also given education and training. They had access to health services and were given job placements and income tax reliefs. A disabled service fund was also set up. The Ministry is looking into implementing the plan of action in phases (See plan of action in Annex I).

3. Information

Information is vital for proper planning. However, information on person with disabilities is scanty, as the collection of data has been sporadic and partial. Very few research studies have been conducted and whatever research that has been done is inadequate. For instance, the findings of a sample survey of person with disabilities conducted in 1980 showed three in 100 people were disabled, which did not tally with the 1.5 per 1,000 population in the 1971 census. Similarly another survey of person with disabilities done in 1995 showed a higher disability prevalence rate of 4.5 per cent compared with the sample survey of 1980. Some smaller sample studies reported that the proportion of person with disabilities could be as high as 13 per cent of the population, which is even higher than the WHO ratio of 100 per 1,000. So the precise magnitude of disability is still not clear.

Disability is found predominantly in illiterate households and amongst the poor. More than 50 per cent of person with disabilities are gainfully employed. Such vital information is beginning to come forth although slowly and in a scattered manner. A proper system of information gathering should be set up. The information collected should be shared among the different organizations involved with person with disabilities. The Ministry of Women and Social Welfare is committed to improving its data collection and analysis.

4. Public awareness

The issue of disability is of major concern in the development of the country. Public awareness of the disability issue is seriously lacking. It should be brought to the forefront through campaigns backed fully by the Government of Nepal.

The estimated population size in 1996 is about 21 million, out of which about 2.6 million are disabled. It is certainly a huge task to provide health care, education, training, and rehabilitation to such a large group of people. The government cannot do it alone. Although the role of the government is vital, participation from ordinary citizens and private organizations is highly needed.

The Ministry of Women and Social Welfare is trying to launch different activities to raise public awareness of disability. Television news is already delivered in sign language. More awareness programmes should be aired on radio, television and printed in newspapers.

Books and statistical bulletins on disability should also be published and art exhibitions and cultural events performed by person with disabilities staged. Coins and stamps with a disability theme should be issued from time to time and sports activities at the local, regional and national level should also be arranged for disabled persons.

5. Accessibility and communication

The exact size of the disabled population is still not known. Current estimates range from 5 to 12 per cent of the total population or between 1 to 2.6 million people. Yet, there are very few special education schools (see Tables 1.3 and 1.4). So the lack of access to education is a serious problem and it needs to be addressed. The solution, however, is not simply to set up special education classes. It must be done through an integrated approach, starting with special training for teachers and the provision of special teaching apparatus.

Similarly, in the areas of health care and employment for person with disabilities, policies and programmes should be planned. There is a lack of general awareness among the common people of the feelings and needs of person with disabilities. Person with disabilities should be involved in the planning and implementation of self-help programmes through seminars and workshops. These seminars should be conducted in villages where most person with disabilities live.

National Disabled Persons' Day should be celebrated, not just as a ritualistic ceremony, but with purposeful programmes involving mass participation by both disabled persons and non-disabled persons.

6. Education

The Constitution has special provisions for the education of person with disabilities. Much can still be undertaken to improve the special education of person with disabilities and is provided free to person with disabilities.

Currently Nepal is implementing the Ninth Plan (1997-2002). In the Ninth Plan concept paper, one of the objectives of education is to provide educational opportunity to persons with disabilities and bring them into mainstream society. Thus the provision for special education will not be minimized. Nepal will strive to provide higher education opportunities to person with disabilities. It is also the government's policy to encourage the involvement of NGOs and the community-at-large in the development of special education.

The Ministry of Women and Social Welfare has already developed a detailed policy on the education of person with disabilities. In the Ministry of Education, a council for special education has been established. There is however a great need to coordinate policy matters between the two ministries.

Special education in Nepal started in the sixties. The first effort was made in 1961 to provide education for blind persons at Jawalakhel in Lalitpur, and an integrated education programme was initiated in 1964 at the laboratory schools in Kirtipur. Subsequently, schools for the deaf persons, blind persons, physically disabled persons and intellectually disabled persons were established.

According to the report titled "Situation Analysis of Disability in Nepal", there are presently 26 special schools with 245 blind students, eight with 396 deaf and hearing-impaired students, 17 for the intellectually disabled students and seven with 145 physically disabled students. Apart from this, with the assistance of the DANIDA Special Education Unit (SEU) of the Basic and Primary Education Programme (BPEP), the Ministry of Education runs 60 resource classes for 600 students in 19 districts. It also runs special education classes for intellectually disabled students in 11 districts and has provided aid to 36 schools.

Several NGOs are also involved in providing education to person with disabilities with assistance from the Council of Special Education. Teacher training in special education is also provided.

Further expansion of special education in the country is of vital importance. The master plan (1997-2002) recommends some programmes, including training teachers in special needs education, setting up a special needs education directorate in the Ministry of Education, strengthening the special education unit and setting up an institute of special needs education and rehabilitation service. Approval of these programmes must come from the government. Their goals are to:

(a) Provide educational opportunity to all primary school children with special educational needs;

(b) Integrate children who have mild and moderate learning difficulties into the mainstream primary school system;

(c) Provide education in resource class and home-based settings to children with extensive special education needs;

(d) Consolidate the existing programme of NGOs for the education of the special needs children.

The target is to educate 90,000 disabled children (see enrolment target for disabled population in Table 2). In addition, school buildings will be made more accessible to children with physical disabilities.

7. Training and employment

In Nepal, most people with disabilities have little opportunity for training. However, training, is essential to enhance the functional skills and employability of person with disabilities, especially vocational training. As such, plans are being drawn up to set up a disabled training academy.

Employment gives person with disabilities self respect and allows him to be integrated into mainstream society. Nepal may have to make revisions to its laws to provide equal job opportunities for person with disabilities.

It should also be mandated that every school has at least one teacher qualified to provide special education for person with disabilities.

8. Prevention of the causes of disability

Prevention is better than cure is a concept that also applies to disability. The following have been identified as causes of disability: poverty; accidents; lack of health care; education, pre- and post-natal care; and Vitamin A and iodine deficiencies; hereditary factors; inadequate child care; diseases; improper use of medicine; natural calamities; traditional and cultural taboos; and smoking, drinking and drug abuse. Preventive measures must therefore be taken.

Nepal has developed five major policies to prevent disability among its people. They are:

(a) Laws, rules and regulations for the rights, interest and livelihood of person with disabilities;

(b) Preventive measures during pregnancy, proper nutrition for children, and effective traffic rules to prevent road accidents;

(c) Public awareness arising through the mass media;

(d) Free education for person with disabilities from pre-primary to higher education;

(e) Updated information on the number of disabled persons.

Nepal has also arranged to provide free health services and sports and entertainment programmes for disabled persons.

9. Rehabilitation services

Rehabilitation programmes are essential for disabled persons, with social integration and gainful employment being the main aims. In Nepal, emphasis will be given to family-centred rehabilitation and the necessary steps are being taken to provide opportunity for employment in government and non-government agencies.

Education is the foundation for rehabilitation. As rehabilitation for an educated and trained disabled persons is easier, there is a need to expand vocational training for them. The National Federation of the Disabled Persons (NFD) Nepal has thus recommended that a national vocational rehabilitation centre (NVRC) be established.

In Nepal, medical rehabilitation is equally important because, with proper health education, the occurrence of disability can be reduced by as much as 50 per cent. In addition, about one-third of people with disabilities can be received full medical rehabilitation.

However, there is a great need for vision and planning in this area. Some of the recommendations provided by the NFD are to organize mobile workshops to develop positive attitudes towards this form of rehabilitation among medical practitioners and to make provision for free and low-cost medical services for disabled persons.

In this country, community-based rehabilitation (CBR) is a relatively new and evolving concept. The Bhaktapur CBR programme is probably the first, but there are other CBR programmes in 12 districts in Nepal. The Bhaktapur CBR programme is comprehensive; it covers both visible (physical, hearing, mental and visual) and hidden disabilities like epilepsy, leprosy and malnutrition related disabilities. It has three main components: rehabilitation of home-based; education of deaf children; job search and integrated vocational training.

This programme also conducts comprehensive training over seven weeks for CBR workers. It is the main training programme for CBR workers in Nepal and has been very effective although currently it is only conducted in 12 districts in the country. The CBR programme should be further expanded to other districts in Nepal.

10. Assistive devices

Assistive devices can play a vital role in supporting people with disabilities. The Government of Nepal should provide such devices at low costs. It may have to subsidize them to ensure quality. If they must be imported, no taxes should be levied on these devices.

11. Self-help organizations

Nepal is interested in promoting self-help organizations and tools to the Economic and Social Commission for Asia and the Pacific as the team leader for promoting such groups.

12. Regional cooperation

There is a need for regional cooperation to share experiences, exchange ideas and provide mutual support to prevent disability and rehabilitate disabled persons.

ANNEXES

Annex I

Plan of Action
first phase programme
(1996/1997 – 1997/1998)

	Description of activities	*Implementation agency*	*Supporting agency*	*Areas to be covered*	*Period of work*	*Achievements and outputs*
1	Revision of the Disabled Protection and Welfare Act, 1982, and the Disabled Protection and Welfare Rules and Regulations, 1982	Ministry of Women and Social Welfare (MOWSW)	Secretariat of Council of Ministers, Ministry of Law and Justice (MOLAJ) and other concerned Ministries	Kathmandu	January 1996	Preparing legal basis for rights and protection of blind and disabled
2	Revision of the following rules and regulations for employment, facilities and other welfare activities of blind and other disabled persons: (a) Civil Service Act, 1992, and Rules and Regulations, 1993. (b) Public Service Procedural Act Rules and Regulation (c) Education Act and Regulations (d) Act, Rules and Regulations related to Company and Company Worker (e) Industrial Business Act, 1992 (f) Income Tax Act, and Rules and Regulations (g) Act and Rules and Regulations related to Sports and Entertainment	MOWSW	Secretariat of Council of Ministers, (MOLAJ) and other concerned Ministries	Kathmandu	August 1997	Preparing legal basis for rights and protection of blind and disabled

(continued)

(continued)

	Description of activities	Implementation agency	Supporting agency	Areas to be covered	Period of work	Achievements and outputs
3	Conceptual frame work of disability	MOWSW	Ministry of Health (MOH)		August 1997	Basis of preparation to distribute identity card related to the disabled
4	Registry of disabled persons in the country	MOWSW	Ministry of Local Development (MLD) and Ministry of Home	Five Districts	August 1997	Availability of statistics
5	Distribution of identity cards to disabled persons systematically by rules and regulations	MOWSW				People with disabilities getting their identity cards
6	Preparation of inventory of organizations related to blind and disabled persons	MOWSW	Various organizations		August 1997	Preparation of updated inventory
7	Necessary works done to include national policy and sectoral programmes related to disabled persons in Ninth Plan	MOWSW	National Planning Commission Secretariat		1996/ 1997	Conduct of welfare programmes for disabled persons
8	Arrangement of separate agency related to blind and disabled persons	MOWSW	Ministry of General Administration, Ministry of Finance (MOF) and Secretariat of Council of Minsters		1997/ 1998	Conduct of activities related to disabled persons smoothly
9	Construction of service building for disabled persons	MOWSW	MOF, Ministry of Housing and Physical Planning, Ministry of Land Reform and Secretariat Council of Ministries	In the capital (Kathmandu)	1997/ 1998	Providing services easily for disabled persons

	Description of activities	Implementation agency	Supporting agency	Areas to be covered	Period of work	Achievements and outputs
10	Implementation of awareness programmes through radio, television and newspapers	MOWSW	Information and Communication		1997/1998	Raising high moral to disabled persons
11	Broadcasting new through television in sign language	MOWSW	Information and Communication		1997/1998	Raising moral of disabled persons
12	Providing judicial assistance freely to blind and disabled persons	MOWSW	MOLAJ	All districts	1997/1998	Providing free judicial assistance
13	Conduct of sports, cultural, literacy programmes for disabled persons	MOWSW	Ministry of Youth, Sports and Culture and MOE	All districts	1997/1998	Physical, mental and intellectual development of disabled persons
14	Provision of free health service to every disabled persons	MOH	MOWSW	All districts	1997/1998	Availability of free health services for disabled persons
15	Provision of mobile health clinic service for blind and disabled persons in remote	MOH	SWC/NGO/INGO	Based on the needs	1997/1998	Availability of health services for disabled persons at the local level
16	Making available text books in braille and sign language interpretation	MOE			1997/1998	Providing educational opportunity
17	Identification of possible areas of employment opportunity for disabled persons	MOWSW	Various agencies		1997/1998	Preparation of basis for employment
18	Arrangement of necessary revision in the concerned rules and regulations to provide employment for disabled persons on the basis of their academic qualification and capability in private corporations	MOWSW	Ministry of Industry, Ministry of Labour and private corporations		1997/1998	Providing employment opportunities

(continued)

(continued)

	Description of activities	Implementation agency	Supporting agency	Areas to be covered	Period of work	Achievements and outputs
19	Inclusion of information on prevention of causes of disability and subjects on disability in school curriculum	MOE	MOWSW	Kathmandu	1997/ 1998	Public awareness raising
20	Provision of counselling programmes for disabled persons and their families	MOWSW	SWC/GO/NOG	Nationwide	1997/ 1998	Provision of counselling for disabled persons
21	Provision of education freely in government ans private schools for disabled persons and their children	MOE	MOE	Nationwide	1997/ 1998	Providing educa- tional opportunities for disabled persons
22	Provision of traffic signals suitable for blind persons and disabled persons	Ministry of Home and Ministry of Construction and Transport	Police Headquarters	Kathmandu valley	1997/ 1998	Providing safer traffic facilities for disabled persons
23	Provision of special education, skill deve- lopment and special health programmes for disabled persons staying at home	MOE	MOE	Based on needs	1997/ 1998	Providing educa- tional opportunities
24	Provision of inclusive school programmes with adequate supervision	MOE	MOE	Based on needs	1997/ 1998	Providing educa- tional opportunities
25	Establishment of a training academy for disabled persons	MOWSW	MOE	Kathmandu	1997/ 1998	Providing training in an integrated setting
26	Provide training in necessary skills to improve capability of disabled persons	MOWSW	Various agencies	Based on the needs	1997/ 1998	Providing training for disabled persons
27	Provision of adult education and skill- oriented literacy programmes for disabled	MOE	MOE	Some districts	1997/ 1998	Improvement in literacy of disabled persons

	Description of activities	Implementation agency	Supporting agency	Areas to be covered	Period of work	Achievements and outputs
28	Provision of loan without collateral and with a minimum interest for disabled persons to start business or to prepare for employment	MOF	Banks and financial corporation or institutions	Some areas	1997/ 1998	Assistance in income generation
29	Human resource development for to special education programme	MOE	NPC	Some areas	1997/ 1998	Human resource development

Second phase programme
(1998/1999 – 2000/2001)

	Description of activities	Implementation agency	Supporting agency	Areas to be covered	Period of work	Achievements and outputs
1	Registration of all disabled persons with all village development committee, district development committee and municipality	MOWSW	MLD	75 districts	1997/ 1998	Update of data-base
2	Launching of distribution programmes of necessary assistive devices, including white canes, wheelchairs and crutches	MOWSW	MOH/SWC/NGO	Some districts	1998/ 1999	Provision of assistive devices for blind persons and other disabled persons
3	Inclusion of disability statistics in the population census in 2001	MOWSW	Department of Statistics	75 districts	2001	Improvement of disability statistics
4	Distribution of identity cards to those who did not obtain them at the first phase	MOWSW	MLD/Ministry of Home Affairs	Based on the needs	1998/ 1999	Provision of identification cards
5	Completion of construction of a home for disabled persons which was initiated in the first phase and provision of education, medical rehabilitation and training for disabled persons in the home	MOWSW	MOF/MHPPP/ MOE/MOH	Kathmandu	1998/ 1999	Provision of various rehabilitation programmes

**Third phase programme
(2001/2002)**

S.N.	Description of activities	Implementation agency	Supporting agency	Areas to be covered	Period of work
	Based on the outcome of the first and second phase programmes, new programmes will be formulated and implemented	Concerned ministries	All concerned agencies and organizations	Kathmandu and other areas	2001 and 2002 onward

Source: Ministry of Women and Social Welfare.

Annex II

Table 1.1. Estimates of disability

Agency	Ratio
CBS	1.50 per 1,000
IYDP	30 per 1,000
WHO	100 per 1,000

Table 1.2. Distribution of schools for disabled persons by category and region 1980

Region	School for blind persons	School for deaf persons	School for physically disabled persons	School for intellectually disabled persons	Total
Eastern	1	–	–	–	1
Central	1	1	1	1	4
Western	–	1	–	1	2
Mid-western	–	–	–	–	–
Far-eastern	–	–	–	–	–
Total	**2**	**2**	**1**	**2**	**7**

Table 1.2.1. Number of programme beneficiaries

Year	Total	Blind persons	Deaf persons	Physically disabled persons	Intellectually disabled persons
1991	848	173	225	99	351
1996	1,567	347	406	71	743

Table 1.3. Distribution of special education units by category and region 1991

Region	School for blind persons	School for deaf persons	School for physically disabled persons	School for intellectually disabled persons	Total
Eastern	2	1	1	1	5
Central	10	1	1	10	22
Western	3	1	1	2	7
Mid-western	2	1	–	–	3
Far-eastern	1	–	1	–	2
Total	**18**	**4**	**4**	**13**	**39**

Table 1.4. Distribution of units for disabled persons managed by NGOs by category and region 1996

Region	School for blind persons	School for deaf persons	School for physically disabled persons	School for intellectually disabled persons	Total
Eastern	5	2	1	1	9
Central	13	1	2	14	30
Western	4	2	–	6	12
Mid-western	2	1	–	1	4
Far-eastern	2	–	1	–	3
Total	**26**	**6**	**4**	**22**	**58**

Table 1.5. Budget for SEC over the years

Fiscal year	Budget for special education council
1993-1994	5 million
1994-1995	13.2 million
1995-1996	19.8 million
1996-1997	30.7 million

Table 1.6. Implementation of NSEP over the years

1993-1994	1994-1995	1995-1996	1996-1997
Jhapa	Uda	Clitsan	Morang
Dhanakuta	Sarlahi	Kanchanpur	Llam
Tanhun	Kapailvastu	Sunssari	Nuwakot
Kaski	Kalikot	Rukum	Nawalparasi
Dang	Doti	Baghang	Rautahat
Surkhet			
Mustang			
Dadeldhura			

Table 1.7. Description of primary teachers for integrated education of blind persons

Training agency	Year	Teachers		
		Male	Female	Total
FOE	1985-1986	7	2	9
	1986-1987	6	3	9
	1987-1988	4	2	6
	1988-1989	9	1	10
	1989-1990	3	4	7
Total	5 Years	29	12	41

Table 1.8. Description of teachers trained for teaching deaf students

Training agency	Year	Number of teachers trained
FOE and WSHI	1981	7
	1987	12
	1989	9
	1991	7
	1995	5
	1996	6
Total		46

Table 1.9. Training of teachers for intellectually disabled persons over the years

Area of learning	Year	Total number of teachers trained
Introduction to intellectually disability	1984-1995	357
Implementing strategies for school curriculum	1988-1995	295
Implementation strategies for home-based curriculum	1987-1990	18
Specific teaching techniques	1984-1990	31
Training of trainers	1990-	7

Table 2. Enrolment target for the disabled population

Year	Disabled population aged 6-10	Enrolment target age 6-10	Enrolment percentage
1995-1996	116,800	9,972	8.55
1996-1997	120,000	13,000	10.76
1997-1998	124,000	20,000	16.12
1998-1999	128,000	30,000	23.43
1999-2000	131,200	45,000	34.29
2000-2001	135,200	65,000	48.07
2001-2002	138,769	90,000	64.84

(The source of all these tables is the Basic and Primary Education, Master Plan 1997-2002)

CHAPTER XIX

Pakistan

A. National overview

In Pakistan, the existence and prevalence of disability, the need to take preventive measures and to make curative efforts are well recognized at both the governmental and non-governmental levels. Efforts have been made to carry out nationwide programmes for the prevention of disabilities and for the rehabilitation of people with disabilities.

A Directorate General of Special Education, under the Ministry of Women Development, Special Education and Social Welfare, and a number of institutions and centres focusing on various aspects of the problems relating to impairment, disabilities and the handicapped, have also been established.

In Pakistan, data on people with disabilities, their sex-age distribution and other characteristics are collected mainly through population censuses and surveys.   However, they have their limitations.   As these censuses or surveys are conducted only during certain times, the patterns of disability collected only represent the prevalent conditions at that particular point in time.

The collected data from Pakistan's 1961 census covered only persons who were totally blind, deaf or physically disabled.   Then, the number of people with disabilities under these three categories formed about 0.34 per cent of the total population.

The 1973 Housing, Economic and Demographic (HED) survey, which collected data on blind, deaf, physically disabled and other disabled persons, found the number of people with disabilities totalled 0.8 per cent of the population.

The 1981 census, in addition to the other categories mentioned, included two more categories, intellectual disability and mental illness. That survey found that people with disabilities formed 0.45 per cent of the total population.

The 1973 HED survey had reported the highest rates among the three because of the quality of its coverage and also because it was based on a large sample and thus was not a complete census.

From 1984 to 1985, Pakistan carried out a national survey of disabled persons, which estimated that the disability rate for Pakistan was 4.9 per cent.

A survey of disabled persons in Rawalpindi and Islamabad, carried out in 1986 by the Directorate General of Special Education, reported an estimated prevalence rate of 2.5 per cent. The most common form was physical disability.

Disability type	*Prevalence rate (per cent)*
Physical disability	33
Mental disability	21
Multiple/complex disability	19
Visual impairment	15
Hearing impairment	9
Not classified	3

The Government of Pakistan is aware that the actual level of disability prevalence in the country is much higher than the figures reported in the 1981 census.

In its Sixth Five-year Plan, the Government stated that people with disabilities are 4 to 6 per cent of the total population, particularly the children and the older person.

A more up-to-date nationwide information and data on the prevalence of disability in Pakistan will be available after the national census is completed in October or November 1997. In this latest survey, a column on disability with variables has been added in the national census form.

B. Progress made in the first half of the Asian and Pacific Decade of Disabled Persons

1. National coordination

A national coordinating committee (NCC) was formed to implement the Agenda for Action for the Asian and Pacific Decade of Disabled Persons, 1993 to 2002 (hereafter referred to as the Asian and Pacific Decade Agenda for Action).

In September 1995, the NCC held its first meeting in Islamabad to discuss the measures the country could take to implement the Asian and Pacific Decade Agenda for Action. The meeting also discussed NCC membership. The National Council for Rehabilitation of Disabled Persons (NCRDP) and the National Trust for Disabled (NTD) were included in the NCC as these organizations play very important roles in the rehabilitation of people with disabilities. Other prominent non-governmental organizations (NGOs) were also included.

During that meeting, it was decided that Pakistan should adopt a tripartite approach, involving the Health, Social Welfare and Education Departments, to look after the welfare and rehabilitation of people with disabilities.

The meeting also decided that the community would be involved and that there should be more community-based integrated programmes addressing the welfare, education and rehabilitation of people with disabilities.

The NCC meets once every three months to review the progress made. At the provincial level, the government has set up provincial coordinating committees and divisional coordinating committees.

Overall, the NCRDP is responsible for formulating policies on the employment and rehabilitation of disabled persons and these plans are carried out by the provincial committees. The NCRDP is also responsible for implementing the aims stated in the Disabled Persons (Employment and Rehabilitation) Ordinance of 1981.

2. Legislation

Pakistan has two legislation on people with disabilities. They are:

(a) Disabled Persons Employment and Rehabilitation Ordinance of 1981;

(b) Voluntary Social Welfare Agencies (Registration and Control) Ordinance of 1961.

3. Information

The NTD has compiled a directory with the complete addresses and telephone numbers of importers, exporters and manufacturers of aids, accessories and appliances for people with disabilities. Pakistan's National Institute of Special Education has also compiled a directory of the special education programmes available in the country.

4. Public awareness

The Directorate General of Special Education, under the Ministry of Women Development, Social Welfare and Special Education, established a national library and resource centre in Islamabad, to provide the following special education services:

(a) Foreign books on Special Education;

(b) Overseas journals;

(c) Audio and video tapes on special education, mainly for course participants and teachers at the national institute of special education;

(d) Content page service (CPS) of overseas journals;

(e) Reports and bulletins.

5. Accessibility and communication

The momentum of providing better accessibility to, and communication for, disabled persons gathered speed after the International Year of Disabled Persons (1981).

Pakistan has implemented the following projects to promote accessibility to, and communication for people with disabilities:

(a) Huge publicity of white canes and observance of White Cane Day every year;

(b) Wide availability of assistive devices and artificial limbs;

(c) Duty-free import of equipment and vehicles used by people with disabilities;

(d) Provision of concessionary fares for travel by rail and by the national airline for blind persons, and special passengers services;

(e) Allotment of small residential plots to people with disabilities at concessional rates;

(f) Provision of facilities such as ramps, and accessible lifts and toilets, at public places to enable disabled persons to visit those places;

(g) Drafting of a law to ensure that new buildings and other places are easily accessible by disabled persons;

(h) Provision of free postal services in the case of Braille literature;

(i) Provision of training in mobility and communication.

6. Education

The Directorate General of Special Education has established 46, and the National Trust for the Disabled has set up three special education centres for people with disabilities. They all provide: assessment and diagnostic services; special education services; provision of personal aids and appliances; curriculum development; sports and recreation.

The Directorate General of Special Education runs 11 visually handicapped centres (VHC), 12 intellectual disability centres (IDC), 12 hearing impairment centres (HIC) and 11 physically handicapped centres (PHC).

	HIC	*IDC*	*PHC*	*VHC*	*Total*
Islamabad	1	2	–	–	3
Punjab	14	11	3	14	42
Sindh	6	8	3	9	26
NWFP	5	2	9	6	22
Baluchistan	2	–	2	–	4
Northern areas	1	–	4	–	5
Total	**29**	**23**	**21**	**29**	**102**

The provincial governments have also set up such special education institutions.

	HIC	*IDC*	*PHC*	*VHC*	*Total*
Punjab	2	3	14	34	53
Sindh	2	–	–	2	4
NWFP	9	–	–	7	16
Baluchistan	1	1	1	1	4
Total	**14**	**4**	**15**	**44**	**77**

In addition, there are also special education institutions established by the NGOs throughout the country.

(a) *National Institute of Special Education (NISE)*

The NISE was established in 1986 with the following objectives:

(i) Develop a manpower training programme in special education by organizing short- and long-term courses;

(ii) Collaborate with universities and international agencies;

(iii) Develop and publish materials for guiding special education teachers, parents and other professionals;

(iv) Promote research activities;

(v) Establish standard policies on the admission, assessment and placement of children with disabilities into the special education programmes countrywide;

(vi) Develop a curriculum for special education;

(vii) Evaluate the children's educational progress.

The NISE has also published the following journals and books:

	Year
Research study on "consanguineous" marriages and disability in children in Pakistan	1991
Pakistan sign language with regional differences [sponsored by United Nations Children's Fund (UNICEF)]	1991
Pakistan sign language based on primary schools course vocabulary (sponsored by UNICEF)	1994
Directory of special education and welfare services for disabled persons (sponsored by UNICEF)	1994
NISE brochure	1995
Modified syllabus for primary classes of hearing-impaired children (Class I to V) in Urdu for the Federal Capital Territory, Punjab and Sindh	1995
Curriculum on speech development for hearing-impaired children	1996
Report on the training courses conducted from July 1995 to June 1996	1996
Pamphlet on "Common Hearing Aid Problem and Solutions"	1996

(b) *National Trust for the Disabled (NTD)*

The NTD was established under Pakistan's Charitable Endowment Act and is headed by the Prime Minister. Its Executive Committee, led by the Minister for Social Welfare and Special Education, and the chief ministers of all the four provinces, is responsible for forming the policies of the NTD. Under the supervision of the Committee, a managing director is responsible for running NTD's day-to-day operations and implementing its policies.

NTD's aims include the following, to:

(i)   Establish model institutions for the care, education and rehabilitation of people with disabilities;

(ii) Prescribe and undertake specialized training programmes for people with disabilities;

(ii) Conduct research on the nature and extent of the problems faced by people with disabilities at the national level;

(iii) Arrange financial assistance and advisory services for individuals and families;

(iv) Deal with, and enter into agreements with, national or international organizations in special education.

The NTD has claimed success in establishing three special education multi-purpose complexes for people with disabilities at Naushahroferoze, Orangi Town in Karachi, and Mianwali.

These complexes in the rural and slum areas are providing services such as early identification of disability, treatment, specialized education, training and rehabilitation.

At Nausharoferoze, the centre started as a rural set-up and was housed in a building acquired with the help of the Government of Sindh. It is now being modernized into model institution. Construction of a purpose built premise is now ongoing and will be completed by 1997 at a cost of Rs18 million.

The special education complex in Orangi Town, Karachi, is a purpose-built centre, and is housed on rented premises. At Mianwali, the special education complex is housed in a rented building and has the state-of-the-art equipment and a skilled team to impart education and training to children with disabilities.

7. Training and employment

The National Training Centre for the Disabled (NTCD) conducts specialized skills training programmes. NTCD objectives are to:

(a) Provide vocational training and rehabilitation services: training is conducted on skills in welding, bench fitting (machinists), knitting, tailoring and making electrical and electronic equipment;

(b) Facilitate and provide placement services;

(c) Educate the community about the contributions of disabled persons to society;

(d) Help the people with disabilities contribute to, and become productive members of society.

Besides the NTCD, two vocational training centres, which offer the same services, have also been established in Karachi and Lahore.

8. Prevention of the causes of disability

The National Institute for the Handicapped has been set up in Islamabad and it provides the following services to people with disabilities:

(a) Coordinate national efforts to prevent disabilities, plan and develop an integrated referral system throughout the country and serve as a training centre for those involved in the prevention of disabilities;

(b) Plan and develop a system of early detection of disability in children;

(c) Plan and develop a multi-professional assessment and diagnostic system at the district and divisional level;

(d) Plan and develop a health surveillance system through the existing institutions;

(e) Coordinate and support services for people with disabilities by various institutions at different levels in the country;

(f) Provide treatment to people with disabilities with various disabilities: the institute employs medical specialists in various fields of disabilities and highly trained paramedical staff to treat and care for people with disabilities;

(g) Provide medical rehabilitation services for persons with extensive disabilities;

(h) Carry out research on artificial limbs (manufacture and assembly) and hearing aids, as well as conduct research on all aspects of disabilities;

(i) Provide stay bays and convalescent facilities to 120 hospitalized patients.

9. Rehabilitation services

To provide treatment and rehabilitative services to people with disabilities, the National Institute of Handicapped coordinates nationwide efforts on the early detection and prevention of disabilities, and also provides treatment to people with disabilities.

Disabled persons of all categories who are physically mobile and able to pursue vocational training are entitled to receive benefits from the Institute. The NTCD provides vocational training and rehabilitative services to people with disabilities in various trades, and also helps successful trainees find suitable jobs.

The National Council for Rehabilitation of Disabled Persons was established in 1982 to form policies on the employment, rehabilitation and welfare of disabled persons. As stated under the Disabled Persons Employment and Rehabilitation Ordinance, 1981, it also evaluates, assesses and coordinates the implementation, by the provincial councils, of this policy.

Community participation in the vocational rehabilitation of disabled plays a vital role in enhancing the economic and social functioning of disabled persons. A project started in 1992 by the government and the International Labour Organization, helps fulfil the aim of ensuring continued development of a national programme of community-based rehabilitation assistance.

10. Assistive devices

With the help of provincial councils, the National Council for Rehabilitation of Disabled Persons, provides to many special persons, locally-made and available assistive devices, such as wheelchairs, tricycles, callipers, crutches, walkers and artificial limbs.

11. Self-help organizations

The Government of Pakistan alone cannot solve the problems faced by people with disabilities. Therefore, it enlists the support of the NGOs and the community. Disabled persons should be treated as national assets. The Government of Pakistan has started the process of mainstreaming and integrating people with disabilities.

In order to promote special education programmes in the private sector, the Government has extended more financial and technical assistance to NGOs around the country. The NGOs providing welfare, education, training and rehabilitation to diverse disability groups are as follows:

Disability groups	Number of NGOs providing services
Physically handicapped	37
Hearing impairment	56
Visual impairment	52
Mental retardation	35
Total	**180**

12. Regional cooperation

The SAARC Ministerial Conference on Disabled Persons was held in Islamabad from 16 to 18 December 1993.

After three days of deliberations, the Conference recommended the following:

(a) The community should be made aware of the right of people with disabilities to participate in the mainstream life, and to meet their medical, educational, social and employment needs. Awareness creation should begin in school through the introduction of a suitable module in the secondary school curriculum. Both the electronic and the print media should also be made full use of in the campaign, and NGOs, including those of people with disabilities, should be mobilized to support the programme.

(b) There should be opportunities for people with disabilities to show their capabilities and to reduce the stigma attached to the state of disability. Disabled persons should be encouraged to hold exhibitions, concerts and competitions to demonstrate their abilities. Both the electronic and the print media can play very important roles in this regard.

(c) Focal points should be established for research and the dissemination of information at the SAARC and country levels. Research should also be conducted on community-based rehabilitation, special education needs, and other relevant aspects. Information on national CBR and special education programmes, new methods of rehabilitation and therapy and low-cost assistive device should also be disseminated.

(d) Primary health care staff should be trained in the early diagnosis and referral of disabilities.

(e) Disabled persons should be integrated into mainstream life. They should be educated in regular schools and universities and special events should be held during regular sports meets. Public utilities, such as transport, buildings, airport and railways stations, should be modified so that they are also accessible by people with disabilities. For example, buildings can be built such that it is wheelchair accessible. Sign language facilities should be made available at the reception desks of public facilities such as railway stations and airports.

(f) Marriage and genetics counselling should be available at sub-national levels.

(g) Demonstration centres should be set up to show the activities of daily living, such as cooking, toilets use and bathing.

(h) Representatives of people with disabilities should be included in national and subnational intersectoral committees of the CBR programme.

(i) Legislation should be enacted to promote and protect the rights of people with disabilities in areas such as education, employment, social welfare and rehabilitation.

(j) Day-care centres should be established.

(k) Specially earmarked resources should be allocated in the budgets of sectors such as health and education.

(l) People with disabilities should be encouraged to organize themselves into associations to voice their opinions, needs and rights.

(m) There should be networking and interaction among related programmes such as primary eye care programmes, the primary ear care programmes and programmes for older persons.

C. Activities planned for the second half of the Asian and Pacific Decade of Disabled Persons

The following activities are planned for the second half of the Decade:

1. Completion of purpose-built building complexes of special education at Islamabad, provincial headquarters and divisional headquarters in Pakistan to provide rehabilitative services through extended professional approaches;

2. Continuation of ongoing special education programmes at both the federal and provincial levels in an integrated way for people with moderate to severe intensities of disability;

3. Revitalization and improvement of the special education centres by provision of sophisticated and modern disability-specific equipment and literature;

4. Expansion and improvement of special education services by NGOs in the private sector;

5. Psycho- and socio-economic rehabilitation of disabled individuals;

6. Inclusion and integration of the education of disabled children into regular schools, in collaboration with the Ministry of Education;

7. Strengthening of community-based programmes for the education and training of disabled;

8. Training and development of master trainers in special education;

9. Development of legislation for the protection of the human rights of disabled persons;

10. Vocational training and rehabilitation of disabled adults to enable them to be financially self-reliant;

11. Promotion of co-curricular activities for special persons;

12. Alleviation of poverty among disabled persons through various supportive aids and measures for training;

13. Development of strong links in terms of providing professional equipment, latest literature research material, and participation in workshops, seminars and symposia, in collaboration with international agencies such as JICA, UNDP, ILO and UNICEF;

14. Conduct of miscellaneous welfare activities;

15. Implementation of the Prime Minister of Pakistan's relief package for people with disabilities.

The Government of Pakistan is committed to the well-being of the masses, including people with disabilities. It announced a special relief package for people with disabilities which covers the following aspects:

(a) Free medical treatment for people with disabilities;

(b) Grants for subsistence allowance;

(c) Stipends for covering the educational expenses of disabled students;

(d) Quota reservation for disabled persons in jobs, professional and technical institutions;

(e) Plot allotments to disabled persons at concessional rates.

The Ministry of Women Development, Social Welfare and Special Education has prepared an action plan to achieve the above targets. The action plan is part of the Prime Minister's relief package for people with disabilities in Pakistan, in collaboration with all relevant governmental bodies and NGOs during the second half of the Asian and Pacific Decade of Disabled Person, 1993 to 2002.

CHAPTER XX

Papua New Guinea

A. National overview

The exact number of people with disabilities in Papua New Guinea is not known. However, based on United Nations estimates, there are approximately 400,000 disabled persons in the country.

Most of the people with disabilities live in their villages with their families. As such, the current trend is more towards community-based and integrated services through ordinary delivery systems such as the health, education and social welfare systems.

Until the International Year of Disabled Persons, 1981, and the United Nations Decade of Disabled Persons, 1983-1992, services for disabled persons were mainly provided by non-governmental organizations (NGOs) with grants from the government. However, the state became more involved towards the end of the United Nations Decade of Disabled Persons.

Since then, a number of national plans and programmes for people with disabilities have been formulated and implemented. Among them are the National Health Plan, the National Special Education Plan and National Plan for the Prevention of Disability – all of which to some extent address some of the 12 major policy categories under the Agenda for Action for the Asian and Pacific Decade of Disabled Persons, 1993-2002 (hereafter referred to as the Asian and Pacific Decade Agenda for Action).

For example, under the national special education programme, primary school teacher colleges are offering disability courses and disabled children are being enrolled or integrated into ordinary schools. Eight of 13 disability NGOs or private agencies in the country have been included as resource centres. The focus is now on the secondary school teacher colleges.

However, in terms of actually observing the Asian and Pacific Decade of Disabled Persons, the country's responses have been late and its progress very slow.

B. Progress made in the first half of the Asian and Pacific Decade of Disabled Persons

Papua New Guinea was present at the meeting in which the Asian and Pacific Decade of Disabled Persons was declared in December 1992 and in several follow up meetings, including the Meeting to Review the Progress of the

Asian and Pacific Decade of Disabled Persons held in Bangkok in June 1995. However, there has not been many follow-up activities.

This is because the country had sent different representatives to those meetings and as such, there was little coordination among them. As a result, the country activities for the Asian and Pacific Decade of Disabled Persons have not been organized and carried out as expected until 1996, when, for the first time, a big delegation attended the Intercountry Seminar on Multisectoral Collaborative Action for People with Disabilities in Kuala Lumpur held in December 1996. It was in preparation for that meeting that more awareness about the Asian and Pacific Decade of Disabled Persons was created.

Since that meeting, the Department of Home Affairs has taken on the coordinating role and the following has been achieved:

1. The Asian and Pacific Decade Agenda for Action and the Standard Rules on Equalization of Opportunities for People with Disabilities have been reproduced for internal circulation, and are now being printed.

2. Documents on the Asian and Pacific Decade of Disabled Persons have been sent to national departments and agencies whose areas of responsibilities are directly related to the 12 major policy categories. Representatives from those departments and agencies, including disabled persons, will form the national working team which will later be replaced by a national coordinating committee.

3. The signing of the Proclamation is now set for 3 December, although earlier attempts were made in 1994 and September 1996.

4. A national conference on disability is organized from 26 to 29 March 1998, when a national policy on disability and national plan of action from 1998 to 2002 will be discussed.

It can be seen that Papua New Guinea is just beginning to implement action towards the fulfilment of the goals of the Asian and Pacific Decade of Disabled Persons and will proceed and make progress at a pace permitted or set by its own socio-economic conditions.

C. Activities planned for the second half of the Asian and Pacific Decade of Disabled Persons

Papua New Guinea is experiencing the effects of the World Bank and IMF structural adjustment programmes which have cut its budget allocations for social services drastically, and raised the cost of living. Therefore, the country's activities towards achieving the aims of the Asian and Pacific Decade of Disabled Persons will be directed towards enhancing existing programmes and, where required, programmes will be revised to include the Asian and Pacific Decade Agenda for Action.

Papua New Guinea will certainly need assistance in the planning and coordination of activities, human resource training and production of assistive devices. The country thus seeks assistance from those with relevant experiences and expertise.

CHAPTER XXI

Philippines

A. National overview

The Government of the Philippines recognizes that people with disabilities have the same rights as their able-bodied counterparts and that they have the rights to take their proper place in society. Every effort to insure their protection to these rights and provision of services to meet their needs are being undertaken to hasten their integration into the mainstream of society.

The United Nations estimates that there are around 6.8 million Filipinos who have some form of disability, either physical, sensory or mental. This means that one person out of 10 is estimated to have a disability. Some 75 per cent of people with disabilities live in rural or semi-urban areas and the remaining 25 per cent in the urban areas.

The vast majority of people with disabilities have very little opportunity to be included in the schemes and programmes that provide services because these are almost always found in the urban areas. For a long time, disabled persons have been segregated and their rights to development and ability to contribute to their families and communities unrecognized. Their access to front-line government services is limited and rehabilitation services inadequate.

Influenced by the developments that occur in the international arena, there has been a major change in the philosophical, social and developmental approach to helping persons with disabilities. A disabled person is no longer seen as a different kind of person. Services for them are now viewed in the same framework as those provided to other citizens in the country.

Disabled persons are viewed as ordinary citizens with special needs and like all other members of society are entitled to the same rights and equal opportunities. Their intrinsic worth as human beings and fundamental rights as citizens are now the basic principle contrary to the ancient practice of hiding or segregating them from their counterparts.

The declaration of the United Nations Decade of Disabled Persons, 1983-1992, brought about a new kind of consciousness among Filipinos. It witnessed a revolutionary change in the efforts of the government and non-government sectors in undertaking programmes and projects on disability prevention, rehabilitation and equalization of opportunities.

While the United Nations Decade succeeded in promoting the rights of disabled persons and advancing disability issues, the goals of equalization of opportunities and their full participation in day-to-day concerns have yet to be fully realized. Much more has to be done to enable people with disabilities to develop their full potential on the basis of the provisions of the Standard Rules on the Equalization of Opportunities for People with Disabilities which embodies their rights and obligations just like their able-bodied counterparts.

1. National coordination

The National Council for the Welfare of Disabled Persons was designated as the lead agency in observing the Asian and Pacific Decade of Disabled Persons, 1993-2002, as embodied in Proclamation 125 of President Fidel V. Ramos. In line with its mandate, the council, including its member agencies was directed to disseminate the Agenda for Action for the Asian and Pacific Decade of Disabled Persons (hereafter referred to as the Asian and Pacific Decade Agenda for Action), as widely as possible to the private and public sectors nationwide. It is also given the responsibility to coordinate and monitor all programmes, projects and activities pertaining to the Asian and Pacific Decade Agenda for Action.

The President also enjoined non-government organizations (NGOs) and self-help groups among people with disabilities to take full cognizance of the Asian and Pacific Decade Agenda for Action and to fully cooperate in the attainment of its goals, objectives and activities by gearing their policies and aligning their programmes with the Agenda.

In line with the Asian and Pacific Decade of Disabled Persons, a Philippine Plan of Action for the Asian and Pacific Decade of Disabled Persons of Disabled Persons was developed and adopted to set into motion the directions for implementation of programmes and services by the concerned sectors. It is within the context of the current development efforts enunciated in Philippines 2000 or the Philippine Medium Term Development Plan. This plan ensures full participation and equalization of opportunities for persons with disabilities. It seeks to institutionalize the prevention of the causes of disability and the rehabilitation of disabled persons within the Decade of Disabled Persons in the Asian Pacific region. Strategies for the programme and project implementation are in line with the 12 policy statements of the Asian and Pacific Decade of Agenda for Action.

2. Priority issues and concerns

In formulating the Philippine Plan of Action, the following issues and problems have been given priority attention:

(a) Absence of a comprehensive and scientific compilation of baseline data which can serve as a basis for sound policies and effective programmes to reduce the incidence and prevalence of disabilities, as well as for equalization of opportunities. Good planning and management policy should be based on accurate statistical data;

(b) Inadequate implementation of existing laws and policies due to the absence of a vigilant monitoring system and the indifference of the government officials in enforcing them due to the low priority assigned to issues on disability;

(c) Lack of effort on existing mechanism designed to push for the implementation of current laws which are sufficient to meet actual needs;

(d) Non-availability or insufficiency of funding for NGOs, lack of programmes and, in most cases, low prioritization of disability-related programmes;

(e) Limited outreach of existing programmes, which do not yet adequately cover rural areas where 75 per cent of the people with disabilities are located; the situation is further aggravated by shortcomings in the devolution process of some vital government operations from national to local levels, as a result of which crucial services have been at a standstill;

(f) Absence of a comprehensive, integrated and continuing campaign to improve public awareness, especially of the families of people with disabilities on the importance of the problems of disabilities and their prevention;

(g) Inadequate government regulatory activity or body resulting in the proliferation of certain NGOs that exploit people with disabilities and the general public;

(i) Lack of proper representation of disabled persons in the various legislative and executive branches at all levels of government, resulting in inadequate support services;

(j) Negative attitudes of persons with disabilities and their family members towards self-development.

3. Guiding goals and objectives

As a response to these identified priority issues and concerns, the Philippine Plan of Action for the Asian and Pacific Decade of Disabled Persons of Disabled Persons, 1993-2002, has the following goals and objectives.

The Philippine Plan of Action contains national priorities directed towards the maximization of opportunities available to people with disabilities in all aspects of life in the community. The target goal of the Plan is to upgrade, strengthen, expand and sustain activities aimed at realizing the full participation and equality of disabled persons.

In pursuit of this goal, all disability-related programmes and services shall aim to:

(a) Strengthen, expand and sustain programmes and policies geared towards better access to education, health/medical, vocational/technical training, employment, social and other services;

(b) Implement existing laws and enact more laws which will protect the right to full and equal participation of people with disabilities;

(c) Organize grassroots associations and organizations of, and for, people with disabilities and provide venues that will involve them in the formulation of policies, development of programmes and projects geared towards improving their welfare;

(d) Provide self-directed, community-based services where priority must be directed towards independent living;

(e) Develop the sense of responsibility of people with disabilities towards themselves, their families, their community and the environment;

(f) Establish comprehensive baseline data on disability for effective programme planning, implementation and monitoring.

B. Progress made in the first half of the Asian and Pacific Decade of Disabled Persons

1. National coordination

The target is to establish a national coordination committee on disability (NCCD) or strengthening of an existing one.

The NCCD of the Philippines was established through Presidential Decree 1509 under the Office of the President of the Republic of the Philippines. From being a commission, it was reorganized in 1987 into the National Council for the Welfare of Disabled Persons (NCWDP) as an attached agency of the Department of Social Welfare and Development. The NCWDP serves as the national focal point on all disability issues. It has a governing board composed of line departments responsible for the translation of the policies into programmes, projects and services.

To further strengthen the NCWDP, the following were undertaken:

(a) Reactivation of the NCWDP Executive Committee composed of technical experts in the major areas of disability concerns to serve as the think-tank and clearing-house relative to issues which need board action;

(b) Organization of a Regional Committee for the Welfare of Disabled Persons (RCWDP) to serve the NCWDP machinery in addressing disability issues in 16 regions of the country;

(c) Creation of action teams in all the member agencies of the NCWDP Board to act as the point persons for all disability issues concerning their departments;

(d) Organization of the Parallel Executive Committee composed of leaders with disabilities representing the different disability groups to identify and discuss issues affecting them for policy development and/or programme coordination;

(e) Development of a monitoring scheme which is being pilot tested by the RCWDPs to monitor and assess the implementation of the Philippine Plan of Action in line with the Asian and Pacific Decade Agenda for Action;

(f) Inclusion of people with disabilities as one of the sectors in the Philippine Human Rights Plan, 1996-2000;

(g) Inclusion of disabled persons as a sector in the concern on human and ecological security;

(h) Regular conduct of consultation dialogues with leaders of self-help groups in the 16 regions to generate issues and concerns for policy formulation, coordination and monitoring;

(i) Creation of a task force to address the concerns and needs of people with disabilities, and gaps in programmes and services;

(j) Inclusion of the sector with disabilities in the Social Reform Agenda (SRA), the government's programme for poverty alleviation and appointment of a representative of the sector in the Social Reform Council – the policy-making body for the SRA.

The NCWDP served as a member of the technical panel during the budget hearings of the 1998 budget proposals of the executive departments to make sure that specific fund allocations are made in compliance with the Magna Carta for Disabled Persons.

2. Legislation

The aim is to enact basic laws to protect the rights of all people with disabilities, and prohibit their abuse and neglect, and discrimination against them.

To achieve the aim, the following were implemented:

(a) The Magna Carta for Disabled Persons, enacted by the Philippine Legislator in 1991, serves as the landmark legislation that provides for the rehabilitation, self-development and self-reliance of people with disabilities and their integration into mainstream society;

(b) Rules and regulations have been formulated and disseminated for enforcement to concerned agencies; advocacy campaigns, such as orientation seminars, brochures, television and radio plugs, have been conducted to support its implementation;

(c) Strengthening the Accessibility Law (Batas Pambansa Lg. 344) which is an act to enhance the mobility of people with disabilities by requiring certain buildings, institutions, establishments and public utilities to install accessible facilities and other devices, including transportation and communication; the implementing rules and regulations (IRR) have been amended to increase the penalty for violation, and to provide for stricter identification of specific individuals and offices liable for the violation; the amended IRR also provides for the accessibility requirements with regard to public transportation;

(d) Tax exemption and benefits for the employers of disabled persons and those that provide accessibility facilities in the work place;

(e) Submission of position papers, in consultation with the sector with disabilities, on a total of 17 bills and resolutions proposed in Congress and in the Senate.

The list of bills and resolutions are annexed.

3. Information

The target is to initiate a national sample survey in 1998. That same year, a national resource centre with an accessible information and database on disability will be established.

In this segment, the following have been achieved thus far:

(a) Conduct of a national registration of people with disabilities;

(b) Inclusion of disability questions in the 1990 and 1995 national census;

(c) Installation of an international communication network for Internet service with homepage and e-mail for data base and information exchange both at the national and international levels;

(d) Dissemination of the Asian and Pacific Decade Agenda for Action to all concerned sectors;

(e) Regular updating of the directory of rehabilitation resources which includes organizations of people with disabilities.

4. Public awareness

Immediate action is needed to ensure that the national and local mass media, including the private sector and folk media, feature disability-related issues through regular and accurate coverage. These will help improve public awareness and attitudes.

The following have been achieved thus far:

(a) Regular conduct of IEC and advocacy campaigns on disability issues;

(b) Annual conduct of the National Disability Prevention and Rehabilitation Week, as a vehicle for the promotion and advocacy of disability issues;

(c) Utilization of puppetry to generate public awareness of disability issues and positive attitudes towards people with disabilities;

(d) Inclusion of the sector with disabilities in the Philippine National Games, a national Olympic style sports event, to showcase the potentials of disabled persons as world-class athletes;

(e) Inclusion of students with disability in the *Palarong Pambansa*, a national school-based sports competition;

(f) Regular weekly broadcast of the following radio programmes nation-wide, anchored by disabled persons and with a focus on disability issues:

　(i) *Ako'y Ikaw rin,* (one hour);

　(ii) *K-Forum,* (two hours);

　(iii) *Mano-mano,* (one hour).

(g) Participation of organizations of disabled persons in national celebrations and religious activities.

5. Accessibility and communication

The immediate task is incorporation of barrier-free features as a standard requirement of designs and plans for all new construction, renovation and expansion of buildings and facilities used by people with disabilities.

Thus far, the following have been achieved:

(a) Conduct of accessibility talk shops and seminars for public utility jeepneys (PUJ) and bus operators;

(b) Monitoring of the implementation of the Accessibility Law by an inter-agency committee comprising disabled persons, the Department of Public Works and Highways and the NCWDP;

(c) Architectural students, as a course-requirement, act as surveyors to collate an inventory of accessible and inaccessible public and private buildings;

(d) Installation of curb cuts in the major streets of Metro Manila and other key cities;

(e) Provision of fare discounts and parking spaces to people with disabilities in buildings, parks and other similar establishments;

(f) Development of a manual titled "Assisting Disabled and Elderly Persons Who Travel (ADEPT) in sea, land and air transportation".

(g) Conduct of ADEPT training for personnel and the crew of sea, land and air transportation companies;

(h) Issuance of policy guidelines on the provision of drivers' licenses to disabled persons;

(i) Installation of corrugated lines and signage in the light railway transit, reserved seat stickers on buses and jeepneys for hire;

(j) Installation of accessible features and facilities in all domestic airports;

(k) Conduct of accessibility talk shops in the regions with architects, building officials, owners and contractors as participants;

(l) Conduct of seminars for PUJ and bus drivers, conductors and operators regarding the Accessibility Law; and Inclusion of the Accessibility Law in the curricula of architecture and engineering courses;

(m) Provision of sign language interpreters during national events, conferences and meetings and to develop a Philippine Dictionary of Sign Language which contains the standard sign language interpretation of Filipino words;

(n) Availability of telecommunication devices for the deaf (TDD) to people with hearing impairment;

(o) Establishment of a library for blind persons at the National Library;

(p) Availability of closed caption television sets, and films with subtitles for people with hearing impairment.

6. Education

By 1997, the aim is to encourage girls, boys, women and men with disabilities to participate in formal and non-formal education programme on an equal basis, through progressive enrolment and with appropriate support services. They will also be included in all policies, plans and programmes to ensure education for all with adequate financial allocations as well as appropriate technical and human resources.

There are also plans to introduce, by 1997, early intervention programmes for children with disabilities in both rural and urban areas.

The following are being established:

(a) Conduct of SPED training for regular teachers to complement the existing SPED teachers;

(b) Conduct of summer classes for regular teachers;

(c) Conduct of the Mobile SPED Training Programme for regular teachers in the regions;

(d) Promotion of inclusive education;

(e) Inclusion of SPED education in the curriculum for regular teacher training;

(f) Conduct of early detection, prevention and intervention of disability services among children in selected municipalities and cities (pilot tested by the DSWD);

(g) Development of resource materials for the community-based SPED programme for blind and deaf persons who are out of school;

(h) Development of educational materials for persons with low vision, visually-impaired persons and children with autism;

(i) Inclusion of subjects on disability in elementary, high school and college curricula;

(j) Provision of funding assistance to deserving students with disabilities through scholarships by utilizing 5 per cent of the private education scholarship funds;

(k) Development of an integrated programme package on autism focusing on the education of autistic children, early detection and intervention of autism.

7. Training and employment

The aims include full participation by 2000, of people with disabilities, in all schemes of assistance to engage in informal income generation and self-employment in the rural and urban sectors and to provide, by that year, appropriate training and employment opportunities for them.

By 1998, the Philippines plans to develop and strengthen the curricula and support training sites and equipment to enable disabled persons to participate fully in regular vocational training schemes leading to gainful employment. By that year, the country also plans to establish production centres that employ people with extensive disabilities and those who require a supportive environment.

The following have been achieved thus far:

(a) Development of a national programme that provides employment and livelihood opportunities to disabled persons, the *TULAY* 2000 (means "Bridge 2000" in Tagalog) and Self Employment Assistance – *Kaunlaran* (means progress in Tagalog) (SEA-K);

(b) Conduct of a national skills competition for people with disabilities integrated in the regular National Skills Competition conducted by the Technical Education and Skills Development Authority (TESDA);

(c) Participation in the Abilympics in 1991 and 1995;

(d) Assessment and upgrading of vocational training courses provided by the existing vocational and sheltered workshops relative to the needs of the labour market;

(e) Creation of an inter-agency committee on employment promotion, protection and rehabilitation of persons with disabilities, though Executive Order 261 of the President of the Philippines;

(f) Installation of accessible features in the vocational and skills training centre of TESDA;

(g) Provision of social and vocational rehabilitation which includes vocational counselling, training and job placement in sheltered, self- and open employment in centre-based and community-based facilities;

(h) Conduct of market and skills surveys to serve as a baseline for the development of employment programmes for people with disabilities;

(i) Establishment of production centres in selected areas that employ disabled persons;

(j) Provision of support to the livelihood projects and activities of self-help groups of disabled persons;

(k) Strengthening of existing government and sheltered workshops in National Capital Region (NCR), Region X, XI and XII.

8. Prevention of the causes of disability

The aim is to initiate, by 1997, public education campaigns directed at the prevention of the five most prevalent preventable causes of disability

Thus far, the following have been achieved.

(a) Utilization of the tri-media in the public education campaigns towards prevention of disabilities such as blindness and iodine deficiency;

(b) Intensive immunization programme for children as a measure to prevent disabilities such as polio and Vitamin A deficiency;

(c) Promotion of maternal and child health care and primary health care;

(d) Implementation of the following to prevent the causes of disabilities:

  (i) Hearing conservation programme by conducting orientation seminars on hearing conservation in work places such as factories;

  (ii) Blindness prevention programme which includes Vitamin A supplementation, primary eye care and cataract extraction in coordination with NGOs;

  (iii) Iron and iodine supplementation programme for pregnant and lactating mothers and infants;

  (iv) Polio eradication programme and conduct of a National Immunization Day;

  (v) Hansen disease prevention, treatment and rehabilitation programme;

  (vi) Observance of Leprosy Control Week.

9. Rehabilitation services

The aims are to include people with disabilities, especially women and their families, as active participants in the formulation of community-based rehabilitation (CBR) strategies, and in the implementation of government and NGO-based CBR programmes and projects.

So far, the following has been achieved:

(a) Development of a comprehensive national CBR programme in coordination with Christoffel-Blinden Mission (CBM) piloted in one municipality prior to national implementation; the programme utilizes a multisectoral approach in the delivery of services to people with disabilities with the local government units as the lead actor and implementing agency; it includes the participation of disabled persons in the planning, implementation and evaluation of CBR projects;

(b) Utilization of the CBR approach by a number of departments in the delivery of services to people with disabilities;

(c) Provision of centre-based rehabilitation services by government and non-government agencies;

(d) Development of a training curriculum on CBR which will be pilot-tested in one municipality.

10. Assistive devices

The targets are to increase availability by 1998 of assistive devices, repairs and maintenance services, and to conduct training programmes for the manufacture of such devices.

The Philippines has to date:

(a) Printed and distributed a catalogue of assistive devices to guide concerned sectors;

(b) Mobilized resources by tapping NGOs, and government and international organizations to meet the needs of disabled persons for such devices;

(c) Established and improved upon workshops in the manufacture of assistive devices by providing funds and technical support;

(d) Conducted counselling sessions, dialogues and seminars to motivate people with disabilities to use assistive devices;

(e) Conducted research and development to make available assistive devices that are durable and inexpensive, utilizing indigenous materials.

11. Self-help organizations

Here, the target is to establish, in 1997, a national forum of self-help organizations from the rural areas as well as those representing women and children with disabilities, users of psychiatric services, persons with intellectual disabilities, persons who are HIV positive and persons affected by leprosy or autism.

These self-help groups also focus on rural people with disabilities, providing mutual support, advocacy and referrals to programme and services. They would also collaborate actively with NGOs engaged in rural and urban development issues.

The following has been set up to achieve the goals:

(a) Institutionalized Forum 100: National Consultation with Leaders of Organizations of People with Disabilities;

(b) Conducted a national meeting of women with disabilities (WWDs) for advocacy in line with the government's gender and development programme;

(c) Organized WWDs into "Circles of Advocates" in the regional areas;

(d) Strengthened KAMPI as one of the national organizations of diverse disability groups that provide services to other people with disabilities;

(e) Strengthened disabled persons' organizations by providing funds and support as well as linkages with resource partners and allocated a budget for such purposes;

(f) Conducted a study to test the approach of utilizing organized self-help groups in the organization and strengthening of other similar groups;

(g) Conducted regular consultations with regional groups to identify gaps and issues for programme coordination and policy development;

(h) Conducted leadership and entrepreneurial management training for disabled persons;

(i) Conducted training on the operation and management of cooperatives in Iloilo;

(j) Developed a resource mobilization and management network to guide self-help groups sourcing for funds and resource partners for their programmes and projects.

12. Regional cooperation

Here the tasks are to develop information materials and organize programmes on approaches to the achievement the goals for technical cooperation among developing countries.

In this area, the Philippines has achieved the following:

(a) Preparations for the concerning of a regional conference titled "Asia-Pacific Issues and Strategies Concerning National Coordination Committees: Towards a More Effective Implementation of the Asian and Pacific Decade of Disabled Persons for Persons with Disabilities" (Manila, 9-12 December 1997);

(b) Information exchange with international organizations and experts concerned with people with disabilities on the latest developments in the field of disability;

(c) Participated in international conferences and meetings as a means of technical cooperation and support for which funds are allotted annually;

(d) Conducted professional exchange programmes;

(e) Hosted several foreign experts and professionals and conducted observation tours of rehabilitation centres and facilities.

C. Activities planned for the second half of the Asian and Pacific Decade of Disabled Persons

The Philippines believes that its goals of equalization of opportunities and full participation of people with disabilities in all aspects of civil life still have to be fully realized. The Government of the Philippines, in partnership with the NGOs and disabled persons, has to do more to enable Filipinos with disabilities to rise above their disability and develop their full potential.

All programmes and activities will be reviewed by all concerned agencies in relation to the targets set and to identify and assess strengths and weaknesses in implementation. Adequate funds will be allocated to programmes and projects in line with the thrusts of the Asian and Pacific Decade of Disabled Persons.

The country will further pursue opportunities that allow people with disabilities to play active roles to help achieve the objectives of the Asian and Pacific Decade of Disabled Persons. The Government of the Philippines will ensure the participation and/or representation of disabled persons in the decision-making process for issues affecting them.

Most importantly, the NCWDP will be further strengthened as the national coordinating centre for all disability-related concerns. It will be responsible for guiding, monitoring and evaluating the implementation of Philippine Plan of Action and the Asian and Pacific Decade of Disabled Persons.

The Philippines will continue to further expand its networks and linkages with both local and international organizations to keep abreast with developments in the field of disability as well as promote regional and global cooperation for the full integration of the sector into mainstream life.

ANNEX

List of Bills and Resolutions for People With Disabilities

Senate Bill (S.B.) No. 378

An Act creating the bureau of special education in the Department of Education, Culture and Sports, providing for its powers, duties and functions and for other purposes.

S.B. No. 1904

An Act penalizing the negative portrayal of a person with disabilities in movies, television, stage and other forms of mass communication.

S.B. No. 1376 and No. 572

An Act giving priority to disabled individuals in the operation of vending facilities in government property. To enlarge the economic opportunities of disabled persons and for other purposes.

S.B. No. 296

An Act providing for the representation of the disabled sector in the House of Representatives for the manner of their nomination and appointment and for other purposes.

S.B. No. 1267 and No. 1678

An Act providing for the creation of municipal special education centre for deaf and blind children appropriating funds thereof and for other purposes.

S.B. No. 92

An Act providing for the design and construction of public buildings to accommodate persons with physical disabilities.

S.B. No. 476

An Act authorizing the SSS to establish and maintain an adequate programme for the retraining and re-employment of covered handicapped employees, incorporating for this purpose a new section 14-B into R.A. 1661 as amended otherwise known as the Social Security Law.

S.B. Nos. 1745, 1766, 1757 and No. 7526

An Act requiring all franchise holders or operators of television stations, producers of television programmes, home video programmes and motion pictures to have their programmes and films broadcast with closed-caption and providing penalties thereof for violation.

S.B. No. 1604

An Act requiring employers in the private sector to have in their employment people with disabilities and providing additional incentives therefor, and amending for the purpose R.A. 7277, otherwise known as the Magna Carta for Disabled Persons.

S.B. No. 5465

An Act granting other privileges and incentives and further amending the purpose of R.A. 7277.

S.B. No. 6105

An Act requiring all government agencies to procure 5 per cent of their annual office supplies from manufacturing firms operated by people with disabilities and providing penalties for violation thereof.

S.B. No. 79

An Act amending Article 78 and Chapter I, titled "Three Book Three" of the Labour Code. As amended, it gives additional protection to disabled workers.

S.B. No. 3002

An Act requiring mall owners to allot space for groups of disabled musicians and vendors and providing for the tax exemption of a percentage of the imputed value of such allotted space.

S.B. No. 4923

An Act establishing special schools for blind persons, deaf persons, and other physically and mentally disabled and disadvantaged persons.

Senate Resolution No. 485

Directing the Committee on Health and Demography, Social Justice, and Justice and Human Rights to conduct an inquiry, in aid of legislation, into the implementation of R.A. 7277, otherwise known as the Magna Carta for Disabled Persons, and B.P. 844, known as the Accessibility Law, and to recommend appropriate measures therefor

Senate Resolution No. 10

Urging the Senate to ratify Convention No. 159 concerning Vocational Rehabilitation and Employment (Disabled Persons) as adopted by the General Conference of the International Labour Organization during its sixty-ninth session on 1 June 1983.

CHAPTER XXII

Republic of Korea

A. National overview

Since the United Nations Decade of Disabled Persons was proclaimed in 1982, the Republic of Korea has endeavoured to extend the rights of disabled persons by establishing several policy measures such as the disabled persons registration programme, the comprehensive welfare plan, and the enactment of the "Disabled Persons Employment Promotion Law". In addition, the Republic of Korea hosted the 1988 Seoul Paralympics and the annual Day of Disabled Persons to promote public awareness and understanding of disabled persons.

The first national meeting was held to review the objectives and recommendations of the Agenda for Action for the Asian and Pacific Decade of Disabled Persons, 1993-2002 (hereafter referred to as the Asian and Pacific Decade Agenda for Action). The meeting appraised the achievements and procedures with regard to the Asian and Pacific Decade Agenda for Action.

This report examines, at the mid-point of the Decade, the country's endeavours to implement the Asian and Pacific Decade Agenda for Action, and it explains the concrete plans required for successful implementation of the programme over the next five years.

B. Progress made in the first half of the Asian and Pacific Decade of Disabled Persons

1. National coordination

The Welfare Policy Committee for Disabled Persons was established in August 1996 with a Secretary-General as the head of the committee to coordinate and integrate the functions of various ministries concerned with the welfare of disabled persons. The committee established a five-year welfare development plan for disabled persons which covers the fields of welfare, employment, and education. It aims to achieve the objectives and recommendations of the Asian and Pacific Decade of Disabled Persons, and to meet the increasing needs of disabled persons in the Republic of Korea.

The committee is composed of several ministers and representatives of non-governmental organizations (NGOs) concerned with the welfare of disabled persons, with the Secretary-General as the head of the committee. The committee takes charge of deliberating and coordinating policies and pro-grammes, including confirmation of policy directions, improvement of various systems, and cooperation among the various ministries.

2. Legislation

The Republic of Korea has pursued full equality for, and the participation of, persons with disability in society by providing self-support facilities and employment, and by improving their rights through the enactment of laws and regulations. In future, the Government of the Republic of Korea will give more attention to issues concerning disabled persons by broadening the legal definition of disability.

The Welfare Law for the Mentally and Physically Handicapped (December 1989), the Employment Promotion Act for Disabled Persons (August 1995), and the Special Education Promotion Law were fully revised to generate legal provisions concerning equal opportunities and rights for disabled persons.

A few measures have been formulated for eliminating barriers restricting employment and the independent living conditions of disabled persons. During the past five years, 37 of 38 regulations which prevented disabled persons from obtaining various job qualifications have been revised. In the meantime, the remaining regulations are being considered for revision.

In January 1995, the Convenience Facilities Installation Act was formulated to provide disabled persons with increased access to buildings and facilities. In April 1997, the Convenience Promotion Law for Disabled, Elderly, and Pregnant Women was enacted to secure social access for disabled persons, including older persons and pregnant women, and not only to physical facilities, but also to legal facilities. With the enactment, and revisions of laws and regulations, the Government of the Republic of Korea established legal provisions to improve the welfare of disabled persons.

3. Information

The Republic of Korea has constructed an integrated information network for the rehabilitation of disabled persons by operating the rehabilitation information centre and conducting national surveys on disabled persons every five years, to collect and use more accurate and expansive data on the conditions of disabled persons. In the future, the Republic of Korea plans to collect information and data concerning disabled women and disabled persons in the rural areas, as the Economic and Social Commission for Asia and the Pacific (ESCAP) has emphasized. The Republic of Korea also plans to exchange information and data with other countries in the Asian and Pacific region.

Since 1980, national surveys have been conducted on disabled persons every five years to collect basic data for efficient welfare policy measures for disabled persons. The survey results have given broad information on the number and characteristics of disabled persons, and facts on various types of disability. The data is used for establishing long- and mid-term welfare development plans and programmes.

The Republic of Korea is operating an integrated network to provide immobile persons with disability with information and the necessary services at home, such as those related to remote consultation, education and public administration.

The Korean Public Broadcasting Company (KBS) started a special channel for disabled persons entitled Voice of Love in December 1995, which uses sign language and explanatory captions to provide information to persons with disabilities. Specialized libraries for visually disabled persons are financially supported by the government. All these were set up to increase access to information by persons with disabilities.

4. Public awareness

The Republic of Korea will endeavour to improve public awareness of disabled persons through cultural events, sports, mass media activities, institutional provisions, and education.

The country has designated 20 April as the Day of Persons with Disability, to increase public awareness of disabled persons and to enhance love and concern for them. There will be various events, including arts and sports events, festivals, meetings, and competitions to encourage the active participation of persons with disabilities in social activities and to remove society's prejudice towards disabled persons.

In April 1996, approximately 230 organizations and agencies participated in a Disabled-Person-First-Campaign which was organized to encourage citizens to pay more attention to the concerns of disabled persons. On the International Day of Disabled Persons (3 December), the Government of the Republic of Korea awarded prizes and honours to organizations and agencies with high achievements in promoting public awareness of disability issues. In addition, cultural activities, such as song festivals and performances by art groups of disabled persons, were organized and were well received by the general public.

Various mass media, including television, radio, and film, have produced programmes concerning disabled persons. Three main television companies broadcast daily news with sign language on screen. In addition, the special channel, Voice of Love in December 1995 gave inspiration as well as information to disabled persons. There has even been a case of a visually disabled student appearing in a television commercial.

The Republic of Korea has revised 37 regulations to ease restrictions on the participation of disabled persons in social activities. Several men of distinction, such as ministers, congressmen, and lawyers, have appeared on television. They have participated in disability simulation exercises to enhance understanding of persons with disabilities. Currently, a few disabled persons are working in high government positions. Meanwhile, city and provincial authorities have set up disability funds and decreased taxes and public fees for disabled persons to financially support them. Local governments also accord disabled persons priority and concession when installing vending machines at public sites.

5. Accessibility and communication

In January 1995, the Convenience Facilities Installation Act for Disabled Persons was enacted by the Government of Republic of Korea to increase the access for disabled persons to buildings and other premises, and to provide them with a comfortable environment. The Act stipulates that it is compulsory for public buildings and other premises to install convenience facilities for disabled persons. Accordingly, buildings and other premises such as parks, government offices, schools, department stores, and religious facilities must install access facilities during construction, as well as during reconstruction or renovation. Installation of convenience facilities must also be reflected in various urban planning projects, as well as direct and indirect investment businesses.

Bus stations and subway stations are gradually installing access facilities to increase the mobility of disabled persons. Currently, disabled persons are exempted from paying subway fares and are given discounts of 50 per cent on railway and air fares.

Welfare centres and welfare facilities have special vehicles for extensively disabled persons who have difficulty in using public transportation. Some local governments provide special transportation services for them.

Considering a car as an assistive device in a broad sense, the Government of the Republic of Korea reduces car-related taxes for disabled persons to decrease their economic burden.

Three main broadcasting companies in the Republic of Korea use sign language on the daily news and during televised national ceremonies. The Association of Deaf Persons plans to offer a sign language qualification examination in October 1997.

With a view to reducing barriers in communication among disabled persons, the Government of the Republic of Korea has installed more than 5,000 telephone booths, with discounts of 50 per cent for domestic telephone calls for disabled persons.

6. Education

The country has a strong commitment towards achieving the basic objectives of education for disabled persons. In this context, special education for disabled children was expanded with the amendment of the Special Education Promotion Law and with a reorganization of the Ministry of Education. Ultimately, the Republic of Korea will secure the right of education for persons with disabilities through various policy measures: increasing educational opportunities for disabled children; developing proper job training programmes; constructing social networks with inter-ministerial cooperation; and supporting life-long educational welfare management systems.

In 1994, the Special Education Promotion Law was fully amended, greatly expanding educational opportunities and increasing the quality of education for disabled persons. With the amendment, the newly-established Bureau of Special Education for Disabled Persons became concerned with the social welfare services and educational affairs of disabled children and youth.

Special classes and special schools have been opened for disabled children and home-based education is given by special teachers for immobile children with extensive disability. In addition, specific vocational education and training are provided for disabled youth who aspire to obtain jobs.

The Ministry of Education has developed and disseminated educational materials and allocated consultants and teachers to ensure the quality of special education for children and youth with disabilities.

7. Training and employment

The Employment Promotion Law for Disabled Persons focuses on enabling disabled persons to obtain employment opportunities. The Republic of Korea is providing financial and institutional support for the construction and management of sheltered workshops and work sites where persons with extensive disabilities are employed. Therefore, to facilitate the employment of disabled persons in the future, the country will continue to support the construction of the vocational capability evaluation system, the improvement of the work environment, the use of campaigns and advertisements, and the expansion of vocational rehabilitation of persons with extensive disabilities.

The Republic of Korea enacted the Employment Promotion Law for Disabled Persons in 1990. Based on this Law, the Government of Republic of Korea has stipulated that it is compulsory that work sites with more than 300 workers must employ disabled persons to the extent of more than two per cent of the total number of employees. Under this regulation, the public sector has a leading role in employing disabled persons.

The Government of the Republic of Korea has also supported 128 sheltered workshops and seven work sites which provide vocational training and employment for persons with extensive disabilities. Four markets in the country are operated to sell products from these workshops. In addition, it has provided financial support for the construction of the first goodwill industry and has provided subsidies and bonuses to raise the spirits of disabled persons, thus strengthening the base for their employment. It has also introduced a networking system among vocational rehabilitation facilities. Several recruitment fairs have also been held and a few public films have been produced in order to improve public awareness of disabled persons.

8. Prevention of causes of disability

To prevent causes of disability, the Republic of Korea has followed to a large extent the recommendations of the Asian and Pacific Decade Agenda for Action in the six fields: information, education, communication, health, safety, and consumption. For this, the country has strengthened education, campaigns to raise awareness of disabled persons, mother and child health (MCH) programmes, traffic safety and industrial safety, as well as the provision of medical treatment at the right time to prevent causes of disability.

The concerned ministry has emphasized MCH programmes for early detection and treatment of diseases at its early stage. Health centres have distributed booklets for pregnant women, and provided regular health examinations of infants and siblings, and regular vaccinations for them. Since early 1997, all new-born babies have received congenital abnormality tests free of charge.

Anti-smoking and anti-drinking publicity materials have been produced and distributed to promote prevention of diseases of adults and older persons. Fluoride tooth-brushing programmes have been carried out in primary schools, and the Government of the Republic of Korea is promoting a 10-year cancer conquest plan, and running a counselling and management programme for older persons with dementia.

The Republic of Korea established the Third Traffic Safety Plan (1992-1996) and the Fourth Traffic Safety Plan (1997-2001), to provide an institutional framework for the early prevention of traffic accidents. It has also tried to promote traffic safety through social education, the mass media and related materials.

The Industrial Safety Enhancement Planning Board, which includes many experts from the government, industrial relations organizations, academic fields, and journalism, was formed to discuss the prevention of industrial accidents. In 1996, the Board published the three-year industrial safety enhancement plan targeting eight issues such as safety at work sites. The Industrial Safety Health Law was amended to improve the current industrial safety and health system in December 1996.

Approximately 330 hospitals have been designated as emergency agencies. These agencies operate emergency care systems 24 hours a day by establishing emergency centres to receive calls. They have also developed special ambulances for the treatment of patients. First aid and other special training will be given to those employees involved in treating emergency patients with disabilities.

9. Rehabilitation services

Welfare policies for disabled persons worldwide have been gradually directed toward community-based rehabilitation (CBR) services, as opposed to institution-based services. The Republic of Korea is also expanding home-based rehabilitation services so that disabled persons are able to receive care, education, and vocational training services at home.

Throughout the country, 43 welfare centres have been opened for disabled persons, providing counselling, treatment, education, training, leisure and sports for them. Eighteen centres have been opened for those with audio-visual disabilities as of 1997. In addition, there are 13 special gymnasiums and sports halls for disabled persons to help in their functional recovery and rehabilitation. Fourteen rehabilitation hospitals are operated solely for this purpose.

In 1996, 10 day-care centres and short-term care centres were established to provide temporary care for disabled persons at home. Since 1997, the Government of the Republic of Korea has operated five homes, where several disabled persons who could not receive appropriate care at other institutions live together.

As a policy measure of CBR programmes, the Government of the Republic of Korea has been establishing volunteer centres at welfare centres for disabled persons since 1994, the number of which reached 28 in 1997.

Three volunteer workers at the volunteer centre provide disabled persons at home with comprehensive rehabilitation services, including vocational education, counselling, medical services, such as physical treatment, nursing, and disability diagnosis. The volunteer centre plays a key role in the provision of CBR services through cooperation with health centres, social workers at local government offices, and mobile treatment teams in the community.

10. Assistive devices

The Republic of Korea has taken various measures to promote the production and dissemination of assistive devices, including free distribution, and supporting manufacturers with tax exemption. In the near future, the Republic of Korea will amend laws and regulations related to assistive devices, systematically managing the production of assistive devices by introducing official notification of items, and conducting research and development on assistive devices.

During the early period of the Asian and Pacific Decade of Disabled Persons, institutional provisions and financial support were so inadequate that only some disabled persons received assistive devices free of charge and they were not exempted from tax and duties.

However, the Government of the Republic of Korea has started to intensify efforts in improving the quality and distribution of assistive devices needed by disabled persons. A survey on the needs and distribution of assistive devices was conducted in 1995, while in 1997 another survey was conducted with manufacturers on government policy implications for them concerning assistive devices.

Since 1995, the Government of the Republic of Korea has paid close attention to the research and development of assistive devices by supporting the research and development programme of health care techniques and G-7 medical techniques development programme to develop high technology devices that conform with the physical conditions of Koreans. As health insurance covers the free or low-cost provision of crutches, hearing aids, orthotics, and artificial larynx, all disabled persons can afford to use these devices.

11. Self-help organizations

The Republic of Korea actively supports programmes which are appropriate to each organization and foundation pertaining to the welfare of disabled persons and with systematic cooperation among ministries. In future, the country plans to expand and strengthen the support for existing organizations to facilitate the activities of self-help organizations of persons with disabilities, and cultivate cooperation among those organizations. The needs of disabled persons will also be reflected in policy measures and their implementation.

Numerous organizations and foundations are active in various fields in trying to improve the quality of disabled persons' lives. Among them, 126 foundations are mainly voluntary organizations helping disabled persons, while others help disabled persons gain employment. All members of organizations and foundations have annual meetings to discuss their programmes.

Responding to the increased needs of disabled persons, the programmes of the organizations and foundations are diverse and include employment, rehabilitation, medical care, education and training, arts and culture, leisure and sports, family support, incentives and allowances. Central and local governments provide support for organizations and foundations to ensure that they carry out their programmes successfully.

C. Activities planned for the second half of the Asian and Pacific Decade of Disabled Persons

1. National coordination

The Welfare Policy Committee for Disabled Persons will actively carry out a five-year welfare development plan for disabled persons with cooperation from the concerned ministries. Those ministries will also implement systematic and efficient policy measures for the plan in the next five years.

The Executive Committee, composed of Directors-General of several ministerial bureaus, will contribute to the development of the welfare of disabled persons in the long term. It will operate as a national coordinator, encouraging the active participation of NGO representatives, systematic cooperation between government agencies, and between government agencies and the private sector, to ensure the effective implementation of policy measures.

2. Legislation

The narrow definition of disability will gradually be broadened. The Republic of Korea plans to establish a law which will include chronic heart diseases, kidney diseases, and mental disorders in the current definition of disability. The country also plans to construct more access facilities to ease restrictions on the social participation of disabled persons as a preparation for the implementation of the Convenience Promotion Law.

3. Information

The Republic of Korea will build a disability statistical database and provide basic data for information exchange in the Asian and Pacific region by adding statistics on disabled women and disabled persons in the rural areas during the national survey on disabled persons to be conducted in 2000.

The country plans to connect the Internet and various internal networks of social security services to increase the use of information on rehabilitation. It will also make available statistics and information on disability so that they are easily accessed by people.

4. Public awareness

The Republic of Korea plans to establish the Association for Campaigning for Disabled Persons, which will plan an annual campaign and monitor campaign activities. Documentaries and public advertisements concerned with the welfare of persons with disabilities will also be produced.

The curriculum of primary and secondary schools includes information on disabled persons to enhance the awareness of youth towards disabled persons. The concerned ministry will coordinate more systematically volunteers from primary and secondary schools who can interact with disabled persons. The Republic of Korea will also create a social environment in which disabled persons live harmoniously with non-disabled persons in the community. Companies are encouraged to include disability issues in their in-house training programmes.

5. Accessibility and communication

As the Convenience Promotion Law for Disabled, Elderly, and Pregnant Women is to come into effect after April 1998, the Government of the Republic of Korea will provide technical, financial and tax support for the installation of access facilities and will levy penalties for failure to comply with the law. Along with this, the access facilities installation programme will be fully implemented until 2002.

Currently, the Government of the Republic of Korea is reviewing the formulation of guidelines to secure access by disabled persons to information and communication.

6. Education

The focus of future policy is directed toward a shift from the enrolment of only young children to the expansion of educational benefits for all disabled children in need of special education. Thus, the Republic of Korea will acquire a model of educational welfare for disabled children which reflects the reality of persons with disabilities in Korean society.

Policy measures include the provision of a welfare network for life-long educational support, construction of educational information centres, and expansion of benefits according to degrees and types of disabilities.

In addition, a special division, which is in charge of vocational training of disabled youth, will be set up in the concerned ministry. Furthermore, the division will develop specific vocational programmes, suited to different degrees and types of disabilities, and emphasize field experiences at work sites.

7. Training and employment

The country will establish 15 vocational capability assessment centres to encourage the vocational skills development of disabled persons by the year 2000. An integrated computer network will be built by 2001 to support organizations concerned with job placement activities for disabled persons.

To develop disabled persons' vocational capabilities, the Republic of Korea will construct two vocational rehabilitation centres for the training of 200 disabled persons annually. Public vocational schools and private vocational training offices will also be established, and financial support for sheltered workshops for persons with extensive disabilities will be strengthened.

The Republic of Korea will provide subsidies or incentives to work sites that employ more disabled persons than is required under the compulsory quota, and will provide loans at low interest or no interest for the construction of facilities.

Various measures will be continuously implemented to improve public awareness, including the employment promotion month for disabled persons, the national and local disabled persons skill competitions, and incentive schemes for successful results in international skills competition.

Trainers will be assigned to sheltered workshops and incentives or allowances will be paid to persons with extensive disabilities. In particular, vocational rehabilitation services will be provided for disabled persons who are cared for at home through subsidizing food and transportation expenses. More centres will be opened for the sale of products from these workshops.

8. Prevention of the causes of disability

Follow-up medical tests which are currently limited to infants of low-income households will be extended to cover all infants. In addition, programmes for the prevention of adulthood diseases will be strengthened. The three-year industrial safety enhancement plan will be promoted to decrease the industrial accident rate to below 1 per cent, and the Fourth Traffic Safety Plan will be carried out to lower the number of traffic accidents. In this context, a national emergency centre will be established by the year 2001 as a prerequisite for the comprehensive emergency system.

9. Rehabilitation services

The Republic of Korea, a member of the Organization for Economic Cooperation and Development, has a strong commitment towards achieving a welfare society for disabled persons. In this context, the country will encourage CBR services. Budget allocation and systematic cooperation among the concerned ministries are prerequisites for the success of the programme.

The Government of Republic of Korea plans to establish 145 welfare centres, 26 special centres according to disability types, 165 community rehabilitation centres, and 31 gymnasiums, in addition to the existing facilities. Professional research institutions should be established to develop special rehabilitation programmes, and the training of personnel in rehabilitation services should be introduced.

10. Assistive devices

The Government of the Republic of Korea will speed up the distribution of assistive devices to all disabled persons free of charge or at low prices. It will introduce an official notification system of assistive devices and establish research institutes and centres. It also plans to lessen the economic hardship of disabled persons by extending insurance coverage to all items, including artificial limbs and wheelchairs. The majority of assistive devices will be fitted at junior colleges to enable their technicians to deepen their knowledge of assistive devices and of the production techniques.

The analysis of the result of the industry survey on assistive devices will help establish an assistive devices system by the year 2002.

11. Self-help organizations

The Republic of Korea will support organizations of mentally disabled persons and those with internal diseases under the revised definition of disability, and will provide financial support to the existing organizations.

The country plans to carry out various rehabilitation programmes for different disability types. To achieve this, more sheltered workshops will be constructed for those with extensive disabilities. Counselling of families with disabled persons will be provided, and half-way houses and day-care or short-term care centres will be built for those with mental disability.

The Government of the Republic of Korea will build and run sign language centres for persons with hearing impairments. For those with visual disabilities, special teacher qualification tests will be supported financially and errand centres and support centres will be established. All these policy measures are expected to help solve the difficulties faced by disabled persons in their social life.

CHAPTER XXIII

Sri Lanka

A. National overview

Sri Lanka established the National Coordinating Committee on Disabled in the 1980s in its Ministry of Social Welfare, with other ministries and other organizations involved in the activities related to people with disabilities. However, the committee did not make much headway, even though an attempt was made in 1989 to activate it. It was revived in 1991, and was reconstituted and activated in 1994 under the Ministry of Social Services.

B. Progress made in the first half of the Asian and Pacific Decade of Disabled Persons

1. National coordination

In 1996, Sri Lanka formed the National Council for Persons with Disabilities in the Ministry of Health, Highways and Social Services. The council comprises 12 members and is appointed by the President of Sri Lanka. The council members are representatives from government, including local and provincial authorities, self-help organizations of people with disabilities as well as other professional groups. The main tasks of the council are to promote, advance and protect the rights of disabled persons in the country.

2. Legislation

In 1996, the Parliament of Sri Lanka passed an Act to Protect the Rights of People with Disabilities. The legislation was based on the basis of the recommendations contained in the Agenda for Action for the Asian and Pacific Decade of Disabled Persons, 1993-2002 (hereafter referred to as the Asian and Pacific Decade Agenda for Action).

3. Information

A National Secretariat for People with Disabilities was established on 3 December 1995 to coincide with the International Day of Disabled Persons. One of the tasks of the Secretariat is to develop a national data bank and a resource centre for collecting and disseminating information. The Asian and Pacific Decade Agenda for Action and the Standard Rules on the Equalization of Opportunities for Disabled Persons have been translated into the local languages and disseminated to government agencies and non-governmental organizations. Steps have also been taken to teach sign language and Braille to government officials, thus enabling them to communicate with hearing-impaired persons and blind persons.

4. Public awareness

The International Day of Disabled Persons is commemorated annually by the Ministry of Social Services with the aim of promoting awareness among the general public and to eradicate negative attitudes towards persons with disabilities. The Sri Lankan print and electronic media have also provided much coverage of the activities and issues related to the World Programme of Action concerning Disabled Persons and the Asian and Pacific Decade Agenda for Action. In addition, the country also promotes the causes of people with disabilities through workshops, seminars, various sports events for disabled persons and during national occasions such as New Year's Day.

5. Accessibility and communication

The Government of Sri Lanka has formed a committee to draft legislation on accessibility. A number of seminars and meetings have been held to prepare this piece of legislation, which will provide the facilities enumerated in the Asian and Pacific Decade Agenda for Action. Recently, a sound signal system was introduced on the country's roads, and this has benefited visually-impaired persons.

6. Education

In Sri Lanka, children with disabilities undergo a special education programme that helps integrate them into the mainstream education system. In certain primary schools, the children are examined by medical professionals to detect impairment and are treated as early as possible. The National Institute of Education has special facilities for teacher training and curricula development to provide education to children with disabilities.

Recently, much effort was made in establishing pre-schools for children who are hearing-impaired. The National Institute of Education has also started a training programme for pre-school teachers on education for children with hearing impairments.

Special arrangements have also been made to develop educational facilities for disabled children in several schools run by non-governmental organizations (NGOs). These arrangements are in accordance with the Asian and Pacific Decade Agenda for Action. In the mainstream education system, action is being taken to develop Braille textbooks and a team of researchers are working on developing a curriculum in sign language for hearing-impaired persons.

7. Training and employment

Both government and non-governmental vocational training institutes in the country provide various training courses for people with disabilities. Special programmes providing pre-vocational training are also in place at special schools and units.

Vocational training is being provided in 26 trades where there are openings for gainful employment. The government has decided to allocate 3 per cent of public sector employment to people with disabilities. In addition, an inter-ministerial committee was set up to seek out and match employment opportunities in the public sector for persons with disabilities. A similar job-search service is being offered for employment opportunities in the private sector. Steps are being taken to provide employment for people with disabilities, in accordance with the recommendations in the Asian and Pacific Decade Agenda for Action.

8. Prevention of the causes of disability

A technical committee is currently developing the national policies and programmes on the prevention of the causes of disabilities. These policies will be incorporated into the national health plan, which the Ministry of Health is formulating. The Ministry of Heath is currently implementing a separate programme on the prevention of blindness and another for hearing impairment is also under way.

9. Rehabilitation services

In 1992, the Ministry of Health introduced the national programme for community-based rehabilitation (CBR), which aims to identify each and every person with disability in the country and to provide rehabilitation services for those who need them.

It is implemented through the various division secretariats in the country. So far it has been introduced in 110 divisions out of a total of 260. The number of disabled persons identified is 61,363. In some divisions, the CBR programme is implemented by NGOs. The Ministry of Health aims to fully implement the CBR programme countrywide before 2000. It is also in the process of expanding rehabilitation centres for persons with disabilities who need life-time care as well as conducting special training programmes for care-givers. A rehabilitation centre is also being set up in each province to provide such services.

The CBR programme is funded by the state and amounts to the following in the annual budget:

Year	1995	1996	1997	Total
SL Rs (in millions)	15	18	18	51

10. Assistive devices

The country provides, free of charge, devices such as wheelchairs, tricycles, spectacles, artificial limbs, hearing aids and Braille equipment to needy disabled persons. These are supplemented by NGOs and donors. Plans are underway to educate manufacturers to produce such devices, according to the special needs of persons with disabilities and to introduce new technology in this area.

11. Self-help organizations

In Sri Lanka, self-help organizations of persons with disabilities are encouraged to expand their services. Both the Ministries of Social Services and of Education work very closely with the self-help organizations that serve blind persons, deaf persons, physically disabled persons, persons with intellectual disabilities and psychiatrically disabled persons. Such self-help organizations are fostered and encouraged.

12. Regional cooperation

Sri Lanka actively participates in promoting, facilitating and sharing its experiences with other countries through various regional training programmes and conferences.

Some of the activities include:

(a) "International Training Course on CBR" held in 1993, 1994 and 1995 organized by the Disabilities Studies Unit of the medical faculty of Kelaniya University: a total of 65 participants from 22 countries in Asia, Africa and South America attended these courses; in October 1997, the university will conduct the WHO regional course on CBR for the South-east Asian and Western Pacific regions;

(b) Training of Japanese and Malaysian CBR personnel in India and of Indonesian personnel in Sri Lanka. The international training programme is also conducted in Sri Lanka;

(c) Setting up of the South Asian CBR network office in Sri Lanka to facilitate regional cooperation;

(d) Holding of the one-day "CBR Network" national workshop;

(e) Hosting of the South Asian CBR network meeting in September 1997;

(f) Hosting of the Bi-regional Social World Conference in 1994, in which participants shared their experiences on the provision of rehabilitation services for persons with disabilities;

(g)　Hosting of a subregional workshop on inclusive education;

(h)　Organization of the 12th Asian Conference (September 1995) by the Ceylon Association of Mental Retardation for the Asian Federation on Mental Retardation; there were 500 participants, half of them from overseas;

(i)　Participation of two representatives in the conference of the Asian Blind Union held in 1994, 1995 and 1996;

(j)　Participation by blind athletes in Abilympics in Australia; they win medals every year;

(k)　Hosting of the World Blind Union Officers Meeting in Sri Lanka in February 1997.

C.　Activities planned for the second half of the Asian and Pacific Decade of Disabled Persons

1.　Policy measures

Sri Lanka's plan of action for the second half of the Asian and Pacific Decade of Disabled Persons will be developed based on past experiences as well as current expectations. The plan of action is still just a draft and has yet to be finalized by the country's newly-formed National Council for Persons with Disabilities. The plan is expected to be finalized in November 1997 and implementation scheduled to begin from January 1998.

When finalized, a committee comprising representatives from the state and provincial governments, private sector and NGOs will draft an implementation plan. A proposal will also be drawn up to secure funding in stages from the government, the World Health Organization and other international agencies.

2.　Information and public awareness

One of the aims of the proposed plan of action is to create public awareness of the needs and abilities of disabled persons and eradicate negative attitudes through implementing awareness programmes, highlighting the abilities of disabled persons through the electronic media and thus generate better appreciation of the abilities of disabled persons. The country can achieve this aim through the following:

(a)　Maintaining a unit where all information about disabled persons is available;

(b)　Broadcasting on television and radio singing, music and dancing programmes meant for persons with disabilities;

(c) Implementing awareness programmes for school teachers with the aim of developing optimistic attitudes towards children with disabilities;

(d) Creating awareness in various institutions such as the urban, road and housing development authorities, the electricity board, ministries of transport and of the mass media, and stress to them the importance of the need to provide special facilities for persons with disabilities;

(e) Issuing first-day covers and stamps;

(f) Holding exhibitions, cultural shows and sports meets to highlight the talents of persons with disabilities;

(g) Presenting awards to talented disabled persons;

(h) Producing television and radio programmes to eradicate the undesirable attitudes that society has towards people with disabilities;

(i) Creating public awareness of mental health problems, controlling the incidence of mental illness and promoting caring for persons with intellectual disability;

(j) Organizing a national mental health week.

3. Accessibility and communication

Sri Lanka's plan of action also aims to create a barrier-free environment for disabled persons. The country plans to achieve this objective by:

(a) Providing access facilities for entry into public buildings and moving about in these buildings and other places: these can be achieved by including the standards for access facilities when preparing plans to construct, repair and upgrade buildings and highways;

(b) Providing enough leeway for the convenient use of pavements and highways and public transport services: these include reserving seats in buses and trains for disabled persons;

(c) Installing signal lights for hearing-impaired persons in public places such as banks, railway stations, airport and hospitals;

(d) Introducing an easy communication system for both hearing- and visually-impaired persons;

(e) Teaching the importance of and need to provide access facilities for disabled persons in the curricula of architects, engineers, and town and country planners;

(f) Legislating into the existing by-laws the provision of access facilities for disabled persons;

(g) Encouraging training in the use of sign language.

4. Education

The plan of action also aims to provide an adequate education for children with disabilities. The government intends to implement these measures to achieve its goal:

(a) Expand pre-school education to include deaf children;

(b) Provide early childhood education facilities for children with intellectual disabilities;

(c) Establish in ordinary schools classes for children with special needs;

(d) Take action to make It more convenient for children who use wheelchairs to receive an education;

(e) Provide educational facilities that can cater to the specific needs of people with disabilities;

(f) Include social education in teacher training courses;

(g) Reserve a certain percentage of places in universities and technical colleges for students with disabilities;

(h) Provide Braille printing machines in schools for blind persons.

5. Rehabilitation services

The country plans to achieve the following under its plan of action:

(a) Operate, at the national level, a community-based programme for the rehabilitation of persons with disabilities and develop this into the main policy on the issue;

(b) Implement a special financial aid system for people with disabilities by establishing funds for their rehabilitation at the divisional secretary level. The scheme could subsidise SL Rs300 per month for those who are extensively disabled;

(c) Provide homes for disabled persons who need residential care: this includes establishing homes at the provincial level for persons with extensive or mental disabilities, or people with multiple disabilities who cannot be looked after by their family members; housing relief assistance can also be provided to families where the head of the household is a disabled person;

(d) Organize leadership skills training and empowerment courses with disabled persons themselves as trainers;

(d) Set up rehabilitation centres at the central and provincial levels for those recovering from mental illness;

(e) Provide accommodation for persons who have recovered from mental disorders, but are not ready to go back to their families, or do not have families to go back to;

(f) Set up a half-way house in coordination with the mental hospitals of Angoda and Mulleriyawa. Private sector and NGOs can be involved in this scheme.

6. Assistive devices

Sri Lanka's plan of action aims to provide the adequate assistive devices to low income-earning disabled persons, encourage the local production of assistive devices and to equip manufacturers with the technical know-how to produce these devices. The country aims to achieve this by:

(a) Providing free assistive devices such as wheelchairs, tricycles, spectacles, hearing aids, artificial limbs, callipers, white canes and Braille equipment to all low income earning disabled persons, especially taking into account the individual's age and the disability type;

(b) Conducting research on the production of assistive devices and vehicles for people with disabilities;

(c) Establishing institutions to produce assistive devices and giving them tax relief and assistance;

(d) Providing technical know-how to the assistive device producers and showcasing their products.

7. Self-help organizations

(a) Set up a committee to coordinate the activities of the NGOs;

(b) Build up and encourage the empowerment of self-help organizations of persons with disabilities;

(c) Encourage the setting up of self-help organizations of disabled persons at the divisional level.

CHAPTER XXIV

Thailand

A. National overview

Thailand covers an area of 198,000 square miles. Its population reached 60 million in 1996, and is still growing at a rate of 1.1 per cent per year. Geographically, the country comprises four regions: the mountainous north, the central plain, a semi-arid plateau in the Northeast and the peninsula in the south. The capital is Bangkok and one in 10 Thais lives in the city. Bangkok is the largest city in the country, about 45 times larger than Chiang Mai, the second most populous city.

The country is governed by a constitutional monarchy with the King as Head of State. Buddhism is the state religion and its values are fundamental in Thai society and life. Although most Thais are Buddhist, religious freedom is warmly embraced in the country. As Head of State, the King is also the patron of all religions. Thai is the national and official language and it has its own distinctive written form and dialects.

In Thailand, 70 per cent of the total population live in the rural areas while the rest live in cities or urban areas. Its population density is about 98 per square kilometre. The life expectancy for a male is 67.7 years while that for a female is 72.4 years.

There are three groups of administrative governments, namely central, provincial and local administration. The administrative units are a hierarchy of village, subdistrict, and province and the country is currently undergoing the decentralization of political, social and economic powers.

An agrarian nation, Thailand is agriculturally self-sufficient. Most of the economic and social developments began in the early 1960s. The country has, since then, undergone seven national economic and social development plans. Thailand also diversified its economy and boosted its agricultural exports, industries and manufacturing. From the late 1980s to the early 1990s, the manufacturing and trade portion of its gross domestic product almost tripled that of agriculture.

Over the past 30 years, the Thais have seen vast changes in their quality of lives and many are enjoying more material comforts. However, rural poverty is still the most pressing problem and the lives of the impoverished, including disabled persons, have yet to show signs of improvement.

Although a number of statistical studies and surveys of people with disabilities had been conducted in the past, the classification of disability adopted in these exercises is limited and also tended to be medically oriented. Hence, it remains questionable whether the samples collected represent the real overall picture of disabled people in Thailand.

In 1991, together with the Ministry of Public Health, the National Statistical Office conducted another survey of people with disabilities in the country. In this survey, there were two classifications for disability, one as a medical condition and the other as a social one.

The first classified disability for treatment and rehabilitation purposes, while the second perceived disability as physical and psychological abnormalities that may be a burden or problem for society.

The survey reported that there were about 1.1 million people with disabilities in Thailand, or around 1.8 per cent of the then total population of 57 million. Out of this figure, 1.1 per cent were male and 0.7 per cent were female.

In terms of distribution, the survey showed that the majority of people with disabilities, some 38.6 per cent, resided in the northeast followed by the north, with 23.5 per cent. As these regions are considered to be the two poorest areas in Thailand, it is assumed that there is a certain correlation between poverty and disability.

In addition, it was observed that there were fewer people with disabilities in the municipal or urban areas than in the non-municipal or rural areas. In the municipal areas, there were 1.2 per cent of people with disabilities compared with 2 per cent in the rural areas.

On the various types of disability, the survey ranked the following starting with the most common:

(a) Limb disability at 19.6 per cent;

(b) Hearing impairment at 13.2 per cent;

(c) Intellectual disability at 10 per cent;

(d) Speech impairment at 5.4 per cent;

(e) Visual impairment at 1.9 per cent.

In terms of age groups, most people with disabilities were aged 60 and above, followed by teenagers and adolescents, with most of their conditions assumed to be resulting from traffic accidents. In addition, the survey found that 64.9 per cent or 713,000 people with disabilities were of working age.

B. Progress made in the first half of the Asian and Pacific Decade of Disabled Persons

1. National coordination

Giving help and support to people with disabilities is part of the Thai way of living. The kind of help offered is generally in the form of mutual aid.

The country's welfare services for disabled persons started in 1941, where the residential home for people with disabilities was established in Samut Prakarn province, near Bangkok. In the early days, people with extensive disabilities who were discharged from hospitals and those who had broken the Beggary Control Act, 1941, would stay in the home. There, they were offered services that met their basic need, for food, clothing, medical care and accommodation.

In 1968, under the supervision of the International Labour Organization, the first vocational rehabilitation centre for people with disabilities was set up in Samut Prakarn. The centre provided vocational training in various fields. Soon after, the Pak Kred sheltered workshop was also set up.

People with disabilities in Thailand were also provided for in the four major areas: medical, educational, occupational and social rehabilitation. In addition there are also various government and non-government task forces set up to provide these services.

(a) The National Committee for the Rehabilitation of Disabled Persons

The 1991 Rehabilitation of Disabled Persons Act stated that Thailand should set up a National Committee for the Rehabilitation of Disabled Persons to be headed by the Minister of Labour and Social Welfare.

Committee members include the Permanent Secretaries of the Ministries of Defence, Labour and Social Welfare, Education, Public Health and University Affairs, the Director of the Budget Bureau, the Directors-General of the Departments of Medical Services, Public Welfare, General Education and not more than six others appointed by the Minister of Labour and Social Welfare.

The minister must also appoint not fewer than two qualified persons representing disabled people's organizations.

The committee will propose and recommend to the minister, the policies and plans involving the assistance, development and rehabilitation of people with disabilities.

These recommendations and proposals will then be submitted to the Cabinet for approval. After that, the committee will designate to the concerned government organizations, the tasks of implementing these recommendations.

In addition, the committee also gives advice to, supports and promotes the work of non-profit private organizations, prepares and approves projects, sets up regulations to ensure compliance with the Act and carries out other matters as designated by the minister.

There is also an initiative to establish subcommittees at the provincial level and other subcommittees that look into specific issues, including medicine, education and community-based rehabilitation. As it is in line with the government's decentralization plan, the work at the provincial levels is given more attention.

2. Legislation

In 1979, Thailand started drafting the Rehabilitation of Disabled Persons Act to protect the rights of people with disabilities and also provided standards for workers. The Act finally became law more than 10 years later in 1991. The Act enhances and protects the rights of people with disabilities and also provides for their development and rehabilitation.

Under the Act, people with disabilities have rights to the following services: medical, educational and occupational rehabilitation, job placement and community support. However, disabled persons who wish to receive such services have to register.

3. Accessibility and communication

The Government of Thailand is well aware of the difficulties faced by people with disabilities when travelling to schools, workplaces or for social activities.

It has already established a committee to draft regulations on accessibility. Committee members include experts in design and construction and people with disabilities. Their work is almost complete and details of the regulations will be announced soon.

In addition, the Committee for the Rehabilitation of Disabled Persons and self-help organizations of disabled persons are advocating together to ensure the access of disabled persons to the public transportation systems to be built in Thailand.

4. Education

According to the Act, people with disabilities are entitled to receive an education from pre-school to university levels.

In Thailand, the school system for disabled persons are divided into special schools for disabled persons (most are boarding schools) with a curriculum similar to general mainstream schools; mainstream schools where people with disabilities have the right to participate at all levels, up to tertiary level; and the non-formal education system in which there is no age limit on participants and whose classes can be initiated by volunteers.

Moreover, there are also classes in hospital for children with disabilities in chronic conditions. The country has also set up the following special education schools:

(a) Thirteen for children with hearing disabilities, 3,233 students;

(b) Eight for blind and low-vision children, 787 students;

(c) Eight for children with intellectual disabilities, 1,381 students;

(d) Two for children with physical disabilities, 463 students;

(e) Six for children with hearing disabilities and intellectual disabilities – separated into different special classes, 463 students;

(f) Five for children with visual disabilities, hearing disabilities and intellectual disabilities – separated into special classes, 1,000 students;

(g) Ten special classes in hospitals or residential homes or foundation, 6,824 students;

There are also 3,466 disabled children studying in more than 200 mainstream schools around the country.

5. Training and employment

There are now 16 government and private vocational training centres in Thailand. To ensure that people with disabilities get jobs, the 1991 Rehabilitation of Disabled Persons Act set up a quota system in the market – employers or private entrepreneurs hiring over 200 employees must employ one person with disability at the ratio of one disabled person for every 200 non-disabled employees.

The employer is entitled to claim twice the amount of wages paid to such persons, as expenses specified under the revenue code. However, if they do not wish to employ people with disabilities, they have to contribute to the National Fund for the Rehabilitation of Disabled Persons. There are now 5,031 people with disabilities working in 1,426 private companies.

All government organizations and public enterprises must employ people with disabilities. For those who prefer to start their own businesses, they can apply for a five-year no interest pay-back loan of not more than B20,000 from the Rehabilitation Fund for Disabled Persons.

On 12 July 1994, a Cabinet resolution declared that all vocational training institutions must accept students with disabilities.

6. Prevention of the causes of disability and rehabilitation services

The Ministry of Public Health has set up 13 kinds of medical rehabilitation services for people with disabilities. These services include diagnostic laboratory examination and other types of special examination, counselling, medicine, surgery, medical rehabilitation and nursing care, physical therapy, occupational therapy, behavioural therapy, psychotherapy, social services and therapy, speech, audio, hearing and communication therapies, and use of equipment or support machines.

The Ministry's policies and plans also focus on the prevention of disabilities. Its preventive programmes include family guidance for married couples about self-care, provision of information about diseases that cause disabilities and vaccination for babies.

There are also various campaigns to promote the use of safety belts in vehicles and the use of helmets by motorcyclists, to suggest the safe use of some toxic chemicals such as pesticides, and safe industrial practices, such as the use of sound protection equipment or light protection masks.

7. Self-help organizations

The Department of Public Welfare and the Association of the Physically Handicapped of Thailand support the setting up of disabled people's clubs at the provincial levels around the country. These clubs mainly provide leadership training courses. The Government of Thailand also contributes some financial support and resource personnel to these clubs.

CHAPTER XXV

Viet Nam

A. National overview

Currently, there are about 4.5 million people with disabilities, or roughly 6 per cent of the whole population in Viet Nam. Out of this, about 1.5 million face utmost difficulty in their daily lives because of their disabilities.

The Government of Viet Nam has, since the 1950s, adopted various specific policies and measures to care for people with disabilities. All its Constitutions in 1959, 1980 and 1992 have regulations that protect people with disabilities.

In 1992, in response to the proclamation of the Asian and Pacific Decade of Disabled Persons, 1993-2002, the Government of Viet Nam set up the Commission for People with Disabilities for the Asian and Pacific Decade of Disabled Persons. The following year, the Government signed the Proclamation on the Full Participation and Equality of People with Disabilities in the Asian and Pacific Region.

B. Progress made in the first half of the Asian and Pacific Decade of Disabled Persons

1. National coordination

In 1992, the country set up Viet Nam's Commission of Global Year for People with Disability. Its activities, which support people with disabilities have brought about important changes. Under one section, the proposed Disabilities Ordinance called for the establishment of a national committee for people with disabilities.

2. Legislation

The Government of Viet Nam has continuously enacted new laws, and expanded existing policies and regulations, for people with disabilities. On 23 June 1994, Viet Nam's National Assembly passed a new labour code. Four sections under this new code advocate the employment of people with disabilities. In addition, seven decrees and a number of circulars passed by the government also advocate and guide the implementation of the rights of people with disabilities in a range of issues, including social benefits, education, health care, assistive devices, rehabilitation, training, employment and business.

Three years later, on 29 June 1997, the Disabilities Ordinance, comprising nine chapters and 47 sections aimed at systemizing and institutionalizing existing documents for people with disabilities, was submitted to the National Assembly for approval.

3. Information and public awareness

In recent years, the mass media has increased its coverage of people with disabilities. There were special programmes produced and articles written on the subject. Coverage also included movies, exhibitions as well as literary activities such as traditional art, songs, dance and drama performed by people with disabilities. Such media coverage, the participants' own achievements and other activities have played an important role towards shaping the right public awareness and consciousness of people with disabilities.

To better help the country draft supporting policies and provide the fundamental data for the Disabilities Ordinance, from 1994 to 1995 Viet Nam's Ministry of War, Invalids and Social Affairs, carried out its first nationwide study of people with disabilities in 53 provinces and cities. In addition, the authorities also conducted in 1994 an in-depth study of the availability of orthopaedic equipment in the country.

4. Accessibility and communication

The Government of Viet Nam and the community in general, help provide an environment that allows people with disabilities to develop their creative potential in the arts, sciences and sports. They are encouraged to take part in all such activities and to participate in competitions both locally and inter-nationally.

Viet Nam's first sports and literary arts festival for people with disabilities held in 1997 at Quang Tri Province saw 600 participants. They, mainly officers, artists and athletes from 40 provinces and cities, took part in six sports and 60 literary arts events. The festival successfully demonstrated the determination of the people to overcome their disabilities and lead normal lives.

In terms of infrastructure, better telecommunication systems facilitated the means for people with disabilities to communicate, receive and disseminate information, and also enabled more of them to take up distant correspondence learning.

5. Education

The education programmes for people with disabilities are integrated with rehabilitation and job training, and are tailored to meet their needs depending on the seriousness of their conditions. Children with minor or mild disabilities do study in the same classes as other children. Those with sight and reading impairments are taught Braille, and sign language is taught to hearing-impaired students. Special schools and classes are set up for children with serious learning disabilities.

Currently, there are 69 schools with 421 classes providing elementary education for children with disabilities and they are aimed at helping them obtain stable jobs and to integrate them into the larger community. There are also 998 schools with 11,000 classes in 37 provinces and cities applying the integration education model in Viet Nam.

Children with disabilities whose families are facing financial difficulties are exempted, totally or partially, from paying school expenses and other contributions. Such benefits and grants are also applicable to those at universities, colleges and vocational training schools.

6. Training and employment

Since 1993, Viet Nam has enacted one law and three decrees, and proposed an ordinance, which promote the rights of people with disabilities to employment and vocational training. Under these reforms, people with disabilities are given vocational training and are exempted totally or partially from paying training fees.

Tax rebates are provided for institutions that provide training to people with disabilities and the government also gives them low-interest loans. In addition, these institutions are also granted land at choice locations to set up their training facilities. The government has set up educational facilities, purchases special training equipment and helps train personnel to teach at these institutions.

Every year, about 1,500 trainees graduate from 16 such training institutions. Besides these 16 institutions, there are hundreds of other training schools that offer courses to and places for people with disabilities. Under the law, administrative offices and economic sector enterprises must reserve suitable jobs for a certain number of people with disabilities. Currently there are about 400 such enterprises in the country.

These business enterprises are given tax rebates and can borrow low-interest loans. They are also given grants on infrastructure spending and offered land for their facilities at choice locations.

People with disabilities can borrow low-interest loans to set up their own small size enterprises. They are exempted from paying taxes and given free management and business consultations. To date, the National Fund has granted D12.127 billion to members of the Blind Association for 218 projects, thereby creating 13,994 jobs.

7. Prevention of the causes of disability

"A stitch in time saves nine" best sums up the Government of Viet Nam's determination to prevent disability. One aspect of this policy is to introduce measures to prevent the conditions from occurring and to lessen the situations that cause them. For example, the government is disseminating through the mass and printed media the causes of disability and some of the preventive measures people can take. It is also carrying out various programmes, including ante-, pre- and neo-natal care, early child health care and extensive vaccination against six diseases namely diphtheria, measles, polio, tetanus, tuberculosis and whooping cough.

The Government of Viet Nam is also executing various nationwide programmes to distribute iodized salt, supply clean and treated water and improve sanitary conditions. It is also setting up clinical points in every commune and precinct to provide better care and treatment for common diseases and to prevent the spread of epidemic ones. In addition, it has enacted laws on labour and transportation safety, sanitation, and environmental protection. These efforts have resulted in reducing the number of people with disabilities, especially when 70 per cent of the cases are due to congenital disability and caused by diseases.

8. Rehabilitation Services

The Government of Viet Nam is determined to provide benefits and help to people with disabilities, enabling them to live in the community and with their families as well as to lessen the woes of those living in nursing homes. It grants monthly social benefits to those with extensive disabilities and who have neither income nor dependable support, or who otherwise have relatives who are too old or poor to help them. The new disabilities ordinance aims to provide higher levels of aid to people with disabilities.

Government clinics nationwide provide medical care and rehabilitation for people with disabilities. Depending on their financial resources and the seriousness of their conditions, they are granted health insurance and are treated according to their needs. Those with serious mental conditions are treated and cared for at other specialist clinics.

9. Assistive devices

The Government of Viet Nam provides orthopaedic equipment and rehabilitation services for people with disabilities. Those facing financial difficulties are granted total or partial assistance in the purchase of orthopaedic and rehabilitation equipment. Since 1993, a total of 245,000 children with disabilities have been rehabilitated and given orthopaedic treatment, with 550 wheelchairs provided for them.

Recently, Viet Nam established the Scientific Institute of Orthopaedic Surgery and Rehabilitation with 13 orthopaedic surgery and rehabilitation centres nationwide. The government sponsored various scientific research projects on people with disabilities and trained orthopaedic and rehabilitation experts.

The government offers low-interest loans to enterprises that produce auxiliary aids for people with disabilities. There are also no import taxes on professional materials, assistive devices for disabled persons, tools and equipment for scientific research on people with disabilities.

10. Self-help organizations

In close collaboration with ESCAP, the country held from 28 to 31 October 1996 in Hanoi, a four-day conference that focused on supporting the self-help initiatives of people with disabilities in Viet Nam. This first conference for people with disabilities has led to the establishment of various self-help organizations and activities.

The Viet Nam Association of the Blind, the most prominent among the organizations of people with disabilities in Viet Nam, has established a central office with branches at the local level. Currently, it has 27 and 202 branches at the provincial and district levels, respectively, with 22,665 members.

The association provide various forms of support for its members, including a Braille newspaper, tapes featuring news, information and current affairs commentaries, as well as various activities, such as poetry recitals and musical performances. It also runs 96 business enterprises for people with disabilities, with a strong workforce of 3,622 and an annual turnover of D5.267 billion. In 1996, the association opened 55 vocational training classes for its members at a cost of D328 million.

The association also proposed granting health insurance cards for 4,072 members and providing regular and case-by-case benefits for 5,760 members. In the same year, the association received 15 visits by international delegations and sponsors.

The Viet Nam Association of the Blind, other self-help organizations, including Disabled Athletes' Group, the Viet Nam Sports Association of People with Disabilities organize their own activities. The Viet Nam Sponsors' Association for People with Disabilities and Orphans, and the Save Children with Disabilities Association provide various effective programmes and activities to support persons with disabilities.

11. Regional cooperation

The achievements of the first half of the Asian and Pacific Decade of Disabled Persons were made possible with assistance from various foreign government agencies and non-governmental organizations from Germany, Holland, Japan, the United Kingdom and the United States of America, as well as United Nations bodies and agencies, including ESCAP and the International Labour Organization. The assistance covered a range of areas, including assistive devices, rehabilitation, job creation, legislation and policies, and technical training.

C. Activities planned for the second half of the Asian and Pacific Decade of Disabled Persons

1. Establish a national committee on people with disabilities, according to the recommendations in the Disabilities Ordinance and expand the role of the committee to review and further implement the Asian and Pacific Decade Agenda for Action for the second half of the Asian and Pacific Decade of Disabled Persons;

2. Expedite the implementation of the Disabilities Ordinance and enhance existing legislation to improve policies for people with disabilities;

3. Disseminate more information through the mass media and adopt various forms of propaganda to raise public awareness of people with disabilities;

4. Expand and speed up the disabilities prevention programme, focusing particularly on the prevention of disabilities caused by diseases and traffic and work-related accidents;

5. Strengthen and expand existing orthopaedic and rehabilitation centres, encourage the establishment of social organizations and the setting up of enterprises which produce orthopaedic equipment to meet the needs of people with disabilities;

6. Establish a Production Association of People with Disabilities and expand training programmes that suit the needs and conditions of people with disabilities and implement policies to achieve goals stated in the Disabilities Ordinance;

7. Consolidate the existing organizations of people with disabilities and coordinate their activities and develop more groupings for people with disabilities, such as the Association of Disabled Athletes;

8. Continue nurturing and enhancing the relationships with international and regional organizations and apply effectively the international assistance offered to people with disabilities.

D. Conclusions and recommendations

This report covered the activities that Viet Nam has carried out, though with limited success, partly because of the country's inexperience and also because many efforts are still in their infancy. Viet Nam remains optimistic that the international community, including governments and non-governmental organizations, will help the country form the necessary policies as well as provide the financial and technical assistance to help implement the goals stated in the Agenda for Action for the Asian and Pacific Decade of Disabled Persons.